Demons of the Inner World

DEMONS OF THE INNER WORLD

Understanding Our Hidden Complexes

Alfred Ribi

Translated by Michael H. Kohn

SHAMBHALA
Boston & London
1990

For Doris

Shambhala Publications, Inc.
Horticultural Hall
300 Massachusetts Avenue
Boston, Massachusetts 02115

9 8 7 6 5 4 3 2 1

First Edition
Printed in the United States of America on acid-free paper
Distributed in the United States by Random House
and in Canada by Random House of Canada Ltd.

Library of Congress Cataloging-in-Publication Data
Ribi, Alfred.
[Was tun mit unseren Komplexen?   English]
Demons of the inner world : understanding our hidden complexes/
Alfred Ribi; translated by Michael H. Kohn.—1st Shambhala ed.
    p.   cm.
Translation of: Was tun mit unseren Komplexen?
Includes bibliographical references.
ISBN 0-87773-579-4 (alk. paper)
   1. Demonology—Psychological aspects.   2. Complexes (Psychology)
I. Title.
BF1543.R5213   1990
133.4'01'9—dc20
90-34345
CIP

But I say unto you, That ye resist not evil. . . .

MATTHEW 5:39

When the unclean spirit is gone out of a man, he walketh through dry places, seeking rest; and finding none, he saith, I will return into my house whence I came out. And when he cometh, he findeth it swept and garnished. Then goeth he and taketh to him seven other spirits more wicked than himself; and they enter in, and dwell there: and the last state of that man is worse than the first.

LUKE 11:24–26

Contents

Preface

Is it possible for a book on demons to be contemporary? Nobody talks about demons anymore, and nobody believes in them anymore. Christianity, in its missionary zeal, has undertaken to save primitive peoples from their fear of demons. Since we Westerners are supposed to have been foremost among the saved, we are no longer allowed to have unfounded fears.

However, our irrational fears don't care a whit whether we think they are or aren't allowed to exist. In point of fact, are we not at least as subject to fears as the men and women of medieval times? But whereas the people of earlier times were frightened by mythical fears, we rationalize ours. We do not recognize our contemporary demons, because they are camouflaged behind a semblance of rationality. Atom bombs and nuclear power plants *are* a real danger—no reasonable person can deny it. However, irrational elements complicate any dialogue between the advocates and the opponents of nuclear power.

Indeed, the demonic component in our technology should not be overlooked. Modern technology has the means to attain un-dreamed-of levels of security. The inevitably present security risk is man himself. Finally we have to admit it—is not the cause of most accidents ultimately "human error"? And the errors do not come purely from inadequate training or lapses in attention, nor from an absence of good intentions. Rather, despite good intentions, a demonic element creeps into the process. It is a typical feature of demons that they foil our conscious purposes and bring to naught the best of intentions.

In everyday life we encounter our demons everywhere; we simply do not call them demons. We are convinced that we are dealing with external dangers. Here is a further characteristic of demons: they conceal themselves and surface in unexpected places. They camouflage themselves with an appearance of reasonableness and objectivity. They manifest in our finest convictions. We make an effort to be objective and rational in our opinions, believing that we can thus elude the demons. Far from it! The craftiest ruse of the demons for evading our grasp is making us identify with them. So long as we are unconsciously identified with something, we are unable to recognize it. Since we place so much stock in being rational, our demons transform themselves into something seemingly rational so that we cannot flush them out. Only when we separate ourselves from something can we deal with it. Until that happens, we remain vulnerable to it.

So if we are of the opinion that demons no longer exist, that is precisely the attitude they require to remain unrecognized. From that point of view, it could be said that we no longer have demons—they have us! They possess us, unconsciously. Modern people are obsessed in their everyday lives with all manner of things: achievement, money, power, social position, drugs, ideologies. All of these obsessions can be convincingly explained. We even delude ourselves into believing that we can escape their fascination. But only when we confess to ourselves that we are not escaping it can we admit that these are the modern demons and that we are their prey. Whoever finds the old-fashioned word *demon* offensive can speak in terms of complexes, for this is the modern psychological counterpart. Everybody "has" his or her complexes—nowadays this is common psychological knowledge. However, how complexes make themselves felt in our everyday lives and how one can deal with them—that is another matter. This is the theme of the present book, which provides both an introduction to the theory of complexes and guidance on how to work with them. At the same time, it offers an easily understandable introduction to the analytical psychology of C. G. Jung.

The attentive reader of this book will hopefully be in a position to join me in recognizing the great extent to which demons constellate our everyday life and the problems of our time, and to realize how critical it is to face them if we wish to deal successfully with these problems. "We are so full of apprehensions, fears, that one doesn't know exactly to what it points," C. G. Jung said in an interview toward the end of his life.[1] He went on to say, "One thing is sure. A great change of our psychological attitude is imminent. That is certain." And why? "Because we need more, we must need more psychology. We need more understanding of human nature, because the only real danger that exists is man himself. He is the greatest danger, and we are pitifully unaware of it. We know nothing about man—far too little. His psyche should be studied, because we are the origin of all coming evil."

Demons of the Inner World

I

The Demons of the Saints

The stories with which I am going to introduce my psychology of demons may seem remote from the events of today's world. Nonetheless, they show us inner psychological movements that we should be able to recognize from our everyday lives. To be sure, they were originally thought of as outer realities. But it is just that flicker of uncertainty over whether something is happening outside or is an inner image that is an earmark of the demons. By no means do all the evil spirits that we generate within us return to us; many carry on their mischief in the world unrecognized. On the other hand, by no means is it so that all the spirits of possession that twist my action and thought against my will are my own. Often enough, the unconscious man seems to be the puppet of these powers. The ancient holy men of whom we are about to speak did not believe, as we do today, that they could subdue demons with rationality. For that they needed a greater power—their faith in God. They are also important for us because they appeared in a formative period of Christian spiritual development where our own roots are to be found. It is far too little known how much early Christianity was concerned with the warding off of demons. To dismiss this feature as outdated would be too hasty. Have we with our rationality really done a better job than the early Christians?

In the fourth century of our era, men of faith, and later women as well, withdrew from worldly life and sought the solitude of the desert on both sides of the fertile Nile valley. In doing this, they followed the words of the apostle Paul in Galatians 5:24: "And they that are Christ's have crucified the flesh with the affections and lusts." They sold their goods and possessions in order not to lose their soul to materialism; for "it is easier for a camel to go through the eye of a needle, than for a rich man to enter into the kingdom of God" (Matt. 19:24). They sought out solitude so that they could serve their God completely. Since time immemorial, the desert has been considered a place of demons. For it is said that when Christianity began to spread in the cities of antiquity, the heathen gods who resided there withdrew into the desert. In this way, in the realm of Christianity they became demons. According to the words of Paul in Ephesians 6:12, "we wrestle not against flesh and blood, but against principalities, against powers, against the rulers of the darkness of this world, against spiritual wickedness in high places."[1]

These pious men and women were seeking just such battles with the unseen forces that we call spirits or demons. They were for the most part uneducated people who had been touched by the Christian message. They were ready to sacrifice everything worldly in order to face this battle alone. At first they went to the uninhabited country in the region of Thebes, to the Scetic Desert to the northwest of Terenuthis and to the mountains of Nitria southwest of it, or to the perilous marshes near Mareotic Lake in the Nile delta. The famous Saint Anthony went into the desert near the Red Sea. Most of the ascetics lived out their solitary lives and died unknown. The story of Saint Anthony, who died in 356, was written down perhaps a year later by Saint Athanasius, who had known him personally.[2]

As a result of this biography, for which no claim of historical accuracy may be made—it was simply intended to glorify this extraordinary man of God[3]—these ascetics became known to the entire Christian world. This biography reached such an enormous readership that now one cannot speak of the saints and their demons without first mentioning Anthony. Of course Saint Anthony has also been depicted countless times in paintings. As

After C. Butler, *The Lausiac History of Palladius*, II, p. xcviii.

a result, his spiritual influence on Christian culture has been very great.

In the following period, anchoritic centers evolved such as that on Mount Kolzim, where Anthony lived. The hermits began to organize themselves in these centers, and finally monasteries developed. (Particularly outstanding as an organizer was Pachomius, who devised a monastic code.)[4] These holy men and women, of whom wondrous miraculous deeds were told, became the object of growing interest. Palladius visited the best-known hermitage sites starting in 388; but it was not until about 419, in his *Historia Lausiaca* (written to Lausus, a chamberlain in the Byzantine court) that he gave an account of them.[5] The author

3

was probably born in Galatia in 364. From 388 until the end of the fourth century, he lived as a monk in Egypt. He describes himself as a student of Evagrius Ponticus, of whom I shall have more to say below. Palladius died in 431. He spent three years in the monasteries in the vicinity of Alexandria, a year in the mountains of Nitria, and nine years in the Scetic Desert. Thus he knew the life of the hermits firsthand. A gastric ailment forced him to leave the desert and to seek the aid of doctors in Alexandria, who sent him to Palestine.

Palladius' *Historia Lausiaca* should also not be regarded as a historical document; rather it is written out of a sense of veneration for the hermits, these "friends of God." It describes the most vivid aspects of the anchoritic life and served until modern times as a textbook of pious instruction. In point of fact, such accounts have a more beneficial effect on the minds of many readers than erudite theological treatises. The *Historia monachorum in Aegypto,* written in 410, in some ways runs parallel to the *Historia Lausiaca.*[6]

Saint John Cassian also merits mention in this context. Born in 365, he early felt the call to the monastic life. After completing his studies, he shared a cell in the monastery at Bethlehem (382–383) with his monastic brother and friend Germanus before visiting Egypt with him, in particular the desert in the region of Panephysis. A further journey, taken with the permission of their monastery, took these two in the course of seven years to the salt marshes near Panephysis, to the Scetic desert, and to Nitria, where they met Evagrius Ponticus. It was not until 420, in his *Collationes,*[7] that Cassian gave an account of the conversations he and his friend had had with the highly esteemed hermit. These *Collationes* have a marked didactic character. They are not merely, like the previously mentioned accounts, expressions of veneration; at this point theoretical formulation of the experiences of the ascetics and of the organization of monasticism begins. Cassian himself established a monastery at Marseilles, where he died in 435. He devoted another of his main works to the organization of monasteries.

The real systematizer and theoretician of the ascetic life is the already mentioned Evagrius Ponticus, who was born in 345 near Jbora in Pontus. He enjoyed friendships with Basil the Great and Gregory of Nazianzius. The latter attracted him to Constantinople, where in 380 he became Patriarch. There also he had an affair with the wife of a high-level functionary, but received a warning in a vivid dream and took ship the following day for Jerusalem. Here he was received at the monastery on the Mount of Olives by the famous Melania the Elder,[8] mentioned by Palladius, and by Rufinus. Melania convinced him to go as a monk to Egypt (in 383). He wrote her a famous letter in which he formulated his boldest thoughts. He settled in Cella, southwest of Alexandria, where he was the only educated monk. Shortly after his death in 399, he was declared a follower of Origen and thus a heretic; he was excommunicated at the Council of Constantinople in 553. For this reason, many of his writings have not come down to us in Greek but only in Syriac or Aramaic. The work of his that is most relevant to our theme is entitled "The Monk, or Concerning Practical Life."[9] In it, Evagrius presents a doctrine of eight vices, including gluttony, promiscuity, greed for wealth, depression, anger, indolence or neglect *(akedia)*, vanity, and arrogance.

However, it is not these theoretical aspects that we are concerned with here, though they had a major influence on later monastic thought, but rather the practical experience of the hermits. From the psychological point of view, as a result of withdrawing into solitary wastelands devoid of human life so as to "mortify the flesh," the unconscious came alive in these men in a process of compensation for the one-sidedness of their conscious outlook. Of course, these men of God saw things differently. For the hermits, their life-style was a provocation to the demons, whose last refuge—the desert—they threatened to conquer. Thus the battle with the dark demonic forces that these pious men had sought was joined. It is this battle, depicted naively in the sources we have mentioned, that particularly fascinates us.

The Devil makes use of trickery to deceive human beings—that was the ascetic's basic assumption in undertaking the struggle with the demons.[10] When Anthony had decided to move yet deeper into the desert, "he saw a silver bowl lying before him. But the blessed Anthony knew," as we are told in the biography by Athanasius,[11] "that this thing was a deception of the Demon; and to let the latter know that even this would not succeed in deceiving him, . . . he turned his gaze toward the plain, that is against the Demon, and replied, 'Where could a bowl come from in the desert? There are no traveled ways nearby, no habitations, no bandits that live in this place! This is an artifice of the Demon! You will not hinder my spirit by this means! Let this be with you for your downfall!' When the blessed Anthony had spoken these words, [the Demon] disappeared and dissolved like smoke in the presence of fire through the words of the blessed one."

Since this work by Athanasius is intended to be instructional, it contains continual allusions to the Holy Scriptures. The first is to the story of Simon Magus (Acts 8). Simon was a great magician who, although he was converted to Christianity, wanted to buy the ability to confer the Holy Ghost through the laying on of hands with a large sum of money. But "Peter said unto him, Thy money perish with thee, because thou hast thought that the gift of God may be purchased with money" (8:20). The second allusion is to the judgment of the godless in Psalm 37:20: ". . . they shall consume; into smoke shall they consume away." And Psalm 68:2 says of the enemy of God: "As smoke is driven away, so drive them away: as wax melteth before the fire, so let the wicked perish at the presence of God."

The saint sees in such visions only a ruse to distract him from his resolve. His resolve is correct—he must undergo yet greater asceticism by penetrating even deeper into the desert. This is meritorious, because it means a further challenge. It is essentially a question of overcoming the worldly (fleshly) person: Asceticism is an *opus contra naturam*. The natural man with his cravings and drives must be overcome. Psychologically, we find it understandable that the natural man should rebel against this. By way of compensation for this unnatural approach to life, the repressed side manifests the hallucinations described in the text. Anthony wants to renounce all the material values that are so close to the hearts of ordinary people; he himself is dependent on them in wishing to undertake a life of privation. Here the repressed aspect of life appears as "temptation."

In our example, the silver bowl stands for all the material values that Anthony wants to give up. They are trying to bind him to the material world, but he wants to divest himself of these bonds so as to devote himself to the spiritual world. Thus he can only construe these hallucinations as hostile, as an attack of the Demon on his resolve, as a trick to undermine his certainty.

From the point of view of Jungian psychology, silver is to be understood not merely as an earthly value, but also, in cases where the object in question is a bowl, a vessel—a hollow shape—as a symbol for the feminine principle. This compensatory vision is telling the ascetic not to forget the feminine principle. It is a reference to the fact that through his solitary spiritual life, inimical to the body, he is repressing not only his sexuality but also everything feminine.

But the temptations were not always as easy to see through as this one. After Anthony had established himself in the ways of a hermit,

> the enemy sowed in him thoughts of material things, concern for his sister and love toward her and his family, and [also] love of money with all the possible cravings and [attachments to] the rest of the comforts of the world. And to conclude the tribulations of this round of temptations—in which Anthony's discipline remained firm but in which, as he said, it was difficult and hard, since [there was also] the weakness of the body and the length of the time span—the enemy whirled up generally and plentifully

7

[the dust] of thoughts against him for the case where he might be drawn on by one of them or be defeated by it or hindered by its enticements."[12]

The previous chapters of the biography recount how Anthony, after the death of his parents, gave all his worldly goods to the poor and withdrew into the desert. In this, he followed the injunction of Jesus, "If thou wilt be perfect, go and sell that thou hast, and give to the poor, and thou shalt have treasure in heaven: and come and follow me" (Matt. 19:21).

Attainment of the "treasure in heaven" motivated these pious men and women to renounce everything earthly. Unexpectedly, however, new obstacles now blocked this path, namely, consideration for family ties. These plunged Anthony into a conflict of commitments. Should he be true to the spiritual path or to his family? These thoughts were once more regarded as instigated by the Adversary, because they had the potential to make him alter his resolve. As we would look at it today, on the other hand, he was in the process of becoming aware of a conflict. A decision only acquires a psychological value when it is consciously carried out. Part of making a conscious decision is becoming aware of the underlying conflict. Only when this has been worked through can a genuine, free decision arise.

Consideration for family ties requires an emotional judgment. Only thereby is the ascetic seen as human. Asceticism does, after all, bear within it the danger of a certain ruthlessness and cruelty. Someone who is not to some degree ruthless toward himself will never feel called to the ascetic life. It is only at a secondary stage that such ruthlessness manifests toward the world, that is, only after the ascetic no longer is subject to sentimentality toward himself. And the "temptations" aim precisely at emotional weakness toward oneself. Such weakness becomes evident in the life of Anthony, for example, in the fact that he did not give away all of his possessions. Instead he considered that he might need something for his old age, when "his body was weakened by the passage of time." Such a consideration was by no means unjustified, but its weakness lay in the fact that he did not give himself over entirely to his *faith of God*. Thus Jesus warns (Matt. 6:25–26): "Take no thought for your life, what ye shall eat, or what ye shall drink; nor yet for your body, what ye shall put on. Is not the life more than meat, and the body than raiment? Behold the fowls of the air: for they sow not, neither do they reap, nor gather into barns; yet your heavenly Father feedeth them. Are ye not much better than they?"

In the instructional stories, one repeatedly finds the warning against exaggerated asceticism. It lacks Eros and humanity. In it one falls prey not only to the ruthlessness of the Adversary. In Cassian, in the account of the second conversation with Abba Moses, we find the story of the old man Heron:

> This last was the victim of a diabolical illusion that plunged him from the summit into the abyss. . . . He had made of fasting an inflexible and absolute law. . . . The angel of Satan was received by him as an angel of light, with great honor [because he was so exhausted from fasting]. Eager to obey him, he threw himself head over heels into a well, the bottom of which the eye could not perceive. In doing this, he placed his trust in the promise that had been made to him that, as a result of his meritorious works and virtues, in the future he would be proof against all danger. . . . Thus, at just the middle of the night, he threw himself to the bottom of the well with the thought of proving his rare merit by coming out in one piece. However, the brothers had great difficulty in pulling him out half dead. He passed away two days later.[13]

The Adversary is a trickster.[14] He seduced the lover of God (*theophilus*), Heron, into rigorous fasting and led him on with the idea of the merit to be gained from it. He even hoodwinked him with the goal of becoming like God. As a result of his excessive fasting he fell prey to the inflation* of being immortal or invulnerable. Putting this to the test proved fatal.

These early Christians recognized the trickster nature of the unconscious mind about which the alchemists were to complain a thousand years later. As a result, they mistrusted *all* manifestations of the unconscious. "The demons have as many different proclivities as humans do. Of this we have indubitable proof," says Abba Serenus in Cassian's account.[15] "Some of them, whom the simple folk call 'vagabonds,' are deceivers and pranksters. They stick stubbornly to particular places or roads. However, they do not desire to torment passers-by if they can trick them. They are content with laughter and mockery and are more interested in tiring them out than harming them."

Let us return to our story of Heron, who suffered inflation through fasting. Heron did not have the right attitude toward asceticism. He wanted to make use of it to attain power and fell prey to delusions of grandeur. These made him inhuman, and he paid for this with his life. The ruthlessness that all asceticism requires must not be allowed to lead to inhumanity. For this reason, Anthony had to work with his sense of obligation to his family before he could go on with his life of a hermit.

"No one doubts," says Abba Serenus,[16] "that the impure spirits know the nature of our thoughts." Anthony was twenty or thirty years old when he withdrew into the wilderness. "The Adversary approached him," says Athanasius,[17] "through the excitability of youth, to which, in accordance with nature, our humanity is bound, and through this temptation, he frightened him at night and tormented him during the day." Further on, he continues,

> And the more the Adversary filled him with impure and base thoughts, the more he took refuge in prayer, for he was very ashamed of them. But the Adversary brought about everything shameful, as is his wont, to the point where the figure of a woman appeared. . . . Or the Adversary multiplied in him the lustful thoughts until such point that the blessed one was no longer angry

---

*Jung used the term *inflation* to refer to a state of overblown self-importance; in this condition the personality is inundated by unconscious, impersonal contents or identifies itself with them.

at the Adversary but became angry at himself, and he fastened on the thought of the threat of Judgment and the torments of Hell, where the worm dieth not (Mark 9:44f.).[18] And when this thought had helped him against the Adversary, then all the other untoward thoughts vanished also.[19]

This ancient saint, whose story we may find outmoded, is ahead of the game at least in one respect: he does not regard himself as the author of his thoughts. They seem to him to come from the outside, to be placed in him by the Adversary. Such a distinction is of the utmost importance. For because of it, Anthony is not identified with his thoughts. This gives him the possibility of asserting himself apart from them and of trying to develop his own independent viewpoint. Only thus is a confrontation with the thoughts placed in him by the Adversary possible. So long as we identify with our thoughts, we are their slaves. We have no freedom of judgment.

If we look at the life of these early Christian ascetics from the psychological viewpoint, we note that as a result of the dearth of sensual stimuli, the unconscious becomes extraordinarily aroused and asserts itself in the form of visual or auditory hallucinations. Behind these, the ascetics saw the deceitful machinations of the Demon, who was seeking to dislodge them from their sacred conduct. The struggle with these "deceptions" of the Adversary strengthened the conscious mind vis-à-vis the unconscious. These men and women had a rich empirical knowledge of psychology; they just called it something else. Developing one's consciousness means discriminating, making distinctions. For these men and women, the point of discrimination lay in not falling prey to the tricks and deceptions of the Demon. These pious men and women were pioneers in the psychology of individuation, of development of consciousness.

We left Saint Anthony in the midst of his struggle with sexual craving. Certainly this struggle was the key one for many a hermit. John of Lycopolis tells the story of a monk who lived in a cave and lived an exemplary life. However, as he grew in virtue, he came to rely increasingly on his good conduct.

> Then the Tempter claimed him for himself as he did Job. One evening he held before his eyes the image of a beautiful woman who had gotten lost in the desert. Since she found the doors to the cave open, she leapt inside, threw herself at the feet of the monk, and bid him give her hospitality on the pretext that nightfall had taken her by surprise. Since he had pity on her—which was not advisable—he welcomed her in the cave and began asking her about her journey. As she told him about it, she intermingled flattering and seductive remarks with her tale and drew the conversation out longer and longer. Gently and skillfully she entangled him in love; ever further themes of conversation arose. They laughed together and began to caress. Through this long conversation she led him astray and finally caught the ascetic in that instant in which she touched him on the hand, on the chin, and on the throat. As bad thoughts proliferated within him—[the thought that] he had matters under control, considerations of the favorable moment, the opportunity to have pleasure without danger—his spirit consented and he began seeking to enter into union with her, now obsessed and become like a stallion at stud, wanting to beguile the damsel. She, however, with a scream slipped out of his hands, became invisible, and fled away like a shadow. In the air could be heard the loud laughter of the demons, who had made a fool of him with their trickery. They mocked him and called out in loud voices: "Every one that exalteth himself shall be abased" (Luke 18:14). "You lifted yourself up to Heaven and have been abased unto Hell."[20]

These simple tales are gripping in their naive realism. They portray bits of everyday psychology that every one of us has experienced. But are we so honest as to confess our self-deceptions to ourselves in this kind of straightforward manner? Such honesty toward oneself is admirable. But precisely because we are identified with our pet thoughts, we are rarely able to acknowledge the deception in them. These old stories seem to acquire new relevance in the light of psychology. We do not need to be hermits or on the path to sainthood to see the validity of this psychology in our everyday lives, to see how our wishful thinking seduces us and makes fools of us.

Palladius, in his *Historia Lausiaca*, tells the story of Pachon, a seventy-year-old hermit in the Scetic Desert, to whom he confided his sexual craving and who recounted the following from his own experience:

> Now, the Devil let me alone for several days but then tormented me worse than before, so that I had almost reached the point of blaspheming God. He took on the form of an Ethiopian maiden whom I had seen gathering corn in the summertime when I was young; she sat down on my lap and excited me so that I thought I would commit fornication. But then I came to my senses and gave her a slap, whereupon she vanished. The result was that for two years I could not abide the evil smell of my hand. I was wandering despondent and beaten through the desert. Then I found a small snake. This I took and held it to my penis so as to die of its bite. But I was squeezing the head of the creature to my member with such force that it was impossible for it to bite me. Then I heard a voice that spoke to me within: "Go your way, Pachon, and continue your struggle! I only let such fell hardship come upon you to prevent you from becoming proud and believing you could attain something on your own; you must be more aware of your weakness and not rely on your own discipline but seek the help of God."[21]

This story vivdly shows how Pachon dealt with his sexual complex. What is touching here is his honesty and consistency. Today we understand such stories still better, because they resemble the experiences of active imagination.* Divested of religious terminology, the ending would read: "We cannot deal with our complexes on our own and should become humble and aware of our weakness. Nevertheless, there is a strength in man

---

*A technique developed by Jung in which significant dream images are reentered in imagination and developed further as a means of learning more about their significance. (Translator's note)

that is greater than that of complexes and able to overcome them. It is the strength of the Self."

Such wisdom keeps its validity over the centuries; it is even helpful for us today. We need not despair because of our complexes. Even if it takes a lifetime to integrate them, they only remind us of our inadequacy so that we may become humble. Making the effort to deal with them is the decisive act, which ultimately leaves the credit for completing the job to the Self, the power of integration and wholeness.

In talking about John of Lycopolis and Pachon, I spoke as a matter of course of the complexes that manifested in their visions. Today the notion of complex has been generally established. Jung introduced this concept. In his word associations, he investigated the structure and behavior of complexes. His understanding of a complex was the *image* of a certain psychic situation which is strongly accentuated emotionally and is, moreover, incompatible with the habitual attitude of consciousness. This image has a powerful inner coherence, it has its own wholeness and, in addition, a relatively high degree of autonomy, so that it is subject to the control of the conscious mind only to a limited extent, and therefore behaves like an animated foreign body in the sphere of consciousness. . . . Fundamentally, there is *no difference in principle between a fragmentary personality and a complex.* . . . Today, we can take it as moderately certain that complexes are in fact "splinter psyches."[22]

The sexual complex of the frustrated hermit is personified as a seductive woman. "Now it is a fact amply confirmed by psychiatric experience," says Jung elsewhere, that all parts of the psyche, inasmuch as they possess a certain autonomy, exhibit a personal character, like the split-off products of hysteria and schizophrenia, mediumistic "spirits," figures seen in dreams, etc. Every split-off portion of libido [psychic energy], every complex, has or is a (fragmentary) personality. At any rate, that is how it looks from the purely observational standpoint. But when we go into the matter more deeply, we find that they are really archetypal formations. There are no conclusive arguments against the hypothesis that these archetypal figures are endowed with personality at the outset and are not just secondary personalitizations. In so far as the archetypes do not represent mere functional relationships, they manifest themselves as *daimones*, as personal agencies.[23]

The hermits' seductive woman does not actually represent sexuality, but rather the anima as seductress. She is the archetypal personality behind the sexual complex of which Jung was speaking in the above citation. She controls the libido charge, that charge of psychic energy that is lacking in consciousness as a result of asceticism. The monastic ideal devalues woman, shuts her out of the sphere of natural life so that she takes on the negative form of the seductress.[24] She imposes herself on consciousness as a visual and tactile hallucination. In this way the Self is trying to bring this one-sidedly ignored element into consciousness. This would lead to the recognition of the natural man, the natural drive in humans.

The objective of the early Christian ascetics, however, was different. They wanted to overcome the natural man. Theirs was an *opus contra naturam*. They wanted to extinguish all drives and worldly instincts. Through their "unnatural" life-style, all kinds of hallucinations were produced. Through overcoming these, "spiritualization" took place. Consciousness thus attained a certain freedom in relation to its instinctive needs. This, however, is the cultural drive,[25] which involves overcoming the merely natural man. Such overcoming corresponds to a reinforcement of consciousness vis-à-vis the powers of nature. Only thereby is consciousness given the space for free decision that we call free will. Free will is not a constant or an a priori quantity; rather it is that libido charge that is at the free disposal of consciousness.[26]

The man of antiquity, if we believe Friedländer's portrayals of his life and customs,[27] was principally shaped by his instincts and drives. Ancient philosophy, with its emphasis on ethics, especially among the Stoics, was an attempt at compensation—an unconscious secular trend to draw humanity out of its unconsciousness. Evagrius Ponticus,[28] the systematizer and theoretician of asceticism, also consciously developed his ideas in connection with those of the Stoics. The *praktiké* of the monk "is a spiritual method that purifies the passionate side of the soul." Its goal is passionlessness (*apatheia*). This is the prerequisite for spiritual knowledge, the mode of access to *gnostiké*. The pair *praktiké-gnostiké* is derived from Plato (*Statesman* 258e–259c). The first is, so to speak, the manual skill of the mind; the second, its occupation. It is only with Philo of Alexandria (*De praemiis et poenis* 51) that the meaning of *praktiké* shifts from the secular to the moral. By "practical life," he understands the asceticism that Jacob practiced before he saw God. It consists, in accordance with the Stoic ideal, in not neglecting any human duty, but also in not sparing any effort or struggle to attain truth. Here *praktiké* has already acquired a primarily moralistic and religious meaning; it is directly governed by the pursuit of a vision of God. At the beginning of his *Vita Contemplativa*, Philo contrasts the Essenes, who led a "practical life" (*praktikos bios*), with the Therapeutics, who devoted themselves to contemplation.

When simple, mostly uneducated, pious people, who sometimes knew the Bible by heart because they could not read,[29] went into solitude to lead a life pleasing to God by struggling against their own demons, this was only a first step. The admirable decision to take that step can still make an impression on us today and cause us to take an analogous step under completely different external circumstances. The individuation process, the popularized and often misunderstood process of self-realization, requires a resolve similar in its radicalness to that of the hermit. Indeed it involves a total "revaluation of values," a turning away from collective external values and a turning toward inner images and the Self (the ascetic's vision of God). The "denial of the world" here consists not in withdrawing in an outer way from the hustle and bustle of the world, but rather in orienting oneself toward the inner values, toward the Self. To be sure, in doing so one often also ends up in a desert, but in one's own. One often then finds oneself in an utter solitude, because one is not part of the mainstream. Ultimately, one is exposed to all the demons that one bears within oneself. And when one has struggled long enough with one's own thousand devils, one ceases projecting them on one's neighbors and finds an inner calm.

Once Makarius knew the singular grace of seeing within his own eyes how the demons play with men:

> During the night service, he saw a kind of small Ethiopians flitting here and there across the whole church while the monks sat on their benches singing psalms. Makarius saw the little devils playing a thousand pranks on the monks. The eyes of some they pressed closed together with their little fingers, and these fell asleep; in the mouths of others they stuck their fingers, making them yawn. Afterward, as the monks kneeled to pray, Makarius saw the little devils going from one to the other, appearing to one as a woman, making as if to set something up in front of another or hold it aloft, and other pranks of a similar sort. At the same time, they put thoughts in the head of each one corresponding to the way in which they were deceiving him. Certain monks immediately shooed the demons away so that they did not dare to come back. But Makarius saw the demons romping about on the necks and backs of other monks, especially those who had not been attentive enough during prayers.[30]

Who is not acquainted with such things from personal experience? When one is tired, relatively superficial levels of the unconscious can break through in the form of hypnagogic images.* If one deliberately strengthens one's attention, then they disappear. They are complexes become visible, in a disorganized form, to be sure. One particular school of modern art lives from

---

*Before falling asleep, hypnagogic hallucinations can arise (Gr. *hypnos*, "sleep"). They are shortlived, vivid, disconnected, often bizarre sensory experiences, especially of an optical type.

such images. "The Devil took advantage of a slight distraction during prayer and sprang astride Hilarion's back, poked him in the sides, flogged him across the neck with the whip, and shouted 'Onward, why are you falling asleep?' Almost bursting with laughter, he asked him if he would like a handful of barley."[31]

It could be no more clearly depicted that Hilarion was "devil-ridden." Any lapse in attention exposes us to the danger that a devil, a complex, might jump on us. Psychiatrists or analysts know this particularly well. Devils are infectious. Often we only notice it when one has gotten hold of us, when we are in a bad mood and carrying on like the devil.

Such demons are for the most part still easy to see through if one is just able to be a bit critical toward oneself. It becomes difficult, however, when the terrible paradoxical quality of the demons comes to the fore. I mentioned previously the example of Anthony, who was oppressed by thoughts of his family responsibilities. Such thoughts do not appear diabolical on the surface. They arose in this case, as was shown, from a conflict of commitments. John of Lycopolis[32] was so sorely vexed by hallucinations one night that he could neither pray nor sleep. In the morning the apparitions threw themselves at his feet and begged him mockingly: "Forgive us, father, for the hardship we created all night long." He, however, answered them: "Depart from me, all ye workers of iniquity" (Ps. 6:8), for "thou shalt not tempt the Lord thy God" (Matt. 4:7).

The Devil appeared to Saint Anthony another time in a gigantic form. Accompanied by the din of a large crowd of people, the Devil placed himself before him and dared to say, "I am the ruler of this world. Whatever you ask of me, I will give you; ask and take" (cf. Luke 4:5–6).

> Another time, as I was fasting, the Deceiver appeared to me in the figure of a hermit, who offered bread and then gave me the following advice: "Hold yourself upright, sustain your heart with bread and water, and rest a little from the multitude of your works; for you are a human being, and no matter what pretensions

you may have, you are burdened with a body. Be fearful of suffering and unpleasantness." I, however, considered his sympathy and held back my words. I turned in the silence to my steadfast way and began to supplicate my Lord in prayer and said: "Lord, make him as nothing, just as throughout all times you have been wont to make him as nothing." And when I have finished these words, he was consumed and vanished like dust and in the manner of smoke (cf. Ps. 37:20) slipped away through the doors.[33]

The advice of his "fellow hermit" was undoubtedly reasonable. *The Devil can even give reasonable advice.* Only the purpose of this advice—to cause the blessed one to end his fasting—betrays the diabolical ruse behind it. The Devil can even transform himself into an angel of light, as Paul tells us in the second epistle to the Corinthians (11:14). Palladius recounts in the *Historia Lausiaca* the sad story of the Palestinian Valens,[34] who went into the desert. After living there for a few years he became so arrogant that the devils began to deceive him. The Adversary "transformed" himself into the Savior and came as a nocturnal illusion, surrounded by a thousand angels carrying burning lamps. He himself, in the midst of the glowing light, looked like the Savior. He sent forth a messenger, who said to Valens: "Christ has taken a liking to you because of your conduct and the openness of your being; now he is coming to see you. Go out in front of your cell! As soon as you glimpse him, throw yourself down on your face, pray to him, and go back into your cell!" So he went out, beheld the radiant company and, a distance off, the Antichrist; he fell on his face and prayed to him. The next day, his deludedness had so greatly increased that he came into the church and called out to the assembled brothers: "I have no need to participate in the secrets, for today I have seen Christ himself." Then the fathers tied him up and set fetters on his feet for an entire year and brought him to his senses. Through prayer, humiliation, and strict treatment, they healed his madness: "For often even virtue becomes the occasion for a snare if it is not carried out with the right intention, for is it not written: 'I saw the righteous man perish in his righteousness, and this also is vanity' " (cf. Eccles. 7:15).

Not everyone who has fallen prey to inflation has such helpful companions to bring him back down to earth and reality in such a healing—albeit rude—way. Not every inflation is as grotesque as that of Valens, and thus may not be recognized by the victim's companions. All the same, if it goes unrecognized, the victim loses his chance of being healed.

In the last example, the subtle temptation consists in setting oneself in the place of the secrets. This latter phrase requires an explanation. Religion deals with the divine secrets. The church is the administrator of such secrets. Now if a man sets himself in the place of the secrets, he has fallen into delusions of grandeur. For this reason, the church has always emphasized the historical objectivity of the life of Christ and the objectivity of God beyond the realm of man—in order to protect the latter from inflation. As long as ego consciousness is weak, it runs the risk of not distinguishing itself from the contents of the unconscious. When unconscious contents break through, the conscious ego is dissolved. Such a dissolution can, as in our example, take on psychotic proportions. Only today, following Jung's discovery of the objective psyche, are we in a position to see this problem in a suitable light. The secret or mystery in fact has not all been done away with by modern depth psychology. It has, however, shifted to the place from which the power of the numinous has always emanated—the psyche or soul. This latter is quite definitely *not* identified with the conscious mind, but rather is, to an almost frightening degree, independent of it. It is related to consciousness as an autonomous partner. Every communication with the divine and every religious feeling comes to consciousness only via the psyche. The psyche is thus the bearer of the *imago dei* (image of God), although we are not in a position to affirm scientifically what causes this image. We know only that it is the vessel for the highest values and the strongest sense of numinosity.

It was important for the church to insist on preserving the objectivity of the secrets. In the days of our hermits and for centuries thereafter, the way consisted in establishing the secret outside of man. For a long time, the only way to deal with demons remained to cast them out of oneself and take refuge in external secrets. This had the effect of shielding men and women from the danger of inflation and pointing them toward their humble place in the divine cosmos.

Has analytical psychology made possible another means of dealing with demons? We can no longer categorize demons simply as "evil." Even if we did so, we would be far from being rid of them, despite what people once thought. The ascetics in the region of Thebes have not been the only ones menaced by demons. We are just as menaced by them today as they were then—with the difference that we are far less aware of it than the hermits were. They knew that "we wrestle not against flesh and blood, but against . . . powers . . . against spiritual wickedness" (Eph. 6:12). Although modern depth psychology could teach us better, we continue to see the danger too much as on the outside. "The only real danger is man himself," said Jung in an interview,[35] referring to the unconscious psyche. We are no longer in the ascetics' enviable position of having merely to expose the demons and their deception to get rid of them. They plague us so heavily that it is no exaggeration to say that our survival depends on them.

The monks in the region of Thebes died out long ago, but they left us with a problem that they resolved in a way that was possible for them in their time.[36] We of today must continue to work on this problem and find a new, modern solution for it. We are far from having found it yet.

2

Demons in Early Christianity

Christendom shared its belief in demons with the Mediterranean peoples of antiquity. Judaism had already taken on a great deal of it from neighboring peoples. Nevertheless, the religious teachings of the Old Testament are distinct from those of Near Eastern demonistic religions.[1] Yahweh's demand for exclusivity (Exod. 20:4; Deut. 20:10f.) certainly shows that he had assimilated the demons of folk religion into himself. As a result, Yahweh developed a highly variable character that incorporated many contradictions.[2]

The apocryphal Book of Tobit has preserved for us the story of the demon Asmodeus, by whom Sarah, the daughter of Raguel of Ecbatana in Media, was possessed.[3] This story teaches us how to deal with demons and how to free people from possession. By means of a kind of incense, Tobias drives out the demon who had killed all seven of Sarah's previous grooms on their wedding night (8:2). In fact he is guided in this successful exorcism by his mysterious companion Raphael (5:4). On the banks of the Tigris River, Raphael advises him to grab hold of a fish that is trying to swallow him up and to throw it up on the land. In order to drive out the demon, Tobias is told to place the heart and liver of the fish on burning coals. He is told to rub the gall of the fish on his blind father's eyes and in this way succeeds in restoring his sight.

Without undertaking a detailed psychological analysis of the *Book of Tobit*, we nevertheless cannot fail to note the central role of the wondrous fish. It is the *alexipharmacon*, the medicine that cures all ills; the demon quails before it and it cures blindness. The blindness of Tobias' father and the possession of the daughter Sarah may well have a hidden connection, since a strong father complex often gives rise in the daughter to a markedly negative animus. She becomes so strongly bound up psychologically with the father that she unconsciously wards off any man who tries to become her husband. The individual in whom this is going on knows nothing of these unconscious processes and as a result becomes the victim of the constellation. The unconscious powers are experienced as demonic because they cheat one's intentions. The more unconscious a person is, the more defenseless he or she is against the demonic powers. Thus Sarah has no choice but to conditionally accept the accusation of the maids that she has strangled her seven grooms (3:8). She feels both powerless and guilty, for which reason she wants to end her life. But because she is her father's only child, she decides against this, not wanting to disgrace him.

The demons who possess us in fact do often drive us to the verge of suicide, because they continually thwart our best intentions. We cannot seem to prevent ourselves from doing what we do not want to do. The only thing that preserves us from suicide is a religious disposition that sees in that which does not comply with our will something powerful—divine, or demonic. A person can cope with this only *concedente deo*, with God's help. And in fact Sarah's fervent prayer is heard "in the presence of the glory of the great God" (3:16). By sending his angel Raphael, he comes to the aid of the frail human being. Here man seems to be no more than a counter in the cosmic struggle of opposites. But in fact the angel does not save Sarah directly. He provides only indirect help as the miracle-accomplishing companion of Tobias, the real hero of the story. It falls exclusively to the lot of human consciousness to perform the crucial action, even if consciousness fundamentally lacks the power to do so without the help of the almighty helper. This is the cosmic role that is allotted to the conscious mind in spite of its frailty. For this reason suicide is no solution to the problem; the real solution requires an expansion of consciousness. Consciousness has become too narrow and is therefore possessed by a content of the unconscious. Release brings not just liberation from possession; it also expands consciousness. Mere exorcism does not accomplish this. Thus the Book of Tobit portrays a more mature level in the development of consciousness.

In his book *Aion,* Jung investigated the symbol of the miraculous fish and its meaning in detail. A dangerous, ravening fish attacks Tobias as he is bathing in the Tigris. The same negative aspect of the fish receives prominence in the story of Jonah, who in order to escape an obligation laid upon him tries to flee in a ship to Tarshish. In the storm that arises, he ends up overboard. Then "the Lord . . . prepared a great fish to swallow up Jonah." (Jonah 1:17). The fish vomits him up onto the land (2:10), here again conveying him toward the destiny he was trying to escape.

The fish symbol is just as ambivalent as destiny, which carries the willing along, but drags those who fight against it." Yet the fish is also the savior: Christ is referred to as *ichthys,* the fish. Already in the Jewish tradition, fish was considered a food for the ailing. Leviathan, the sea monster, is equally ambivalent; on one hand, it is the symbol of the devil; on the other, it is the substance of the Eucharist, connected with the Messiah.

If the conscious personality resists the dangerous side of the fish, then the blessed side comes to the fore. For the fish symbolizes that living content of the unconscious that the conscious attitude lacks. This deficiency makes it vulnerable to possession. Whenever the conscious is lacking a factor essential for its completeness, a weak spot emerges that makes it vulnerable to possession. In the Book of Tobit, Sarah, a symbol of Eros, is possessed by an earth demon.

The Book of Tobit dates roughly from the third century before Christ, the time of the Exile. It portrays not only an individual but also a collective problem—a deficiency in the Eros factor of the homeless Jewish people. The Jewish culture and religion was quite onesidedly masculine-patriarchal. The feminine side was represented by Israel, Yahweh's bride, the Jewish people. Between the two a tense marriage existed, characterized by jealousy and resentment on the part of Yahweh (2 Sam. 24:1, 1 Chron. 21:1). In consequence, the people could not undergo a natural emotional development; important feelings were demonified.

Such demonification is a process that is actually striving toward healing and a higher level of wholeness. Thus in the unconscious a counterpart to the demon developed in the form of the angel Raphael and the wholeness-restoring, healing fish—a new Eros that reconciles the opposites. In the New Testament, Jesus is the conqueror of the demons, the exorcist, who at the end of time will render the Devil and his demons powerless (1 John 3:8). The gospel of love seems to bear within it all the seeds necessary for the continuation of the development introduced in the Book of Tobit. In early Christianity, baptism had an exorcistic function:[4] it was meant to keep demons from the child being baptized (Col. 2:12–15). The holy spirit that is conferred through the baptism gives the gift of power over evil spirits.[5] The notion of baptism as rebirth (John 3:3–7) corresponds quite well with the miraculous healing fish of the Book of Tobit. The baptismal font is the *piscina* (fish pool); those dipped in it are the *pisciculi* (little fishes). This symbology has the following meaning: the human being who has shed the old natural humanity (1 Cor. 15:44) and become connected with the living primal source need no longer fear demons; for wherever demons arise, a factor of healing and wholeness also arises as an antithesis to them and is available to him.

In the course of its confrontation with the world around it, the young Christianity of the first centuries underwent a considerable transformation.[6] Its monotheism overcame the Hellenism of antiquity. In the process it became "infected" with polytheism. The conquered ancient gods were demonified; they were relegated to the unconscious—as an immortal reality of the human soul that the prevailing approach to consciousness could find no place for. The ancient gods of Olympus had indeed been dethroned, but now they exercised their demonic power in a hidden way.

In the second century, the demon belief within paganism surged up from the dark lower strata to the surface, even in literature.[7] This religiosity of antiquity had lost its liveliness and efficacity. Into the gap, young Christianity leaped. In doing so, it did not destroy the culture of antiquity—which had already been undermined—but simply took advantage of its weak points. Christ's conjuring of the demons precisely suited their intimidated state of mind. The early church placed its own exorcist in every community, who had his own status in the lower hierarchy.[8] This exorcistic penchant on the part of early Christianity brought it not a few followers (James 2:19).

The official teaching of Christianity was that the demonic powers had been overcome by the death and resurrection of Christ (Eph. 1:21). But the polytheism that was supposed to have been conquered now established itself in a new form. The cult of saints and the veneration of relics grew and developed, both of them accommodating polydemonic tendencies. Monotheism constitutes a higher development to the extent that it brings opposing tendencies into a synthesis. However, the complete synthesis of *all* opposites in *one* image of God failed to develop. For this, precisely that complex yet integral Eros that was problematical in the Judaism of the *Book of Tobit* would have been necessary. With the Old Testament providing the precedents and pointing the way to the New, Christianity became heir to this problem. Beneath the surface of monotheism lies a concealed dualism of good and evil, and beneath that, even a polydemonism. The desert ascetics contributed not a little toward the polarization of the divine image. In the first centuries of Christianity, there raged a battle over the integration of evil into the image of God. Especially Gnosticism focused intensively on this primary problem. However, it had to give way to the institutionalized church, because of the inadequacy of its organization.

Early Christianity exerted itself especially in its confrontation with ancient philosophy. Its apologists were able to point to the prologue to the Gospel of John in asserting that the Logos had incarnated itself in Christ, that very Logos that was the object of all philosophy. In this way Christianity could be proposed as a primal philosophy,[9] the one philosophy in which all the other philosophies originated. True philosophy was also true religion (Posidonius; Seneca, *Epistula* 90:3). Genuine religion, according to Posidonius, was the same as moral probity. Seneca says that philosophy has but a single task—to find the truth of the divine and the human.[10] Lucan recounts[11] that Zeus took pity on the ignorant human race and sent down personified Philosophy with the charge of making sure that human beings ceased being unjust toward one another, using violence, and living like animals, rather than heeding the truth and living peacefully with one another.

Thus Christianity as a primal philosophy tendered itself for adoption on an already prepared ground. The job of the apologists was to prove to the educated world of antiquity that it was only a short step from its own spiritual approach to that of the new religion, that both actually rested on the same foundation, and even further, that the ancient philosophies were derived from the truth revealed by Christ.

The missionary efforts of Christianity first took hold on the lowest social levels, those of slaves, freedmen, and artisans.[12] Thus Paul could write in his first epistle to the Corinthians (1:25–29):

> Because the foolishness of God is wiser than men; and the weakness of God is stronger than men. For ye see your calling, brethren, how that not many wise men after the flesh, not many mighty, not many noble, are called: But God hath chosen the foolish things of the world to confound the wise; and God hath chosen the weak things of the world to confound the things which are mighty; and base things of the world, and things which are despised, hath God chosen, yea, and things which are not, to bring to nought things that are: that no flesh should glory in his presence.

Now the apologists were attempting to make Christianity accessible to the learned classes as well. In doing this, they set the irrational religion of revelation on a rational footing. Scholarly theology even attempted to show itself the equal of philosophy. Over the next centuries the Christian mystery was rationalized, amid bloody battles, into a systematic doctrinal edifice. The original immediacy vanished into formulary confessions of belief and dogma. Religion was externalized and institutionalized into a church. The power of an established organization manifested and proved itself in the suppression and extirpation of the Gnostic movement, which is an introverted, intuitive undercurrent in many official religions. (It already existed in pre-Christian Judaism; today we find it in Islam.) All introverted movements must inevitably give way before a powerful extraverted church. In consequence, much has been suppressed and externalized that might have formed part of a unified image of God. This has opened the gates to the demons. On the outer walls of Gothic cathedrals, they appear as waterspouts (gargoyles), a representation of all that has been thrust aside and down by institutionalized Christianity.

The demons always insinuate themselves at the point where they are least expected. In a decaying culture like that of imperial Rome, in which the demonic forces of chaos, despotism, disrespect for human life, and instinctive blindness prevailed, the young Eastern religion was the spiritual force that could cast the demons out. It was the expression of a new order and new living values. Perhaps with the exception of Seneca, the philosophy of the imperial period was no longer creative, and it was dominated by moral considerations. It had to function as a counterpoise to the violence and instinct-driven quality of the time. Although philosophy often spoke of God, very few philosophers had real experience of God. Pascal's "God of the philosophers" was a conceptual construction and not a numinous experience. Among the people, a living relationship to religion was no longer to be found. People fulfilled their religious obligations toward the gods out of habit. It is true that the cult of the state was still maintained, but there was no longer anywhere a genuine spiritual reference point.

Christianity was successful in this spiritual vacuum precisely because it did not preach high ideals and abstract concepts, but knew how to reach the living psyche of the individual. It succeeded in expressing the psychic realities. In particular, in accordance with the Pauline epistle cited above, all that was weak, lowly, and inadequate was accepted and exalted before God. That must have meant salvation for millions of people of the antique world. Especially if we construe the words of the apostle as an expression of an inner reality, they mean an appreciation of everything weak, imperfect, and lowly within us. That is true exorcism: to accept everything in oneself that one is ashamed of before the eyes of the world. By doing this, one pins the demons down where they can do the least harm and where they are able to transform—and in this way casts them out.

Not least because of its exorcistic capabilities was Christianity able to spread in the antique world. But it distanced itself increasingly from this approach, and at the same time narrowed ever further its image of the divine. Thus it became incapable of providing a satisfactory answer to the question of evil, which Gnosticism, for example, had come to terms with. The more rational its image of God became—for instance, taking the form of the *summum bonum*, which was adopted from Greek philosophy—the more demonic all the neglected elements became, and the more irrationally they behaved.

The relationship to nature and Eros is only one example of this among many. Ancient religion still possessed many animistic features. Nature swarmed with nymphs, dryads, Pans, Satyrs, and sileni. Though Christianity did not abhor this wondrous quality of nature, it focused on the Creator who stands above his creation rather than on the worship of nature itself. Covertly, a certain sense of hostility toward nature is present here. Part of nature is also Eros, which is more than just sexuality. Christianity reduced it to *agapé*, the love of one's neighbor, and thereby expunged its cosmogonic function. Not only was the narrowing down of the God image a loss; worse yet, the unacknowledged part of it was relegated to the unconscious, because it found no place in the prevailing religious doctrine. Whatever is relegated to the unconscious, whatever is without some kind of representation in consciousness, threatens to become a demon. The psychotherapeutic function of religion—and at the same time the oldest psychotherapy—consists in providing through its myths and symbols an expression of the wholeness and unity of the psyche.[13] To the extent that it does this and we relate to it in a vital way, religion protects us from demons. Still today, though with ever decreasing success, the Christian cross is being raised against the demons.

Over the centuries, the Christian church has neglected to keep up the development of its mythos in a way that would have kept it alive.[14] The image of the divine that it proposes has become ever more rigid and constricted. In consequence, everything that lies outside this image has come to life once again in an aberrant manner—in the realm of the demons.

Demons draw their power primarily from the fact of not being represented, honored, or indeed, even mentioned in the conscious world. They remain an unknown and menacing power. This in turn—like everything unconscious—is projected onto external factors, and as a result we lose sight of them entirely. In this way, they become much more dangerous. The demons make a fool of man and mislead him into seeking them everywhere except where they really are: right there within him. On the other hand, the most unwelcome of undertakings is looking into oneself. The fact that in Christianity the image of God is still projected and we do not search for it within ourselves has as its counterpart the fact that we have lost the knack of tracking down the demons within us and unmasking them. Whatever happened to the "Christ . . . in you" (Rom. 8:10)? Or what of the other passages in Paul that make it clear that he is not identifying himself with Him, but rather is referring to His spirit or His force within himself (1 Cor. 3:23; 2 Cor. 12:9)? As the image and likeness of God, with Christ within him, man is not only exalted, he is also charged with the responsibility of becoming aware of his thousand devils. For each one has his cross to bear and must suffer from the tension of opposites. This is the true, the archetypal suffering of humanity.

3

The Dissociability of the Personality

"If we take the hypothesis of the unconscious seriously," says Jung,

> it follows that our view of the world can be but a provisional one; for if we effect so radical an alteration in the subject of perception and cognition as this dual focus implies, the result must be a world view very different from any known before. This holds true only if the hypothesis of the unconscious holds true, which in turn can be verified only if unconscious contents can be changed into conscious ones—if, that is to say, the disturbances emanating from the unconscious, the effects of spontaneous manifestations, of dreams, fantasies, and complexes, can successfully be integrated into consciousness by the interpretative method.[1]

As practical psychology has adequately proven, there do exist, in addition to the conscious mind, unconscious contents that can, in principle, be incorporated into consciousness. Of course, consciousness must be properly prepared for this. Also the unconscious contents must exhibit a form that consciousness "understands." This is the task of psychological "interpretations." Though dreams do already exercise their own effect on consciousness, only interpretations of them can "translate" from the language of the unconscious into the language of consciousness. This of course presupposes that the language of the unconscious is different from that of consciousness. And in point of fact, the unconscious does express itself for the most part in symbols.

Fantasies and complexes also require adequate interpretation in order to become integratable. The conscious mind often rejects fantasies as nonsensical or meaningless, because it does not understand them. Only when fantasies are enriched with parallel material from our cultural history, that is, when they are amplified, does their meaning become accessible to the consciousness. The situation is even more difficult with complexes, which at first strike consciousness as totally alien. In order to integrate them, a considerable psychological effort, coupled with a definite expenditure of energy, is necessary. In the process, the conscious mind simultaneously changes and expands. Because of this required expenditure of energy and its fear of changing, consciousness often resists such a task.

Assuming that the unconscious psyche is a reality, what aspect of the psyche constitutes the ordinary subject of perception and knowledge? In the nineteenth century came the first elucidations of the nature of multiple personalities.[2] One of the first scientifically investigated cases was that of Mary Renold, who at the age of nineteen suddenly fell into a curious condition in which she was blind and deaf for several weeks and lost her memory. After five weeks, she awakened just as suddenly into her previous condition and had no idea what had happened to her in the interval. For fifteen years, she alternated between a normal condition, in which she was a quiet, sober, pensive person with a tendency toward depression, and a second condition, in which she was happy, fun-loving, extravagant, and gregarious and inclined toward mischief, practical jokes, and the composition of poetry. Her handwriting in the two conditions was markedly distinct. In each condition, she was aware of the other condition and afraid of falling back into it.

Another famous case was that of an eleven-year-old girl, Estelle, who was treated and described in detail by the elder Dr. Despine.[3] After being knocked down at the age of nine by another child of the same age, Estelle had complained of increasingly unbearable pains, which finally became crippling. Under hypnotic treatment, a condition of double personality appeared, whereby she was still crippled in her "normal" condition but could walk in the other, hypnotized, condition. In the "normal" state, she hardly ate at all; under hypnosis she ate abundantly—even snow. As a result of treatment, the "illness" subsided to such an extent that she was able to return home with her mother. Back home, her cure was applauded as a miracle. She was called *la petite resuscitée*, the little one who had been resuscitated again.

Even though such phenomena had already been looked into and described in the nineteenth century, a painstaking investigation of the biographical data of the subjects and the products of their unconscious was still lacking. Meanwhile, the occult movement of the early twentieth century also stirred up interest in the phenomena that today we call unconscious. In this context it is understandable that Jung's medical school dissertation dealt with occult phenomena.[4] In it, he described Fräulein S.W.,[5] whose personality was seemingly possessed by spirits during her somnambulistic attacks,* as they were called at that time. First it was the spirit of her grandfather, whom she had never known, and later other "spirits" also came. Among these was also the dead brother of one of the participants in the séances.

In somnambulistic states, Jung's medium adopted the name Ivenes and "changed" into a spirit among other spirits. During many of the séances, Ivenes undertook distant journeys with several spirits, not only in this world but also in the beyond, where numerous spirit worlds were supposed to exist. Jung portrays her somnambulistic personality as that of an adult,

---

Somnambulism (Lat. *somnus*, sleep; *amulare*, walk around), "sleepwalking." Afflicted persons exhibit behavior such as standing up, getting dressed, or performing definite tasks in a unique, sleeplike twilight state. The eyes are open and gaze fixedly forward, seeming to be looking into emptiness. Afterward, there is no recollection of these activities, even when intense dream experiences are reported.

small, black-haired woman of markedly Jewish type, wrapped in white robes with her head covered by a turban.[6] After waking up, the normal ego of Fräulein S.W. was without recollection of the mediumistic phenomena that fell within the realm of the alien personality. By contrast, she remembered clearly all phenomena that were directly connected with her own ego.

After the medium came across Justinus Kerner's book *Die Seherin von Prevorst* (The Seeress of Prevorst), a highly complicated system of previous incarnations appeared, no doubt evoked by Kerner's suggestion. Similar cases were reported from their practices by other psychiatrists. The well-known doctor Max Bircher-Benner published the story of a Zurich housewife named Ikara[7] who spontaneously recalled previous lives—for example, one in which she lived in a primitive hut in the midst of a savage tribe. Théodore Flournoy (1854–1920),[8] of whom Jung thought very highly, occupied himself for five years, starting in December 1894, with the young medium Catherine-Elise Müller, who recounted scenes from her previous lives. (These were published under the pseudonym Helen Smith.) In an initial cycle, she relived her supposed previous life as a fifteenth-century Indian princess. In the second cycle, she claimed to be the incarnation of Queen Marie Antoinette. Finally, in the "Mars cycle," she knew the inhabitants of Mars and their language and was familiar with the planet's landscape. Flournoy presented his results in his book *Des Indes à la planète Mars* (From India to the Planet Mars; 1900). He was able to point to the hidden sources of memory in the medium and to connect specific phases of her life with these cycles.* He analyzed the basis in her personality for her "romances." But he also emphasized the importance of subliminal fantasizing as an ongoing creative activity. He suggested that in all her various subpersonalities, the medium had maintained the fundamental unity of her personality.

---

*Here we may speak of *kryptomnesia* (Gr. *krypto*, "hidden, of unknown or hidden origin"; *mnesis*, "memory"): return of a forgotten memory which seems to be a genuine new impression (cf. CW 1 §180).

What is the relationship of the various personalities in a single subject to each other? They can appear sequentially or simultaneously.[9] They can be mutually aware of each other or not. It is also possible for only one of them to know of the others. Sometimes whole clusters of personalities are present, that is, more than two different fragmentary personalities. Jung showed in the case of Fräulein S.W. that her somnambulistic personality Ivenes embodied what she wished to be in twenty years, namely, a self-assured, influential, clever, gracious, and pious woman;[10] she regularly "dreamed herself into" this higher ideal state. Her various spirits corresponded to two basic types, the serious, religious type and the cheerful, uninhibited type.[11]

Such researches made clear that the unconscious is capable of feats that are impossible for the conscious mind. In particular, it is capable of calling forth memories that the conscious mind has forgotten. In the same way, it also has access to all subliminal perceptions that do not become conscious. Clairvoyant and telepathic phenomena can also occur.

These partly inexplicable and partly contradictory observations were placed on a firm footing by Jung's studies on word association.[12] In a word association test, a so-called evocative word is called out to the test subject, which he has to respond to immediately with the first word that occurs to him. The time required for the response is carefully measured. The initial objective of the test was to gain access to the chains of association involved in thinking. However, Jung soon realized that what was interesting in the tests was not the normal associations but the disruptions of them. Ziehen had already used the test in the same way before him and attributed prolonged reaction times to underlying "emotionally accentuated complexes of ideas" or just "complexes." Today the word *complex* has become a common term, but without it ever having become clear what it means. One widespread misunderstanding is that a complex is a pathological component of the psyche. Complexes are normal building

blocks of the psyche. The ego complex, for example, includes all mental representations that are associated with one's own person.

Jung pointed to and built on the work of his predecessors in this area. In particular, Pierre Janet's "subconscious fixed ideas," which represent unconscious contents that have splintered off, found their experimental confirmation in the concept of complexes. The notion of complexes also essentially clarified the dissociability of the psyche, as observed in the multiple personalities of Miss Beauchamps by Morton Prince.[13] The fragmentary personalities described are not immutable. They change with time, fall periodically into the background, or fuse with other fragmentary personalities. They show how the constituent elements of the psyche lead their own lives. "These fragments exist side by side relatively independently and can replace each other at any time, that is, each fragment possesses a rather high degree of autonomy," Jung continues in his account of the nature of complexes:

> My findings in regard to complexes corroborate this somewhat disquieting picture of the possibilities of psychic disintegration, for fundamentally there is no difference in principle between a fragmentary personality and a complex. They have all the essential features in common, until we come to the delicate question of fragmented consciousness. Personality fragments undoubtedly have their own consciousness, but whether such small psychic fragments as complexes are also capable of a consciousness of their own is a still unanswered question.[14]

That complexes move as a matter of course through our daily lives may be easily overlooked. They are fragments of the psyche that could not yet be brought into relationship with the ego complex or that the ego complex rejects. Following up the remarks cited above, Jung outlines, somewhat humorously, a phenomenology of complexes in everyday life:

> Complexes behave like Descartes' devils and seem to delight in playing impish tricks. They slip just the wrong word into one's

mouth, they make one forget the name of the person one is about to introduce, they cause a tickle in the throat just when the softest passage is being played on the piano at a concert, they make the tiptoeing latecomer trip over a chair with a resounding crash. They bid us congratulate the mourners at a burial instead of condoling with them,[15] they are the instigators of all those maddening things which F. T. Vischer attributed to the "mischievousness of the object." They are the actors in our dreams, whom we confront so powerlessly; they are the elfin beings so aptly characterized in Danish folklore by the story of the clergyman who tried to teach the Lord's prayer to two elves. They took the greatest pains to repeat the words after him correctly, but at the very first sentence they could not avoid saying: "Our Father, who art not in heaven." As one might expect on theoretical grounds, these impish complexes are unteachable.[16]

As this series of examples suggests, we encounter complexes in everyday life at every turn. They can manifest in all kinds of harmless or mischievous coincidences. No one is proof against them. The importance of complexes in our everyday life can hardly be exaggerated. But there are two widespread misunderstandings we should attempt to forestall at once. First, complexes "have" us more than we "have" them. That is, as a consequence of their autonomy, they prove stronger than the repressive tendencies of the conscious mind. Second, we do not create our complexes. Thus, having complexes is not a matter of guilt. It is meaningless to blame ourselves for them or blame them for ourselves. Prominent complexes that have been with us for a long time are easy to look upon with disdain when recognition and elimination of them is long overdue. On the other hand, there are deep-seated complexes that become guiding motifs for individuation and expansion of consciousness. The perpetuation of these could be very meaningful. Behind them is always to be found an archetypal problem.

"Today the hypothesis that complexes are *fragmentary psyches* that have become cut off from the whole can indeed be regarded as assured," Jung continues.

The aetiology of their origin is frequently a so-called trauma, an emotional shock or some such thing, that splits off a bit of the psyche. Certainly one of the commonest causes is a moral conflict, which ultimately derives from the apparent impossibility of affirming the whole of one's nature. This impossibility presupposes a direct split, no matter whether the conscious mind is aware of it or not. As a rule there is a marked unconsciousness of any complexes, and this naturally guarantees them all the more freedom of action.[17]

What does "unconsciousness" mean in this context? For example, I often only know that I have made a slip of the tongue afterward, when people around me point it out to me. And then I still do not know the cause of it. We call something unconscious when we do not know its cause. Of course the conscious mind is a master at conjuring up some rational basis for an unconscious action after the fact—so swiftly that the gap is seldom noticed by others. Everyone can somehow come up with a rationale for his actions when asked about them afterward. For the most part, these are more or less plausible constructs that have nothing to do with the real unconscious motivation. If we were to notice how rarely in our everyday lives we consciously weigh an action in advance and then come to a conscious decision, then we would see to what a frightening extent we act unconsciously. When is an action or an idea actually "conscious"? Posed in this way, this is a misleading question. For consciousness is a relative term,

> since its contents are conscious and unconscious at the same time, i.e., conscious under one aspect and unconscious under another. As is the way of paradoxes, this statement is not immediately comprehensible. We must, however, accustom ourselves to the thought that conscious and unconscious have no clear demarcations, the one beginning where the other leaves off. It is rather the case that the psyche is a conscious-unconscious whole.[18]

The unconscious is accordingly a different medium from the conscious. . . . Consequently there is a consciousness in which unconsciousness predominates, as well as a consciousness in which self-consciousness predominates. This paradox becomes immediately intelligible when we realize that there is no conscious content which can with absolute certainty be said to be totally conscious, for that would necessitate an unimaginable totality of consciousness, and that in turn would presuppose an equally unimaginable wholeness and perfection of the human mind. So we come to the paradoxical conclusion that there is no conscious content which is not in some other respect unconscious. Maybe, too, there is no unconscious psychism which is not at the same time conscious.[19]

Particularly for the psychology of complexes, this insight is extraordinarily important. The complexes owe their existence to an attitude of consciousness that is unable to accept their contents. Looked at in this way, the complexes are unconscious ideas. On the other hand, the phenomenon of splintering would suggest that consciousness has been at some time confronted by these ideas. Thus they could not be alien to it; at the least consciousness must have taken cognizance of their incompatibility with its prevailing attitude. Thus complex and consciousness stand in a relationship of complementarity toward each other. They complement each other mutually—and just as strongly ward each other off.

With these considerations in mind, the saints and their demons appear in a new light. The saints needed their demons in order to become saints, and the demons owed their existence to the one-sidedness of the saints. Was the struggle thus simply a case of tilting at windmills? Something that stands in antithesis to consciousness must, in order to become conscious, become distinct from the unconscious background. If those ascetics had lived like other people around them, they would not have become more conscious. Their one-sided, instinct-resisting life violated the natural man in them and artificially invoked all the demons they needed to prove themselves in their heroic struggle. In this artificially provoked struggle, they became conscious of the mode of functioning of their unconscious. Viewed teleologically, the utility of complexes for the process of consciousness expansion lies in their ability to disrupt a person's normal functioning. Undisturbed functioning is always unconscious. Thus animals fulfill nearly completely the purpose built into them by the Creator. As soon as the miracle of consciousness arises, the harmony of the first day of creation is impaired. From this the complexes—or demons—arise. As soon as consciousness appears, the harmony of the unconscious psyche is disturbed and complexes develop. These are an intermediate product, still partially bound to the unconscious and in dialectical confrontation with consciousness. In virtue of this chimerical nature of theirs, they are often depicted as strange hybrid beings.

But that is only one side. In Jung's work "On the Nature of the Psyche," which I have already cited a number of times, he comes to the conclusion that "the ego consciousness should be conceived of as surrounded by many little luminosities."[20]

Thus the unconscious is by no means simply dark like a moonless night sky, but like the night sky is strewn with countless stars. These multiple luminosities rest on the consciousness-like state of unconscious contents; but not just any contents, but rather archetypal ones. In other words, the archetypes are the real sources, or better, light-seeds (Khunrath) or light-germs (Mani) of consciousness expansion. They represent, so to speak, the excited state of an unconscious content, which is seeking to cross over into consciousness. The complexes are an intermediate form; acting as a go-between, they convey these contents out of the unconscious into consciousness. Thus complexes always have to do with consciousness expansion, but at the same time reflect the antithetical quality of consciousness and the unconscious. They are thus an eternal cross for humanity—but also the *conditio sine qua non* of any expansion of consciousness.

4

The World of Spirits

What is the "Holy Spirit?" Even among believers, very few people know what to make of this principle. It is too remote, too abstract, too unapproachable.

Indeed, we have a hard time trying to define the notion of spirit altogether. In his work on spirits in fairy tales,[1] Jung chose to investigate linguistic usage concerning spirits rather than to begin with some narrowing definition. Since in fact spirit is something that transcends consciousness, consciousness can, in any case, never completely grasp it.

The concept of spirit is a very broad one, corresponding to a variety of manifestations. It includes anything from the animating principle in human beings to paranormal apparitions (about which I will say more in chapter 13). Spirit is always connected with a dynamic quality, as its linguistic affinity with wind (*pneuma*) might suggest. Such a wind might be the one at the beginning of the Chemical Marriage of Christian Rosencreutz,[2] or the wind of the alchemistic parable[3] that drives the hero on to new adventures; or it could be the new spirit that poured forth as a rushing wind on Pentecost and made the old house shake (Acts 2:2). Wherever something is set in motion, spirit is the driving force. Thus it is an inalienable part of human life, which keeps it from becoming rigid. Analytical psychology sees in spirits the dynamic aspect of complexes. Hieronymus Bosch found images for the dynamism of the spirit: In his triptych *The Hay Wagon* (Prado, Madrid), complexes, in the form of demons, are the force propelling the wagon.

As fragmentary personalities, complexes have not only a form but also a certain charge of psychic energy (libido), which can sometimes be greater than that available to consciousness. Because complexes are autonomous, out of this charge an independent dynamics of spirits develops. Since spirits are no more subject to the control of consciousness than complexes are, they are experienced as alien and objective. The discussion as to whether spirits exist in and of themselves independently of people is an idle one, inasmuch as spirits always appear as something outside of us. On the other hand, we also have the notion, found through all the cultures of the world, of a personal spirit inherent in man. This spirit is never identified with the conscious personality, although there is a connection between the two. The objectivity of the spirit makes it possible for man to step out of the limitedness of his consciousness and enter, in ecstasy, into unbounded states. Of course he remains the same human person, but a spirit has taken over his ordinary consciousness. He is *possessed*.

The concept of possession in Western culture has almost an entirely negative connotation. We are so identified with our conscious minds that to lose touch with this conscious role seems tantamount to catastrophe. Clinical tests compared the reactions of white Americans to the ingestion of peyote (mescalin) with those of American Indians who were accustomed to the drug.[4] The whites exhibited extreme mood changes, restless depression, fear, and euphoria. By contrast, the Indians reacted with relative stability of mood, followed by religious ecstasy and fear, with a tendency toward feelings of religious awe. With the whites, social inhibitions dissolved; they exhibited immodest sexual behavior or aggression. The Indians, on the other hand, remained socially adjusted. The white Americans complained of feelings of alienation from reality, depersonalization, personality fragmentation, and meaninglessness. The Indians, by contrast, enjoyed a feeling of encountering something new and meaningful, a higher order of reality. The white Americans drew no benefit from the experience and underwent no enduring changes. The Indians, on the other hand, experienced therapeutic benefits—chronic fear was reduced, feelings of self-esteem increased, and social contacts were experienced as more satisfying.

We may conclude that stepping out of the customary realm of consciousness requires first, a religious attitude and, second, a suitable outlook toward new experience. Members of Western cultures have a hard time fulfilling these two conditions. In their case, forces are clearly unleashed that their conscious minds have hitherto strenuously repressed for the sake of social adjustment. Of course, such exceptional states as drug experiences cannot produce long-term changes in the personality. Thus Jung deliberately avoided using psychedelic drugs in therapy.[5] In any case, it remains questionable whether they actually expand consciousness; rather it seems that they remove barriers—the natural defenses of the ego against the unconscious. If consciousness is disabled, contents breaking through from the unconscious cannot be assimilated by it. This "organic psychosis" cannot fundamentally change the personality. Consciousness can only expand and develop lastingly when it takes a morally responsible position toward the contents coming in from the unconscious and makes an effort to assimilate them. For the conscious mind, this means nothing less than bringing together two disparate ways of seeing the world: the conscious and rational one and the entirely different one in which the laws of the collective unconscious hold sway. In order to do this, it must be able to relativize both outlooks. Otherwise, the traditional consciousness might well be flooded by the contents of the unconscious with serious risk of psychosis. Psychiatrists see how rare it is for a schizophrenic collapse of the personality really to improve. At the best, it tends toward what Jung called regressive restoration of the persona.

In order, in the pages that follow, to investigate the significance of spirits and of possession by spirits, we must set aside our, as it were, Western approach to consciousness. Among primitive tribes, consciousness is not yet so radically separated from the unconscious. For members of these tribes, possession by a spirit means a state of trance. For them, this is a divine and excellent state, certainly not a pathological one. In these states, feats are possible that are normally out of the question. Such a state has cultural significance not only for the individual involved, but even more for the community as a whole.[6] The medium brings to the community the messages of the spirit that has possessed him. He or she is a mediator between the spirit world and the human world. Sometimes a translator is necessary to make these messages understandable in everyday language. The phenomenon is quite complex and varies with the cultural context. Women seem to be more apt than men at becoming the host of a spirit. Possession is heralded by nonspecific general symptoms of varying duration, such as inexplicable loss of well-being, accidents, frequent illnesses without an assignable cause, and sometimes also dreams.

Then the spirit abruptly chooses its instrument—and possesses it. The possessed person falls into a state of dissociation, which can last several hours. In the first short period, the person is dazed and inaccessible; in the next, he or she is seized by excitement, which may lead to dancing, singing, hopping, jumping, making faces, and speaking oracles. The initial states of trance can be wordless. Then, in communicating, the spirit declares its name, where it came from, and what kind of being it is, which is important for the listeners and their reaction. In this way they can tell which spirit they are dealing with. Their traditional view tells them what attitude they should take toward this particular spirit and how it fits into their world.

Among the Tonga of Zambia, ghosts arise from the forgotten and neglected local dead and take possession of people. Other spirits are under the control of a sorcerer.[7] Sudden grave illnesses are said to be their work. The shades or ancestral spirits (*mimizu*) do not possess living persons, but they can bring illness and misfortune on their relatives in order to make the latter remember them (see chapter 9). *Masabe* is a word that is used both for spirits and for the dance in which they are conjured. The *masabe* seek a host through whom they can express their wishes and their real nature, for often they represent the quintessence of a new experience.

Possession can arise spontaneously. This happened to a Tonga woman when, in 1954, the first airplane flew over her village. The village women fled from this incomprehensible menace into the bush, out of which they returned when the supposed danger was over. Only one woman had to be brought out. The "airplane spirit" had seized possession of her. After a little while, she began a dance that this spirit had taught her. The dance soon began to spread. Others began to dream of airplanes, which was considered a sign that they, too, were possessed by the airplane spirit. A complete cure was the sign that the airplane spirit had wanted to express himself through the patient, and that the latter had now learned to work with the spirit.

This example seems to me to make the psychological process underlying it clear. The plane was an entirely new, unknown, and therefore threatening, experience for the Tonga. This one woman was not able to integrate the emotion connected with it in a straightforward manner. She was possessed by it. The dreams and visions that arose while she was in this condition instructed the possessed woman what dance she had to perform in order to throw off the possession. This shows the self-healing quality of the Self, which manifests itself in the products of the unconscious. The emotion that had disturbed the psychological balance found an opportunity for expression in the excitement of the dance. Through this, the new experience could be incorporated into consciousness and the woman was able to find her equilibrium again.

The social aspect of possession is illuminated by a case investigated by S. G. Lee. A married woman of about thirty, who had become a seeress eighteen months previous, recounted the following.

> I had been sick for over six months. I chiefly suffered from pains in the sides. They said the spirits of my ancestors were angry

about some unbecoming behavior that was taking place at my
home, so that they were stabbing me (sharp pains in the sides). A
goat was killed to propitiate them. This had no effect. A young
ox was killed. I thought I was recovering after this. I could even
sit up by myself. I could walk with the help of a stick. Two weeks
later it came back on me again, now worse than before. I was
already a bag of bones. I had a very deep sleep after going several
nights without. I dreamed that I saw my grandfather and great-
grandfathers. I felt afraid and bowed myself down. My grandfather called me and told me: "We are your ancestors. We have
long tried to make your people understand (by illnesses) that we
want you to be our house—to speak for us. We have decided to
come ourselves as we see you in danger of death. Wake up! Dress!
Go out quietly, and as soon as you are outside the homestead,
run fast before your absence is discovered. We shall then guide
you where we want you to go." I woke up. It was a dream. Yet to
my surprise, I felt my bones strong. I felt I could walk, bag of
bones as I was. I dressed quickly and slipped out of the hut. . . .
I came to a big homestead. I felt something like a voice saying:
"Go there!" I went into one of the huts—a very big one. In it I
found a number of seeresses (*izangoma*) sitting. . . . I went straight
to the chief-woman of the seeresses. . . . She simply looked at me
without saying a single word. Without asking me any questions,
she jumped up, howled, and began to dance. After this, she burnt
some medicine on burning embers and made me smell it. It made
me dizzy and I felt a shiver go through my body and my heart
became painful. Then I began to cry. I cried and cried until, after
a time I was ordered to follow immediately. We went with the
chief-woman into a nearby canal. There I was given some emetic.
We then returned home. Every morning this was done until one
night the spirits of my ancestors came to me and told me to rest
assured that they were with me. . . . After a short time I felt that
I could "smell things out." At meetings of the seeresses people
hid things here and there. I could now follow the thing until I
pulled it out from where it was hidden. [8]

Later in her home village she was initiated as a seeress. In her
case, the vocation came through the ancestors. The land of the

ancestors or the dead is the unconscious. Access to the unconscious comes via possession. Among the properties of the collective unconscious is precognition (see chapter 14). As a seeress, she serves her community.

In many cultures, healers work while in a trance. Lay people from Brazil recounted their experiences of being initiated by the spirit of a certain "Dr. Fritz," who used them as the instrument in effecting extraordinary cures.[9] It seems that trances open the way to capabilities of the unconscious that are inaccessible to the ordinary personality. In investigating such phenomena, one should not be misled by the idea that the host remains the same when this happens. Also, it makes no difference whether or not Dr. Fritz ever existed. The only thing that matters is the effect emanating from the spirit. In many cultures, for example among the Mayotte,[10] it is taken for granted that the same physical person sometimes may be an ordinary person, but when in trance may be the host of a spirit. The idea seems to be that during a trance, the ordinary personality of the host is absent. Such an idea could also help explain the phenomenon of the berserkers, who went raging into battle possessed by the god Wotan, while their bodies lay at home as though sleeping.[11] Here the difference between the two states is so radical that we must speak of a *double*. That is why there is often retrograde amnesia* in relation to the events of a trance and why mediums in a trance speak of their ordinary personality in the third person. In fact the two know nothing of each other.

We can learn much from primitive peoples about the positive function of possession. In this extraordinary ecstatic state in which the ordinary consciousness is more or less disabled, even paranormal feats, which are often used for the welfare of the community, become possible. (Genuine séances with mediums approach this quite closely.) Ecstatic states have always been considered an exceptional religious condition and play a major

---

*Amnesia is a partial or total, temporary or lasting loss of memory. Retrograde amnesia covers the period *before* the event that triggers it.

role in many religions throughout the world. The oracles of the Pythia in Delphi or the soothsaying Germanic seeresses should be seen in this light. The maenads in the retinue of Dionysos were filled with the god, which does not necessarily mean that they were drunk. A long thread connects the Roman Saturnalia and the Carnival festival in German-speaking countries, which was celebrated in the church until the eleventh century. It is obviously of importance for our psychological equilibrium to be able to step out of the everyday ego into a greater world. The techniques for reaching such a state are many and varied—from chemical drugs to monotonous rhythms. In every case, there is an *abaissement du niveau mental*, a lowering of the mental level, which makes it easier for unconscious contents to cross over. Christianity has kept such techniques and tendencies at bay. It banned them from the churches like ball playing and other games. But basically, every emotion leads to an *abaissement du niveau mental* and thus allows a breakthrough from the unconscious. Whether this breakthrough has a beneficial or disastrous effect depends on the cultural setting in which it takes place.

Once a young woman came to me who had taken part in the Basel Carnival and became fascinated by the piccolo player in a small band. He had cast such a spell on her that she had to follow him all through the night, like the children after the Pied Piper, even long after he had left his band and was walking by himself through the lonely streets of the old city playing his piccolo. He was wearing a *commedia del'arte* costume and his face was painted white. As morning approached, he suddenly eluded her. She could no longer find him no matter how hard she looked. This experience made such an impression on her that she thought perhaps she was beginning to have some kind of breakdown. Thus she decided to put herself in the hands of a psychiatrist.

What had happened? An ancient custom had taken hold of her, one whose religious background she was no longer aware of. Through its long tradition, the Basel Carnival has maintained its original authenticity. By dressing up, the piccolo player showed himself as a god who, like Orpheus, cast an enchantment over everything with his music. Even in the course of the days that followed, my patient could not shake off her fascination with him. Something in her had fallen under his spell.

Don't young people of today, in order to get away from the everyday humdrum, work up a similar intoxication by listening to pop music with its exaggerated volume and hard-driving beat? The alcoholic basically becomes the victim of a similar fascination with a state alien to the ego, even if he does not understand his addiction in terms of having fallen under the spell of a god. Otherwise he would have to develop a religious attitude toward it. Many alcoholics have assured me that they don't like alcohol at all. They are just using it as a means to reach, as fast as possible, the desired state in which ordinary consciousness is more or less disabled. Since, however, they do not seek out this state, as did the followers of the bacchantic religion, with a religious purpose, but rather as an escape from reality or a cheap spiritual substitute, the results are for the most part negative.

In chapter 7, we shall look into possession by the demons Animus and Anima; here I should like only to point out that the problem of animus and anima in the relationship between man and woman would lose a great deal of its explosiveness if more emotions could be abreacted in an ecstatic manner. But instead, we conduct ourselves "reasonably," and as a result the dammed-up negative emotions of anger, irritation, hate, and grief transform into destructiveness. We ponder our revenge and fail to notice that we have lost touch with our common sense. Possession is an everyday event—one in which there is a shift in the balance between consciousness and the unconscious. This shift can range from a slight *abaissement* accompanied by a slight overbalance of the unconscious to the total extinction of consciousness characteristic of the trance. In the consciousness of primitive peoples, short-lived, easily curable possessions are frequently observed, as, for example, among the Bushmen of the Kalahari.[12] Our culture wrongly limits possession to specific demonic cases and speaks in milder cases of obsession. Exorcism, meant to treat these cases, involves an interaction between the possessing unconscious content and the exorcist, who tries through his methods—prayer, chanting—to cast it out.

A man of middle age once came to my office who for many years had worked as the reliable executive officer of his company. One night, using his key, he entered the company offices and methodically wrecked everything there. When the first workers arrived around five in the morning, they saw him leaving the offices. He went home to his wife and lay down to sleep. That is how the police found him. At the hearing, he could only confess his deed; about his motive he knew nothing. This was the reason he came to me. He was terrified that he was capable of such a deed without knowing what drove him to it. His motives were so buried that even a thorough investigation brought nothing to light. Psychiatrists speak in such cases of an "oriented twilight state," which explains nothing. This concept merely indicates that consciousness was to a great extent disabled but that nevertheless a goal-oriented series of actions was possible. The man only remembered that it gave him unutterable satisfaction to destroy everything in the office and that he contentedly left off this hard work only when he was disturbed by the first arriving workers. This satisfaction was connected with the emotion that was possessing him: he had to blindly act it out.

"What got into him?" we occasionally ask. Doesn't this expression show that mild cases of possession are an everyday matter? In fact sometimes little, heedlessly made remarks are enough to "infect" us, even when we consciously defend ourselves against them. All that needs to happen is for one of our complexes to be touched upon by such a remark and immediately the arrow is firmly planted.

For the archaic mentality, the world was still filled with spirits. The archaic mentality was never in danger of identifying with any of them. Our enlightened approach, by contrast, is no longer able to perceive the spirits as distinct. We are so identified with our rationality that we dismiss everything irrational as nonexistent. Thus the irrational side is relegated to the unconscious. This can lead to a neurotic splintering of the personality—or to a demonification of the unconscious.

Such demonification of the unconscious seems to me to be a symptom of our times. It manifests in particular schools of modern painting such as surrealism, as well as in modern horror and so-called "fantasy" literature. It deprives the unconscious of its functions of a healthy compensator and spiritual guide. The more one-sidedly the ego identifies with consciousness as the whole of the psyche, the stranger the unconscious becomes. This can go as far as outright polarization, which is accentuated further by the Christian tendency to identify with goodness and light. The unconscious, then, instead of seeking the middle ground in a balanced fashion, becomes only the personal and collective shadow. If we could understand that this reaction on the part of the unconscious is only an effort to heal us of our one-sidedness, we would have a chance. The more we take the part of our light side, however, the more the dark one threatens to swallow us up unawares. For in denying the dark half, we run the risk of unknowingly being possessed by it.

That is the psychological reason why the dark side is on the increase in our civilized world, though we expend so much effort on the light one. But we are in error if we think that goodness must increase if we put conscious effort into it. So long as we do not develop our consciousness of the darkness in us in the same proportions, that darkness will nullify our best efforts. Development of consciousness means discrimination, making distinctions. Before we can integrate something unconscious, we must distinguish ourselves from it. In that way we ward off the danger of being possessed by it. Only then can we begin to work with it as the other in us and attempt to develop a relationship with it.

Possession by the unconscious can be prevented by means of a religious attitude. I am always amazed how little tolerance and understanding modern people have for such a statement. A religious attitude means careful consideration for the other, the alien, the unfamiliar, the unexpected, and the antithetical so as to be able to relate to it with the proper respect. Such an attitude does not deny the antithetical quality of anything, but also does not let itself be possessed by it, because it distinguishes itself from it.

In his essay "Spirit and Life,"[13] Jung calls our attention to the origin of the word *Geist*, "spirit." In its basic meaning, it has something to do with affects; in this sense the spirit is a representation of the personified affect. "Every affect has the tendency to become an autonomous complex"[14]—something that is clearly reflected in our figures of speech. As we know, an affect goes hand in hand with an *abaissement du niveau mental*. It is easy for the affect to take possession of consciousness. "We were beside ourselves with anger" is an expression that means that we were no longer ourselves. Something else took hold of us or even, for that matter, possessed us; something entered into us or came over us. Attitudes and mental dispositions trigger affects. Often these are derived from a model. This model is often unconscious, which strengthens its effectiveness. Mostly, it is our parents, living or dead, who work on us this way, either from the outside or the inside. We might say "he acts in the spirit of his father" or in the "spirit of his mother." Here their "spirit" represents their entire behavior and approach to things, and it continues to live on in their offspring. The less the latter are aware of this, the more vividly it shows itself—in times of fear, with manifest clarity. A spirit or attitude of this type can dominate a whole family for better or for worse. We might say "a good/bad spirit reigns in that family" or "the father/mother is the good/bad spirit of that family." Such a person, even after death, will be a source of positive or negative affects. In this way the living person becomes a spirit of the dead, one who helps—or persecutes.

Great personalities have an influence that reaches beyond the family sphere. They represent a particular mental attitude or disposition that can make them a guiding light for many people or even for an entire epoch. They stand for a certain guiding idea that shapes lives. Such a guiding idea can be anything from a proverb-like slogan to a whole philosophy. In any case, it is only effective as an idea if it can call forth an emotional reaction. Otherwise, it remains no more than a colorless opinion. The living idea, on the other hand, possesses the power to shape situations and lives.

As we know, a proverb is an abstraction of countless experiences. In it manifests, as it were, an age-old personality in us that is the sum of countless lifetimes. In products of the unconscious, this kind of personality is symbolized through the figure of the Wise Old Man. This figure represents the spirit in symbolic form. It might be connected with an insight, a helpful idea, inner composure, critical judgment, fundamental reflection, or even instinctive knowledge.

What is the unconscious foundation of the living idea? The religions provide us with veritable treasure troves of them. As research in comparative religion has shown, these living ideas always group themselves according to the same basic patterns. Jung called these patterns "archetypal ideas." Great personalities seem to be able to draw on the archetypal foundations of mankind. Most of them have conveyed new knowledge to man in the age-old, eternal, true archetypal form. Thus they represented not only a historical uniqueness and particularity but also a living spirit that can continue to work on and touch us through the centuries.

Of course the living idea is by no means dependent on having a historic and outstanding personality to formulate it. Such ideas exhibit their own independent dynamics and might emerge anonymously anywhere. In our intellectual history, there has always been an ebb and flow of ideas that shape entire periods without our being able to trace their origin. Here we encounter the much talked-of Zeitgeist, the "spirit of the times," an unconscious current that can determine the cast of mind of an entire civilization or epoch. And here we touch upon the introverted or inward side of intellectual and universal history, a side of history that has yet to be written. Our extraverted attitude has hitherto made every possible external factor—war, famine, plague, poverty—responsible for the movement of history. That is understandable, because the underground roots of historical movement are much harder to point to. Sometimes there is "something in the air," and only a small push is needed to trigger incalculable effects. The spirit as wind is an unrecognized element that prepares itself invisibly over long periods of time only to erupt suddenly with unexpected force. It is as though a large-scale synchronization takes place unseen within the collective unconscious, so that finally the slightest gesture will set it into coordinated motion.

The spirit as living idea or zeitgeist exhibits, like our point of departure the complex, a very strong tendency toward autonomy. In times of change, there is never any lack of prophets, founders of religions, and world-improvers. The effect of a Jesus of Nazareth could be understood in the sense that he was able to express a new creative content that already lay prepared and waiting. The spirit, inasmuch as it is a new, innovative spirit, draws on still unplumbed psychic potential. In analytical psychology those psychic potentialities that, within the unconscious, free themselves from its pervasive continuity and approach the threshold of consciousness are termed *constellated contents*. In chapter 6, we will look into what constitutes a *creative complex*. Here, I would like to anticipate myself slightly and point to the function of such a complex in the collective, in the human community, where it can transform contents constellated as spirit into a new spiritual movement. In doing this, the spirit is capable of effecting evil as well as good, and the new spirit is not necessarily better than the old.

What all these manifestations of the spirit have in common is that they strive mightily to take possession of an individual, whether for that individual's benefit or misfortune. The spirit is like a powerful earthquake that we cannot escape—even though it is perhaps only in retrospect that we learn to what extent we have been shaped by it.

Possession, in all its varied degrees and forms, is part of the phenomenon that we call spirit. The emotion that is connected with the spirit weakens consciousness which allows the affect to take root. We are then ridden by our emotions. Emotions are also responsible for our being possessed by ideas. As a rule, an emotion will subside after a short time. But ideas make sure that in the process of adjusting to the world around us, new emotions continuously come up. It depends on the nature of the ideas whether the emotions turn out to be sources of good or ill.

Mens sana in corpore sano ("A healthy mind in a healthy body"), we were taught as young Latin students. And in fact today we are very concerned with keeping the body fit and healthy, because we know how much depends on it. Are we doing as much so that a healthy spirit can take its place there? The spirit is essentially a phenomenon of the unconscious. We cannot consciously choose it: it chooses us. But we can cultivate it, test it, foster or reject it—presuming, of course, that we notice at all that a spirit is moving us. We must conclude its nature from its effects, because it is not directly accessible to our mind.

That we are driven hither and thither by various spirits is a fact that cannot be denied. And it is not up to our consciousness to decide which one we accept. We can, however, gradually become conscious of the various spirits so that we man integrate them into the economy of the overarching whole. Of course the conscious will is very feeble in comparison with its spirits. So if we do not want the same thing to happen to us that happened to the sorcerer's apprentice in Goethe's poem, we are in need of a prudent and morally responsible consciousness, and even more, of introspection.

Cases of possession have the unpleasant property that we cannot be directly conscious of them, because they involve unconscious identification with a content. The separating out of contents is the key to the development and expansion of consciousness. In the unconscious state, we find ourselves still in an all-pervasive continuity. The more conscious we become, the smaller that which we refer to as our ego becomes. In its place grows the Self. In the unconscious state, we are still embedded to a great degree in a nondifferentiated connectedness with our surroundings and our fellow men. Through the torment of disappointed expectations, our bloated ego withers. To the extent that it does, it is able to withdraw from the spirit influences of this embeddedness and find itself.

In the group, possession plays possibly even a greater role than in the case of the individual. In the collective mass, cohesion arises through a common unconsciousness—a common spirit. Everything depends on the makeup of this spirit. As part of the mass, one can elude this spirit only with great difficulty. It can lead men to wholesome fulfillment in the community experience or lead them into the abyss. Men become manipulable in the mass, because they are vulnerable to spiritual infection. Only progress in individuation protects us against such infection; conscious critique is only effective to a limited degree. This is because we are dealing with ideas with an archetypal basis, which no one can escape and which do not reach the level of the conscious will. Only on the path of individuation can we find effective protection from possession of every kind—and develop a wholesome spirit.

5

The World of Shamans and Medicine Men

A content from the unconscious can, as a creative complex, initially appear as a disturbance in consciousness. In a case where consciousness is able to assimilate and integrate this foreign body, it removes its disturbing and harmful effect—and consciousness expands. On the other hand, if consciousness is unable to bridge the gap to the complex and incorporate the new content in a meaningful way, then the complex transforms into a pathological complex.

Knud Rasmussen encountered examples of these types of psychological events on his fifth Thule expedition (1921–1924). In the region of King William's Land, he met a young Netsilik Eskimo by the name of Arnaqoaq who had had spirit visions and had become a shaman. This young man had never in his life held paper and pencil in his hand, but Rasmussen asked him to draw his story. For hours Arnaquaq sat with his eyes closed and let the strange experiences arise in him so that they would take a visible form. "From time to time, the relived experiences had so strong an effect on his imagination that his whole body began to shudder and he had to stop drawing."[1] Unique representations of his spontaneous, unconventionalized spirit visions and the way he worked with them arose. Most of the visions of shamans known in ethnological literature have remained within the framework of tribal tradition. The reason for this is that visions are

sought after and then recounted to an older, experienced shaman.[2] The experienced shaman gives them a traditional interpretation, which tends to discard any unique features as insignifi-
cant. The sparse commentary accompanying Arnaqoaq's
drawings indicates that most of the "spirits" attacked him with
hostile intention. The evil spirits in Figure 1[3] came upon him one
night as he was sleeping outdoors under the shelter of a rock.
They wanted to devour him. His dogs managed to keep them at
bay.

These spirits were two restless souls. The big one, called
Listener, has a big maw with two teeth and the tongue hanging
out, and a malformed hand with six fingers. It is shown running.
The other, Long Ear, has two mouths and three legs.

The representation shows demons as distorted figures, most of
whose features are exaggeratedly developed. They lack harmony,
for as restless souls, no harmonious, balanced development was
possible for them. They have not reached their natural objective,

FIGURE I

were unable to realize themselves; and therefore wander about, their existence unresolved. They are looking for a living being in order to harm him, but more fundamentally, to find completion. Since a complex is only conditionally linked to a particular person, it can happen that it begins to look for a "new house." It is said that shamans are able to capture souls in passage. The soul, in accordance with its symbols of bird and butterfly, is in any case something that can easily separate itself from a given individual. These two restless souls are distinguished by an exaggerated sense of hearing, which perhaps points to a special receptivity for voices from the beyond (the unconscious). Listener's mouth and hands show clear features of a devourer—an aspect of the unconscious that we encountered earlier on.

While wandering in the mountains in the summertime, Arnaqoaq met the terrifying sorceress Manilaq ("compressed ice"), depicted in Figure 2.[4] At the upper right, the artist has shown how he fainted with fright and regained consciousness only when

FIGURE 2

his dog licked his navel. This shows how vividly real such apparitions are for those who encounter them. We know too little of the other details of the drawing. The sorceress became Arnaqoaq's helping spirit (*paredros*), who would mediate between him and the Mother of Sea Creatures and provide him with a catch. Notions of a spirit ally who helps with hunting are also to be found among other primal North American peoples, as for example among the Naskapi.[5] The Lord of the Animals appears to the hunter and lets him know where game will be made available for him to shoot. The hunter who has a relationship with such powers will be successful. If, however, he should offend those powers, his luck in hunting will leave him.

Wandering in the mountains another time, Arnaqoaq saw an extremely powerful spirit (Fig. 3).[6] It was mute and so strange that Arnaqoaq ran away from it, without taking it as a helping spirit. In fairy tales, too, sometimes the right thing to do when addressed by a demon is to keep quiet, and sometimes it is better

FIGURE 3

to answer—depending on how strong consciousness is. If it is too weak, it runs the risk of being overpowered by the demon instead of being able to assimilate it and work with it. For the latter possibility there must be a subject with its own viewpoint. Not for nothing do sagas and fairy tales advise us to make the sign of the cross or take other similar measures in order to ward off a demon. The figure in Figure 3 is a typical vision of solitude. It symbolizes the unconscious and follows the solitary wanderer as a shadow (*synopados*).

A similar event took place once when Arnaqoaq was seal hunting.[7] A spirit with immense teeth suddenly leapt up out of the space between ice and water (*wake*), the place where seals come up to breathe (Fig. 4). This monster was as big as a bear, but had long legs with lumps at the joints and two tails. In a fold of the skin, there seemed to be a large ear. Its teeth were as huge as walrus tusks. The giant spirit let out a mighty roar, and the

FIGURE 4

62

Eskimo became so afraid that he ran home without taking it as a helping spirit.

This spirit out of the depths of the sea is even more weird than the previous one. The hairs covering the whole body do not give the impression of a warm pelt, but look more like spines. The menacing mouth with its powerful tusks shows how dangerous it is. The Eskimo did not feel himself up to dealing with it, so he ran away. The drawing, in which Arnaqoaq sought to portray his fear, anticipates in a simple way the function of painting and drawing in psychotherapy. In therapy, drawing and painting make it possible to provide the irrational, the fearsome, and the incomprehensible with a form. At first an emotion is usually expressed by which consciousness is fascinated, obsessed, or paralyzed. If, through painting or drawing, consciousness can free itself from this crippling effect by "objectifying" the emotion, then it can begin to work with it. Arnaqoaq's drawings are like those of children, who also spontaneously use drawing to get a hold on something that is bothering them. Their productions are often moving in their immediacy and expressiveness. Here we hit upon the origin of every representation of a demon, however, grotesque or masterly it may be: the demon's being is captured thereby. For the primitive (this characterization is never meant pejoratively) mentality of aboriginals and children, what is represented in these depictions is alive and present.

Shortly after the death of Arnaqoaq's parents, the melancholy helping spirit Giant Eye (Fig. 5) appeared to him.[8] The spirit consoled him thus: "You don't have to be afraid of me. I also have to struggle with sad thoughts; therefore I will follow you and be your helping spirit." As the drawing shows, the spirit has an abundance of shaggy hair sticking straight up on end. Each eye is divided in two. The large mouth is set vertically in his face; in it are one long tooth on top and two shorter ones on the sides.

Grief following the death of one's parents is a natural reaction. However, sometimes hidden behind it is a parent complex, which prevents the grief from ebbing after a time. If this happens, the

FIGURE 5

dead parent transforms into an obsessive demon. For that reason, it is important to take on sorrow and to work with it—so that one can free oneself from the spirit of the deceased. The spirit Giant Eye represents Arnaqoaq's sorrow over his parents. Since the Eskimo was not afraid of it, it became a helping spirit who helped him to find people who had broken tabu. Such people disrupt the social order, enabling demons to intrude and cause harm. When accident or illness strikes, it is to be suspected that there has been a violation of tabu.[9] Then the shaman or spirit conjurer tracks down those who have committed the breach. Tabu violation is what today we call sin. In primitive societies, a sin is not a merely personal trespass, but one that affects the entire tribe. The breach disrupts the society's order and thus weakens it. In this way, the door is opened to all manner of unwholesomeness. It is the shaman's task to ward off this unpleasant eventuality. In this, he has the support of his helping spirit. When Arnaqoaq got over the death of his parents, they exercised a supportive influence on his life from the beyond. This example shows that a complex that has been overcome not only can be integrated, but can go on to have a fruitful effect on our lives.

Once when Arnaqoaq caught a salmon, the Spirit with Many Holes[10] shot out of the depths of the sea (Fig. 6). "He wanted very much to serve a human being and be his helping spirit." This spirit's specialty was midwifery. The many holes in his body encourage children to come out of their mother's body. The figure in the circle is the Mother of Sea Creatures, the Great Mother who sits down below on the sea floor and ponders the destiny of humanity.

For shamans, there is nothing more difficult than to gain access to the Mother of Sea Creatures.[11] Occasionally, it happens that the old lady is in a bad mood and angry at humanity. Then she sits in her house on the floor of the sea, turned away from the light and from her creatures, her hair hanging disheveled over her face and her eyes cast down. She bewails the sins of man and

FIGURE 6

the thoughtlessness of women in giving birth to children. A sorcerer must use all his arts to pacify her wrath. Only when she has calmed down again does she release all the sea creatures from her house, which means a big catch and a general state of plenty for mankind.

Demons by no means always come to men as enemies, but often also, as in this case, as helpful spirits. The Spirit with Many Holes, as an unseen helper in salmon fishing also occasionally symbolically fetches in nourishment for consciousness. If consciousness understands the content it has been brought and takes the proper approach to it, then it becomes helpful. Fairy tales are full of examples of such encounters. Through a firm consciousness, the shaman succeeds in integrating the demons and allying himself with them as helping spirits. In this way, he becomes the lord of the spirits—not with the help of a great feat of magic, but rather by relating to all the horrors of his psyche, which he experiences incarnated in spirit visions, and including them in his personality.

We cannot tell from Rassmussen's account how renowned Arnaqoaq was as a shaman. For us, he is important because of the spirit visions he knew how to depict so realistically. Discussion concerning the psychological state of shamans and medicine men has found a large place in our literature.[12] Their key feature seems to be that they are more "permeable" than ordinary people to experiences arising from the unconscious—for them a supernatural world—without being victimized by them. If they were unable to resist the unconscious, then they would have to be regarded as sick themselves and incapable of healing the sick. On the other hand, they also could not heal if they were not acquainted with the horrors of the spirit world from their own experience. This permeability to transcendent experiences explains many curious features of the shaman's personality. The psychiatrist and anthropologist Wolfgang J. Jilek sums up his experiences in the following words: "After years of personal and professional contact with traditional healers and shamans in

North America and other parts of the world (Africa, Haiti, South America, Thailand, and New Guinea), I consider this global pathology—the labeling of the shaman as pathological—to be absolutely untenable."[13]

The decisive point in the vocation of a shaman is a coincidental meeting with a semidivine being, with the soul of an ancestor, with an animal, or the occurrence of an unusual event (lightning, accident). The so-called supernatural world gives the final impetus to the vocation and final commitment of the shaman. The psychologist sees in this nothing supernatural, nothing that stands outside the laws of nature. For him, such phenomena are grounded in the nature of man, even when they are numinous in character. Everything that is accompanied by numinous feelings derives from the collective unconscious. The archetypal powers of the collective unconscious have the quality of destiny: they determine the course of individual lives. We are not as conscious as are primitive peoples that the profession of shaman, or in our case, doctor, is not so much a career as a vocation. A "spirit" takes possession of the shaman-to-be and determines the course of his life. Often the souls of great shamans who have died or the souls of the ancestors of shamans choose a successor to serve their tribe. Often the future shaman must die ritually so as to come in contact with the souls of the dead who will share their knowledge with him. To "see the spirits" in a dream or awake is the decisive sign of the vocation of the shaman, whether this happens spontaneously or is freely chosen," writes Mircea Eliade.[14] Such a vision temporarily confers magical power.[15] However, there is a difference here, depending on whether the recipient of this vision is a future shaman or an ordinary person. The shaman-to-be seeks such a vision not for himself but rather for the sake of the general welfare—so that the tribe can live and so that life will be better for everyone. Vocation through contact with the collective unconscious has the effect that the shaman no longer belongs to himself alone, but rather belongs to the community or humanity as a whole.

The medicine man John Fire Lame Deer of the Lakota tribe of South Dakota tells of his initiation in an earthen pit on a mountain, where at the age of sixteen he went on a vision quest:

> Suddenly I felt an overwhelming presence. Down there with me in my cramped hole was a big bird. The pit was only as wide as myself, and I was a skinny boy, but that huge bird was flying around me as if he had the whole sky to himself. I could hear his cries. . . . Slowly I perceived that a voice was trying to tell me something. It was a bird cry, but I tell you, I began to understand some of it. . . . I heard a human voice too, strange and high-pitched, a voice which could not come from an ordinary, living being. All at once I was way up there with the birds. The hill with the vision pit was way above everything. I could look down even on the stars, and the moon was close to my left side. It seemed as though the earth and the stars were moving below me. A voice said, "You are sacrificing yourself here to be a medicine man. In time you will be one. You will teach other medicine men. We are the fowl people, the winged ones, the eagles and the owls. We are a nation and you shall be our brother. You will never kill or harm any one of us. You are going to understand us whenever you come to seek a vision here on this hill. You will learn about herbs and roots, and you will heal people. You will ask them for nothing in return. A man's life is short. Make yours a worthy one."[16]

The "winged ones" are supernatural beings, somewhat comparable to our angels. As spirits of the air, they introduce the aspiring shaman to his shamanhood and provide him with the knowledge he needs. They present an intuitive experience intensified to hallucinatory clarity—a gift indispensable for medicine man and doctor alike. If he follows these destiny-fraught powers, they will show him their helpful side. If he struggles against them, they will turn their demonic, destructive side to him. "A shaman," Eliade explains, "is a person who has a concrete, immediate relationship with the world of gods and spirits; he sees them face to face; he speaks with them, bids them, supplicates them—but he 'controls' only a limited number of them. Not every god or spirit invoked in a shamanic session is on that account already a 'familiar' or a 'helper' of the shaman's."[17]

The helping spirits (*spiritus familiares*) are at the shaman's side in his work, serving and helping him, especially during his journeys into the beyond. Shamans undertake the perilous journey into the beyond in order to bring back lost souls. (See chapter 6 for a consideration of illnesses triggered by loss of the soul.) The archaic journey to the beyond corresponds to the descent of the modern psychotherapist into the unconscious. For this, he needs as helpers the complexes integrated during his training analysis, so that he does not fall prey, along with his patient, to a common unconscious element (demon). (Frequently, analysands spontaneously appear who have the same problem that is occupying the analyst.) The archaic techniques of the shaman are of great interest for modern psychotherapy because they are its precursor. In contrast to modern psychotherapy, they rest on a foundation of thousands of years of experience.

Every integrated complex, as may well have become clear by now, expands the personality through new capabilities. These are the helping spirits, the capabilities, that come to the aid of the personality when it finds the right attitude toward them. Only in the rarest cases can the shaman coerce the spirits to conform to his purpose. As spirits, they maintain a certain autonomy. The psyche integrates a complex by including it in the framework of the personality in such a way that it is no longer antithetical to the personality—and not by somehow dissolving it. A complex could not anyway be "dissolved," because there is always an archetype behind it. Complexes are living elements of the psyche. Not only among medicine men but also among modern men, they represent a part of the personality. Integration consists in bringing the different parts into firm relationship with one another. Otherwise, dissociation results, in which the individual parts of the personality separate from each other, as we saw in chapter 3.

The shaman surrounded with helping spirits is the equivalent on an archaic level of a person who has integrated the various parts of his personality. Only such a person can exercise a healing effect. Only such a person can counteract the dissociative tendencies of the ailing—and restore their lost souls.

6

The Sorcerer's Arrows:
Primitive Conceptions of Illness

In evaluating the accomplishments of shamans or medicine men, we must not neglect to consider their understanding of illness. A number of researchers have reported that among aboriginals, occasionally our Western medicine has failed, while the apparent hocus-pocus of medicine men has proved effective. There are even cases known in which Western ethnologists administered their own medicaments to themselves to no avail but were successfully treated by native medicine men. On the other hand, we also have accounts, such as that of the ethnologist Koch-Grünberg, who was treated extensively by a medicine man with no effect. Does primitive medicine only work because it is ceremonially dramatic and suggestive? Many scientists are inclined to believe this.

In any case, its healing power is to a great extent based on the spiritual premises of a given culture. This is no doubt the reason that medicine men are for the most part, if not exclusively, successful with members of their own cultures. These spiritual premises constitute the archetypal foundation of the culture, its unconscious conceptions. These are the sacred images on whose basis a culture develops. When a religious ceremony or a medicine man's ritual draws on these images, it makes a connection with something very deep in man—the archetype of the healer or divine physician. Whenever this archetype is touched upon and constellated, healing takes place. An old proverb tells us: *Medicus curat, natura sanat* (The doctor cures, nature heals). It is no mere coincidence that the Christian savior is not only a doctor of the soul but also a miracle healer. With his miraculous cures, he proved that he was a "true physician" and healer.[1] At that time, body and spirit had not yet been broken up into two irreconcilable opposites as they are today. Physical illness was not yet separated from its psychological components; primitive medicine still treated body and soul as a unity. Moreover, the well-being of the soul was also intimately bound up with an unimpaired state of the body *(mens sana in corpore sano)*. Only our modern medicine has lost its connection with its religious origins and become a body of purely technical procedures.

Occasionally, the success of medicine men is attributed entirely to their psychological influence. But even today's technologically advanced medicine, including surgery, by no means works purely somatically in the sense of simply repairing physical defects. With its sorcery of hygienic purity and apparatus, it works no less psychologically than the medicine man does. Whether we like it or not, our "gods in white," despite their rational claims, treat and heal just as potently through irrational means. But in doing it, they can make a suitable impression only on patients who, by having the same cultural outlook, bring with them a certain understanding of this "magic."

At the same time, another part of the effect is a mystery. The more "rational" methods of treatment become, the less effective they get—because they do away with mystery. Modern Western medicine makes use of its technical capital to surround itself anew with that sense of mystery that is indispensable if any healing is to take place. In many processes of healing, this mystery is no more than mystery-mongering, intentional obfuscation. Fundamentally speaking, the true mystery in every cure is a kind of archetypal action. This type of action defies all attempts at rational explanation.

No secretiveness would be necessary if we were conscious of

this real mystery in every cure: it is the religious basis of the medical art. All primitive healing derives originally from a religious cultus. The best known examples of this are the ancient Greek schools of Kos and Epidauros. Today, most paramedical healing methods owe their success to religious components. It is idle to speculate as to how much more effective modern medicine would be if it had not lost touch with its religious roots. Associations of Christian physicians nowadays are attempting to reintroduce consideration of those roots. Of course this project is complicated by the fact that present-day patients—and the patient's spiritual outlook is just as important as the doctor's—have also lost touch with their Christian roots. The cultural outlook of doctor and patient must be in harmony.

It is also sometimes possible for the magic of a compelling religious experience to take hold of a totally unreligious person, especially when the leaping spark of the experience is part of a mass-psychological phenomenon. Herein we see the significance of religious communities and the basis of the power of public opinion. In the mass with its *abaissement du niveau mental,* a collective state of shared fervor (essentially a state of awe toward something regarded as more powerful) comes about much more easily. This is not a property of any one culture, but how it may be invoked is culture-dependent.

"Thy faith hath made thee whole," we read in Luke (8:48). What we understand by faith today is no longer the same thing as that which the Gospel writer was referring to. Did he not mean to indicate that the archetype of the healer in the patient was touched upon by the appearance of Christ and that she was deeply moved by it? The word "faith" referred originally to this emotion of religious fervor and had nothing to do with some particular article of belief.

The archetype of healer or savior is ultimately related to the Self or *anthropos*. It points the way to the wholeness of man. Whoever is whole is also healthy. Illness is a lack of wholeness. As soon as the archetype of wholeness is constellated, healing can take place. The cultural outlook of doctor and patient have a decisive effect on whether the doctor will succeed in invoking the archetype of wholeness, and whether the patient will understand the signals and symbols he employs. The archetype and the symbols of wholeness vary from culture to culture, although in themselves they are the common property of all humanity. The healing of a patient is made possible when the doctor succeeds in communicating these symbols to him.

A function such as this is commonly reserved for priests. In fact priests and shaman are often the same person. At Epidauros and Kos, there were priest-physicians.[2] Imhotep in ancient Egypt was considered a physician become god. The functions of priest and doctor were always intimately linked. The modern hospital developed from the medieval *hôtel-dieu*.

What distinguishes the doctor from the priest? The priest's concern is the practice of religion; he regulates the relationship of men with the gods. The doctor works, so to speak, on the shadow side of this relationship. He is concerned with those who suffer from an impairment of the normal workings of this relationship. In addition, it is the function of the doctor to diagnose what is amiss in his time and culture so that remedial action is possible. In sum, the doctor is concerned with perturbations in the normal flow of life in individuals and in the historical period in which he lives. His is the realm of disturbances, deviations from the norm, imbalances, suffering, and illness.

In earlier times, spiritual-psychological and physical pain were not distinguished. Now that materialistic medicine has passed its zenith, we are once again becoming mindful of the unity of body and mind and are attempting to understand suffering more in psychosomatic terms. But centuries-old habits of thought do not disappear all at once.

With the concept of *unus mundus*,[3] Jungian psychology started out on a new path, for it was no longer possible to return to the unitary outlook of antiquity. Matter and spirit in our consciousness are two entirely distinct fields of investigation. (Postulating a spiritual matter in the manner of Teilhard de Chardin does not solve this problem; moreover, no one has ever been able to show empirical proof of such a thing.)

Even without metaphysical acrobatics, we do find that material processes are meaningfully related to psychological-spiritual ones. In the phenomenon of synchronicity, spontaneous coincidences relating material to psychic processes occur. In such "creative acts in the dimension of time," as Jung once called them,[4] a parallelism of psyche and matter that could only be based on a unitary world beyond our consciousness becomes visible in the empirical world. Thus it is not surprising that many physical illnesses are adumbrated long before their appearance by signs on the psychic level. In "body language" psychological processes acquire a physical expression; the binding factor is the emotions, which indicate unconscious events through physical accompaniments. We blanch with horror, our heart leaps with joy, our knees get weak with fear, problems get on our nerves, and so on. Such emotional reactions appear mainly through the action of the autonomic nervous system, which is not under the influence of consciousness—we blush precisely at the moment when it is embarrassing for us.

Jung adduces the case[5] of a seventeen-year-old girl about whom it was initially unclear whether she was suffering from a physical ailment—progressive muscular atrophy—or hysteria. There were points in favor of both diagnoses. The girl was tormented by nightmares. In particular, she had been terrified by a hideous dream in which her mother hung herself from the living-room chandelier. In the second part of the dream, a shying horse jumped out of a fourth-story window onto the street below, where it lay smashed. Interpretation of the dream pointed the way to the correct diagnosis; it also helped in understanding the physical developments through which the animal level of life was destroying itself in the girl.

Modern medicine makes use of dreams as a source of information all too rarely. To be sure, it is extraordinarily difficult to see the meaning of dreams that might be significant diagnostically before the physical symptoms have appeared. In hindsight, it is much easier to pick out the particular dream in a dream series that heralded an impending illness. An illness is not preprogrammed. A constellated problem that has not been recognized and made conscious can, but need not, lead to a physical manifestation or express itself in some other way. Only retrospectively is such a sequence of development determinable, not beforehand. It is impossible to predict in advance, even with a slight degree of certainty, that a pathogenic conflict will manifest in a psychosomatic illness. Only after the illness has appeared can we in hindsight point to the pathogenic conflict and indicate the pathogenesis.

Body and mind are significantly related systems: processes in one are reflected in the other. Simply consider the way we commonly intuit someone's state of mind from his physical posture and unconscious bodily manifestations. Mime is a superb nonverbal communication medium. What is happening in our unconscious is betrayed by our body; someone who can read this language will know more about us than we want to disclose.

The extent to which people generally are unconscious of their physical processes is clearly seen in the daily practice of an ordinary doctor. Patients are seldom able to describe their afflictions, their diagnoses are vague and imprecise—they complain of an ache or a dull pain. They are often not able to say exactly where the pain is. In ancient China, patients were asked to indicate their symptoms by pointing to the parts of a porcelain figure. This was apparently a way to avoid having the patients undress, which was regarded as awkward; but perhaps another reason was that the patients could not give a clear account of their symptoms in any other way. I have been struck by the fact that in primitive medicine, clear symptomological descriptions are hardly ever encountered.

It is harder still to diagnose psychological ailments. Often they

elude precise description simply because the patient is not sufficiently aware of them. Our language is poor in words that
correspond to psychological states; poets must use images and
comparisons. But beside the linguistic problem, there is an
entirely different problem involved in expressing inner psychological states. Up till recently, and still today in some respects,
the events occurring in our psyche were not taking place in an
inner psychological space but were experienced as external. Still
today, we think that a mother complex must refer to the actual
mother, because we experience the suffering related with the
complex in the external world, in relation to the actual people
involved. Still today, we fail to make a clean distinction between
our psychological processes and external happenings. We continue to honor the primitive view that the external world really
exists as it appears to us, as we experience it. We hardly perceive
our psychological processes as such, but rather relate to them as
though they were part of the external world.

The primitive man experiences his psychological activity even
more intensively as a process in the world around him, with
which he lives in a *participation mystique*, an archaic identity. Is it
any wonder, then, that his world is animated with spirits and
demons, some of which are helpful, some dangerous? We are
tempted to try to enlighten him by talking him out of the spirits
and demons, but they are real. It is just as senseless to try to talk
him out of them as to deny the existence of complexes. Among
primitives, these exist not only autonomously as they do with
us, but actually objectively. But we also, and not only the
paranoids among us, identify complexes to such an extent with
objects that nothing can dissuade us from this way of seeing. At
those points where we are unconscious, we are not far from the
primitive mentality; therefore, we are able to understand that
mentality quite well from our own experience.

A distinction made by Glick[6] of three kinds of causality seems
to me helpful in understanding the primitive view of illness:

- The *causa efficiens* (effective or triggering cause)
    1. Illness brought about by another person
    2. Illness brought about by so-called supernatural powers
- The final cause (why the illness arose)
    1. Violation of a social or religious norm
    2. Result of a sorcery or spell
    3. Mischief on the part of so-called supernatural powers
- The *causa instrumentalis* (how technically it arose)
    1. Penetration by a foreign body
    2. Loss of the soul
    3. Possession

This system of distinctions, it seems to me, is superior to previous ones, and is quite relevant here.[7] From the cause of an illness, one infers the treatment. This principle is followed just as logically and with the same rational consistency by the primitive as by our modern healers.

In this context, we are interested only in the instrumental cause of the illness. Everywhere in the world, medicine men suck at the afflicted part of the body, either with their mouths or through a tube, and finish by showing their awed onlookers the noxious foreign body they have drawn forth.[8] Once the extraction of the foreign object has been proved, the cure is as good as assured. The idea here is that the illness has been caused by the penetration of a foreign object. The notion of an infectious projectile[9] is widespread, for example, an arrow shot by an evil sorcerer in order to cause illness in a person or a domestic animal. In many regions, this type of affliction is spoken of as a "stroke" or a "shot." In Australia, "bone-pointing" is practiced.[10] A sharp bone or piece of wood is pointed at an intended victim; it is believed that a piece of the bone or wood penetrates into the victim's body and makes him sick. As suggested by A. P. Elkin, such conceptions might well have originated in Australian aborigine visions and dreams.[11]

In fact, in everyday analytical work, one not infrequently hears comparable dreams even from modern enlightened people. A middle-aged man with a negative mother complex believed that two women of his acquaintance had behaved disloyally toward him in a particular situation that was important to him. The night after the incident, he had the following dream:

> For diagnostic purposes, I have to be stuck in the back with a long needle. I am very afraid of this and shy away. Finally I hold still. One doctor sticks me. Several doctors gather the results. When I wake up, I feel a definite pain in the back.

Because the man distrusted women, he was unable to acknowledge the true situation. He had projected his negative opinion of women—and at the same time, of the witch within himself—onto the two women. The dream had the function of putting him into painful confrontation with the facts. Such dreams indicate that a projection has taken place.[12] Projections are foreign bodies. For linguistic reasons, we are misled into assuming that projections are actively carried out. In reality, the archetype of the Sorcerer shoots his noxious projectile into our flesh. He may even creep up on his victim in sleep.[13] The god of love is another dangerous sorcerer of this type that shoots us with arrows. Job laments (6:4): "For the arrows of the Almighty are within me, the poison whereof drinketh up my spirit: the terrors of God do set themselves in array against me."

The agent of the projection is not the subject, but rather the archetype. It brings about the projection. In other words, behind every projection is an archetype. "Archetype" means an inbuilt way of seeing things. We do not experience the object or the environment as it *is*, but rather as it typically *appears* to us. Its mode of appearance is transformed into a typical form by the archetype that the object constellates. This transformation also calls up emotions that are connected with the object. For example, an unknown cat I see might strike me as weird; if, on top of that, it responds to my gentle attempts to approach it by arching its back and raising its fur, I might get cold shivers up and down my spine; I sense that it might be a witch's cat. By its repellent behavior, the unknown object has constellated in me the archetype of the Witch. We say that I project my witch image on the poor cat. In reality, it is the alienness of the cat and its strange behavior that triggers in me the constellation of the negative Mother archetype. This archetype then causes me to apprehend the cat in a typical way, that is, in accordance with this *type*—as a witch's cat. The projection consists in my experiencing my negative Mother archetype (Witch) not in me but in the cat.

How can a projection lead to illness? Insight into this can be found in the case of a man nearly thirty years old who frequently suffered from nocturnal stomach cramps. No ulcer had been found by his doctor. The man had the following dream:

> I see several shadows in my stomach, where I myself am also represented by a shadow. The stomach becomes a room in which there are about eight people whom I am incessantly talking at. I know that some of the people are traitors, and I also know which ones. I want to get rid of them, so I send them out of the room. But I find that they are still able to hear me. At the same moment, I realize that I will not be able to get rid of them. I gather the other people closer to me and talk more softly.

When the man awoke at two in the morning, he realized that two shadows in his dream were identical with two of the people and also with his stomach pains. He took a pill and drank some lukewarm milk. The pains came back in two hours. In spite of that he was able to relax and go back to sleep.

This person literally has a problem he cannot stomach. It is a shadow problem, a problem involving an opposite, something antithetical, that is manifesting in his body instead of his psyche. For some reason, the patient does not see the shadow, the traitor, as in himself. Generally, we project conflicts, mostly onto the external world, onto a neighbor or a dear one. In this case, the projection was not onto the outside world but instead onto the patient's stomach. Alfred Adler observed that such cases often involve an "organ inferiority." A particular organ reacts especially sensitively to psychological conflicts. This is a particular predisposition. If the conflict is projected onto the body, the "inferior organ" reacts. If over a period of time the conflict cannot be transferred out of the projection into the psyche, where by nature it belongs, then the organ begins to show damage, which finally become irreparable. This is the typical stomach ulcer resulting from stress.

Years ago I was consulted by a man in his fifties who had suffered his third heart attack. My exploration revealed that in his business life he had for years worked as the second highest officer of a firm and that his superior, in order to save money, had the firm's garbage emptied by truck into a nearby gravel pit. Our patient was unable to reconcile this miserly behavior with his conscience about environmental pollution. He had repeatedly spoken to his superior asking him to correct this disgraceful state of affairs and have the garbage taken to a proper garbage dump—in vain. It literally broke his heart to have to look on helplessly as his boss, to save a few pennies, wreaked havoc on the environment. In conversation with me, the patient was very insistent that he was right and that his superior's behavior was shameful. He did not want to look for a new job—he was too old for that. He projected his shadow on the boss, and thereby the possibility of working with it was blocked. This block brought on the feelings of helplessness that attacked his coronary arteries.

Projections are always connected with emotions, because they constitute a deficient adjustment to reality. The patient could not go so far in adjusting to reality that his boss's behavior became a matter of indifference to him; he was much too compulsive for that. But he could have gotten to know his own shadow; then he would have been able to be more tolerant toward the shadows of his fellow men. However, he saw himself in the right: the fault lay with somebody else! Though I was unable to follow his destiny further, I fear that since then he has probably paid for his inflexibility with his life.

As these two examples show, concrete cases of projection are not easy to see through. The therapist must be very wary of oversimplification. Only when he is familiar with the patient's unconscious situation in detail and has thoroughly explored his life story do the deeper connections begin to reveal themselves to him.

Let us now consider the next type of cause of illness, the loss of soul.[14] The notion that one of man's souls or *the* soul may be stolen or can spontaneously wander off is known practically throughout the world. It is frequently the task of the shaman to face the grave dangers of a journey to the beyond to lead or lure the soul back. The shaman portrays these journeys to the beyond in a very theatrical and realistic fashion for his audience. Fundamentally, he is doing nothing other than carrying out an active imagination in his archaic way.[15] In doing so, he interprets the inner images that spontaneously arise quite realistically so that he can come to grips with them. The shaman needs his audience so that a collective-unconscious atmosphere can develop that will work suggestively on his patient. The accounts of shamans[16] lead us to suspect that they not only outwardly portray these journeys but also carry them out inwardly. This evidently helps the patient to regain his soul and get better.

Loss of soul is a phenomenon well known to psychology. Jung recounts in his memoirs a fantasy in which his soul flew away from him, that is, the libido withdrew into the unconscious and was carrying on a secret life there. A process of this type can, as it did with Jung, intensify to the level of ghost phenomena. Ghosts are, as we shall see later, exteriorized unconscious complexes. When consciousness is incapable of accepting or understanding particular highly charged unconscious contents, they manifest in a parapsychological manner. As soon as Jung began to write down the fantasies that had been constellated, the host of spirits was dispelled and the haunting came to an end.

The symptoms of soul loss are similar to those of depression. In both cases, there is initially no illness. It is a kind of reaction that we encounter quite frequently. After the loss of a close relative, the libido tends to withdraw into the unconscious. Since the unconscious is "the land of the dead," we could also say that our soul wanders off into the beyond with the deceased. This fits with the widespread notion that a dead person does not gladly undertake his journey to the island of the blessed on his own. He looks for a companion. The loss of the soul of a relative can become a serious danger for us. For example, a lapse of attention while driving the car can then lead to death by accident.

It is striking how often one marriage partner dies soon after the other: while he or she was still alive, the soul of the surviving partner strayed away with the soul of the dead one.

In the case of soul loss as a reaction to an external life situation where the connection between the situation and the reaction is clear, we speak of a *reactive depression*. Where a clear and simple connection of this type is lacking, we speak of a *neurotic depression*. Here a fragmentary personality remains stuck and unresolved in the unconscious. The so-called *endogenous depression* develops according to the same psychopathological pattern. Here the libido seems to be hidden deep in the unconscious and constitutional factors seem to play some role (hence the name *endogenous*). Many psychiatrists wrongly assume that such depressions do not follow the same psychodynamic pattern as the other types of depression, but are purely physiological. However, the same considerations are applicable in the treatment of endogenous depression as in treatment of the other types.

Senile depressions are not less psychogenic than the others. They may be forewarnings of death, or a preparation for it. I recall a vigorous, well-to-do lady in her seventies who came to me with a depression that had the usual symptoms. She complained that she was not as enterprising as she used to be. In fact, she was an extraordinary woman who had led a very extraverted life, managed a large household, taken many journeys, and had also some noteworthy athletic accomplishments to her credit. The previous summer she had swum across the Lake of Zurich. She could not come to grips with the fact that she was now no longer able to do such a thing. Her libido continued to cling to these extraverted matters. It had become necessary for her, as a preparation for death, to give her attention to the state of her psyche.

Another case of senile depression was recounted to me by Dr. Franz Riklin, the late president of the C. G. Jung Institute in Zurich. He was once asked to treat a man around seventy years of age who was esconced in a serious depression in which he neither ate nor spoke. To begin with, Riklin could not converse with him at all, since he did nothing but stare at the wall. But when Riklin asked him if he saw death there, the question struck the old man like a bolt of lightning. He began to loosen up and ended up by telling Dr. Riklin the story of his life, in which he had been the very proper and conscientious head of a company. He had cared for his parents until their death, because his brother had shown no concern for them. When Riklin asked him about his brother, the depressed old man sighed: this brother was the black sheep of the family. He was full of zest for life, carefree, enjoyed everything, went hunting and fishing, had women—in short, he was the exact opposite of the patient. The patient had not had any contact with him for years. Riklin realized that the brother represented the side of the patient that he had never lived. He also told the patient of this impression of his. The result was that the patient set about making peace with his brother and during his vacation undertook the journey to his brother's house. There with his brother he somehow made up for all the shortcomings of his life. When he returned, his depression was entirely gone. He lived a few weeks longer and then died peacefully. With his brother, he had lived in extraversion of that part of his libido that had withdrawn into the unconscious and so attained a certain wholeness. In this way his life had attained completion.

The modern analyst deals with soul loss in essentially the same way as the shaman. He helps the patient to elevate into conscious-ness fragments of his psyche that have withdrawn into the unconscious or have come to life there. Dream work and the active-imagination technique play an important role in this proc-ess. To be sure, it is important for the soul to be brought back as soon as possible; otherwise the patient will become chronically ill and is bound to die, in the view of primitive societies.[17] In the terms of depth psychology, a simple complex becomes a patho-logical one. This pattern is frequently encountered. For example, one of my patients, when he was a student, had a traumatic experience in which it seemed to him he had been discriminated against. He failed to take advantage of the depression that followed to work with the trauma, which had touched upon a weakness in his personality. In the following decades, he associ-ated every comparable experience with this trauma. A system of associations and an impaired behavior pattern developed that bordered on the pathological. Increasingly the contents of every-day life were incorporated in this system, and in the process their connection to the original causes of the trauma became more remote. This development was reinforced by characterologically based mistrust. In my judgment, the initial problem or trauma was not so terribly overwhelming that this intelligent patient would not have been able to work through it had he only known how.

Soul loss can occur other than by spontaneous wandering away or withdrawal of the soul. More often the soul is stolen by a sorcerer, a hostile shaman, or a vengeful spirit.[18] Sorcerers and sorceresses are not personal figures but archetypes in the sense that, as we have seen in the case of the projectiles, the effect emanates from the archetype. For example, after a meeting with a particular woman, a man can be entirely changed. He thinks of nothing but her, he is unable to sleep, no longer enjoys eating, and he longs for her. For us, this is a matter of a personal romance between the two of them. For the primitive, the woman is a witch who has stolen his soul. The primitive outlook is correct to the extent that the effect that the "spellbound" man is laboring under does not emanate from the woman's consciousness—perhaps she has no idea what she has done. On the other hand, however, the social role of the sorcerer or sorceress hardly rests on possession of real "supernatural powers," as Sherrill Freeman assumes.[19] Rather the analytical psychologist sees here the archetype of the sorcerer, who exercises a *self-regulating function* for society. He is a kind of controlling moral authority; he represents the tribal society's moral code.[20]

But let us return to loss of soul. The example of Jung made clear that when a new content is constellated, it may correspond to something having come to life in the unconscious. This may be called a *creative depression*—a term that is to be found in no psychiatric textbook. This phenomenon is unknown but nevertheless occurs quite frequently. It is not a pathological condition, but can nevertheless be very unpleasant, because the symptoms are the same as in other kinds of depression. "You have to go fishing in the depression"—this bit of practical guidance is applicable to all depressions, but especially to the creative depression. In the final analysis, depression has the function of expanding consciousness by adding to one's life a new content from the unconscious.

The diagnosis of *possession*, the third type of cause of illness, is hardly ever to be found in psychiatric textbooks. Such a term is considered to belong more to the realm of theology.[21] This might create the impression that we are dealing here with a rare phenomenon. This is by no means the case, as has been made clear by T. K. Oesterreich's major monograph.[22] It is also by no means the exclusive domain of ethnologists, who often encounter the phenomenon in simple cultures.[23] Such conditions also appear in the everyday life of modern people, usually in the company of an emotion. Here an unconscious factor dominates, often the anima or animus. In men, they manifest mostly as hostile moods, in women as unfeeling opinionatedness and haggling. The level of consciousness is subject to fluctuation. Fatigue, drugs, and emotions cause an *abaissement du niveau mental* that enables contents from the unconscious to intrude and dominate.

Possession is contagious. Primitive people know this and sometimes avoid taking part in possession dances.[24] We are no longer aware of this; we expose ourselves frivolously and become infected. Who has not experienced suddenly finding oneself in an unaccustomed bad mood? If one thinks back to find precisely when it began, one can see that it came from contact with someone who was not quite him- or herself. Group panic is basically nothing other than epidemic possession resulting from an acute emotion of fear.

The initial disorder arises in a creative person. There is nothing more destructive in the psyche than a creative complex that is repressed; the complex then becomes creative in destruction. This occurs not only in cases where a vocation has not been understood; it occurs especially in cases where an individual, through laziness, complacency, or opportunism, repudiates the creative demon. It goes without saying that creativity is bound up with suffering and privation, because one no longer belongs to oneself but to the demon. Many of us fear this determination of our destiny by the demon and try to hold ourselves back. The story of the prophet Jonah in the Old Testament is an example of this. The creative demon by whom he is swallowed up is the great fish, in whose belly he feels as in "the belly of hell" (2:2). The prayer from the whale's belly is a reflection of a creative depression, in which one feels oneself cast out into "the midst of the seas," closed in by the waters "even to the soul," seaweed wrapped about one's head. One has gone "down to the bottoms of the mountains," "the earth with her bars" is about us "for ever." Only when one has been vomited out on land again by the great fish has the transformation been accomplished that brings readiness for creative action.

In our Western civilization, possession is not at all a rare phenomenon, and also by no means exclusively a pathological one. In my view, one should include here not only the cases of so-called demonic possession that are dealt with by the Catholic Church by means of exorcism.[25] In order to be effective, exorcism, like all archaic methods of healing, requires the participation of an audience. Only with its presence, as in spiritualism altogether, can the atmosphere be generated that is necessary for healing.

Especially the pathogenetic significance of possession is not yet sufficiently known. Possession is a feature of the majority of psychological disturbances. Most of the time a pathological complex is what, in ancient terminology, is described as a demon taking possession of the conscious personality. This leads to abnormal psychological and physical states, as in the following case history.

A woman of about thirty suffering from the most varied physical disturbances was referred to me by a general practitioner after he had treated her without success for frequent headaches, attacks of dizziness, "lumps in the throat," and particularly heart pain spreading to the left arm. The patient had already seen a number of doctors who had told her her problem was "just nerves." This opinion, however, was of no help to her. In addition, she was afraid that some of her brain cells had died, since because of blockages in her veins, her blood was not circulating properly; or that she had a brain tumor. Following an episode of hyperventilation tetany (cramps resulting from excessive exhalation of carbon dioxide), an electroencephalogram was taken that turned out to be normal. This also failed to calm her fears, as did a normal electrocardiogram. Migraine medication was of little help; antidepressants had little effect. Since she herself had already considered psychological treatment, her doctor's suggestion fell on fruitful ground.

When she came to my office, she was full of hope for relief from her years of suffering. She recounted her various anxieties and her fear that she would die young because of her deficient health. She was afraid, despite her doctor's attempts to calm her in this regard, that the cramplike pains in her chest spreading to her left arm meant that she would have a heart attack.

In twenty-three sessions over the course of a year, the following core conflict came to light. At the age of fourteen she had had a boyfriend. Her father continually resisted this relationship and finally made her life so unpleasant that at the age of twenty-one she moved out of the house. A year later the father suddenly and unexpectedly died of a heart attack at the age of fifty-six. They had never made peace. From that time on, the patient heaped guilt on herself: she believed that her inadmissible relationship with her boyfriend had caused her irascible father so much grief that he had finally had a heart attack.

Although she had sought out psychological treatment, she always expressed the fear that it would not really help because an unknown physical process lay behind her troubles. Her symptoms actually emulated those of her father, as though her father could avenge himself by causing her to suffer from the same ailment as himself. She was tormented by persecution dreams. She also dreamed that, in a forest deep in snow, she bumped into a corpse and then encountered a police car.

Through his death, the father became a vengeful demon who persecuted her. Not only had he damaged her Eros to such an extent that she was only able to enter into a relationship with a man again two years before she came to me; when she was a child, he had cast such a heavy pall on the domestic atmosphere that she often became afraid that war was breaking out and pulled the bedclothes over her head. When the father died, she was by no means sad—she felt relieved. But even then she felt a pain in her heart. Just three and a half years before she came to me, the real troubles began, with pounding and racing of the heart (tachycardia), constricted breathing, lumps in the throat. Her mother more than once accused her of being responsible for her father's premature death. Her godmother told her that the father had complained to her of how much he suffered from the tension between himself and his daughter. Nonetheless, whenever she came home he always treated her as though she were hardly there and remained irreconcilable.

Self-sacrificingly, she took care of her mother after the father's death so that she would not have to reproach herself in the same way once her mother died. In spite of all this she dreamed that her mother suffered a heart attack and she arrived too late.

In the meantime, the patient's symptoms have begun to abate, she feels better. But the work on her neurosis continues.

Was the father really a demon who persecuted the patient relentlessly, or did she only experience him that way? This question cannot be answered, because the complex is constituted by a mixture of both aspects. On the one hand, the patient could only experience her father in accordance with her archetypal preconceptions. On the other hand, particular behavior activates a particular archetypal image out of the array that the archetype presents. For this reason, Plato held that demons were mediators between humans and the gods. The gods are the archetypal conceptions, humans represent individual concrete experiences. The active element is the complex—here a father complex—which is constituted by both aspects. It caused illness, because it took possession of consciousness.

Possession is characterized by the inaccessibility of the afflicted individual to any logical argument. All her doctors had assured the patient that her illness was not physical; even she herself was ready to believe this, but again and again she was overcome by doubt. The power of the demon was so great that she altogether lost her ability to breathe when, in an active imagination, meeting her father in the garage, she tried to communicate with him.

That the layman has hardly an inkling of the power and impact of complexes can hardly be held against him. What is worse is that many psychiatrists carry on as though they knew nothing of complexes and try to treat them by suggestion. Their daily practice should provide them with enough examples to convince them that this is not possible. Among the public as well as among professionals, behind the denial of demons is hidden a deep-rooted fear of them, which has existed since the beginning of mankind. The ancients never grew weary of giving expression to the menace of the demons. Since the Enlightenment, Western man has taken pleasure in either negating the existence of demons or ignoring it. Both attitudes are dangerous, for therein speaks psychic blindness or poverty of consciousness.

7

The Demons Animus and Anima

A special position among the demons is occupied by the animus among women and the anima among men. Men quite easily become obsessed by the feminine unconscious and women by the male unconscious.

The psychology of the animus and anima, especially their positive sides, has been presented many times.[1] Here I am going to concentrate on their negative aspect. In brief, the positive anima is the Eros and emotional side of a man, the positive animus is the creative spirit of a woman. However, it is often from the negative side that we see the two archetypes.

It is part of the demonic quality of these two complexes that they conceal themselves, that they avoid being recognized and exposed—any trick is fair. Not for nothing does Jung remark that "if working with the shadow is the journeyman work [of individuation], . . . working with the anima is the masterpiece."[2] Anyone who is possessed by one of these complexes will deny having anything to do with it. I have known several women who, at the very moment they were really being ridden by the animus, expressed the opinion, independently of one another, that they would never again see things with such clarity. In the state of possession by the animus, there is a sense of lucidity that strikes an outsider as unnatural and suspect. The image of an external situation called forth by the animus dominates consciousness without the latter being able to gain critical distance from it— because the underlying affect distorts this image. The image barely corresponds with the external situation, thus the affect and the image fit together all the better. Often this affect originates in an unhighlighted emotional hurt or disappointment, against which the subject did not defend herself in time. (The same goes for the anima with men.) The negative animus of the woman is a lying spirit that shrinks from no distortion or perversion of the truth. It twists one's words in one's mouth, it strikes one with one's own weapons, it uses the truths of the adversary to argue against these same truths. In short, it is a trickster.

I have yet to meet someone who has accepted the statement that he or she was possessed by the anima or animus. However, the more heatedly a person reacts against such a statement, the more on target it is. For the demon will put all its powers of persuasion on the line to convince the critical observer of the contrary and to try to prove that he has no grasp of the subject's psychology whatsoever. The "counterproofs" are usually quite eloquently presented, but the deeper psychological levels do not join in; thus these arguments can create confusion, but they do not convince.

Possession vitiates one's soundness of mind. Animus and anima strike their carrier with blindness—he lets himself be carried away into words and deeds that would be unworthy of his conscious state. I need only recall those unfortunate scenes in a marriage when restraint is thrown to the winds. Totally obsessed by the affect, one sees only red. One is absolutely convinced of being in the right. Creating this kind of blindness is part of the demon's tactics; he can only go on with his game as long as he remains unrecognized.

The negative animus of a woman, like the negative anima of a man, finds many ways of expressing itself. Every expression is one-sided and an incomplete representation. A man experiences the animus from the outside, a woman from the inside. He experiences the anima from the inside, she from the outside. Depending on the point of view, different types of images arise.

Waltraut Körner has given a sensitive account of how women experience the animus, particularly its positive side.

Ultimately, behind the complexes of animus and anima are gods, that is, the archetypes. For basically, these are superhuman powers we are dealing with, powers humans can only cope with by adopting a religious attitude. Only a steadfast consciousness anchored in reality can withstand the assault of these powers from the unconscious. Often these powers take possession of consciousness unnoticed. Those around the possessed person notice a kind of haughtiness and inflation. Every mixture of consciousness with unconscious contents leads to a dissolution of the ego personality and a sense of exaggerated self-importance owing to the force arising from the unconscious. Such a person treats others with lofty superiority. One finds oneself being instructed like an ignorant little child; one feels worthless and small. The animus is taking you in hand because you need it so badly, because you are so weak and dependent. The animus can turn out to be a real power fiend, ordering people around and feeding on their adulation. All means are fair, from sugar candy to the whip. His hunger for power is insatiable. If he senses weakness or a tendency to give in, he becomes more voracious still.

Just as the animus wants to dominate everything outside of him, so does he behave toward his conscious personality. Though women possessed by him may have an arrogant and flashy air, their real personality is a pathetic bundle of depression. They can't take pleasure in anything; the animus snatches anything worthwhile right out from under their noses. Such women suffer terribly. But they are unaware of the cause of the suffering. They believe that those around them reject them, cause them suffering, contradict them, won't leave them in peace. The source of their suffering is not themselves but the people around them. Once again this is a trick of the animus to make it possible for him to carry on with his nasty ways undiscovered. Such cases often withstand all therapy. From the outside it seems that a person could not be so blind and hardened as not to see the real root of the evil. That which one cannot see oneself is more than clear to other people. All reasonable attempts to make the person see the light are crushed by the power of the possession.

The animus has the ability to adapt to changing situations like a chameleon. To him the truth is unimportant, although he may pay it great lip service. It is his goal that is important. Any tactic, any lie, any ostensibly coherent argument, any fallacious conclusion, any deceptive maneuver is all right with him. With his masculine nature, he tries to get his way by showing off, threats, intimidation, even violence. He entangles his enemies in word duels in which he cares only about rhetorical strategy; he is not interested, as he claims to be, in the truth, only in keeping the upper hand. In this respect, he has a strange irritating effect on a man, egging him on to opposition. This perverse reaction in turn goads the animus further to capture the man's attention, string him along, enthrall him, entangle him in conflict. The animus is looking for trouble. He invokes opposition on every hand and sows discord. He provokes those with peace-loving natures until they finally explode and land themselves in the wrong—like the nagging wife who goes on provoking her husband until he finally resorts to violence. Now she has grounds to complain of his boorishness in front of everyone. In the world's eyes, he bears the blame.

Animus and anima are the divine or royal couple. They can't get along without one another. They are the syzygy.*[3] They have a love-hate relationship. They are responsible for the tremendous fascination the two sexes have for each other and also for the bottomless hatred and all the misunderstanding between them. They are also a demonic couple, godparents to all marital strife and hostility between the sexes. The opposition between man and woman is so unbridgeably great that God had to create love to bring them together, so Jung mythologized.[4] And since it

---

*In Gnosticism, this term referred to the sexual union of supernatural beings (cf. C. G. Jung: Aion, CW 9/II).

is not only the conscious man and conscious woman over against each other, but also their unconscious counterparts, the animus and anima, the Babel of confusion is perfect.[5] For the most part, one can hardly sort out who is talking, flirting, or fighting with whom. This is the source of many problems of communication. People think they are talking "reasonably" with each other and yet do not understand each other at all, which only comes out afterward. Each one understands what is said in the way that is typical for him or her, and this is often a world away from what was meant.

A negative anima makes a man effeminate. He begins to wail and complain, becomes absorbed in self-pity: the "stronger" sex becomes weak. He seems to himself to be the poorest, most neglected, unjustly treated, and exploited person around. When he gets depressed, he goes off into a corner to sulk and doesn't talk to anybody for hours, often days. The negative animus makes a woman sullen and easily wounded in her pride. The anima in a man makes him easily sentimental, theatrical, even hysterical. He suffers from his fellow beings and the world—only not from himself. Because in his suffering an inner woman often comes to him and whispers in his ear that he deserves a better lot in life and better treatment, sadness mingles with arrogance. The world has yet to notice what he has done for it and what talents he has to offer.

Since his adjustment to the outer world has been unsuccessful, the libido tends to arouse grandiose fantasies. In the sulking phase, the external world is dismissed, and the libido flows into the unconscious. The gap between inner and outer becomes ever greater: here is the world, which shows no understanding for this poor man, and there is the seductive anima, leading him on with protestations of his importance. This is the posture that he persists in. Any attempts to appease him are in vain. Only if you beg him for forgiveness in the most abject way, taking the blame for what has happened onto yourself and promising never to behave in such a way again, will he perhaps creep little by little out of the corner where he has been sulking.

Any possession by animus or anima leads sooner or later to feelings of inferiority—and behind this lies a real inferiority, the downfall of consciousness. In order not to have to admit this to oneself, someone else is consigned to a lower level—the one who perhaps did trigger the animus or anima attack, but did not cause it. One's own pain and depression is poured out onto this fellow being. Because of the *abaissement du niveau mental* involved, animus and anima possession are connected to affects ranging from harmless defiance to homicide. Feeling is repressed by the affect, as a result of which one can coldbloodedly do or say the most horrendous things. Altogether, where animus or anima are present, people become unfeeling and cold. Warmth and affection toward one's fellows are extinguished. One radiates pure negativity, emits sparks, hurls lightning bolts, spoils every mood, poisons the atmosphere, dampens cheerfulness. Other people try to avoid such a person, because he is "infectious." Not only does he constellate animus or anima in other people, but he infects them with his own negative emotions.

Every now and then, one pulls oneself together and suppresses one's bad anima mood—and infects one's surroundings despite this. In the presence of such a possessed person, one feels ill at ease, oppressed, constricted, fraught with a sense of hidden blame. One lacks the confidence to be spontaneous or cheerful: one's every gesture could cause offense. The atmosphere of this person seems to say, "What do you mean by being cheerful, seeing how badly off I am!" Logic goes haywire: "It serves my father right if my hands freeze, why doesn't he buy me a pair of gloves?" Many a suicide has come about based on this kind of motivation: "It serves you right if I kill myself, why didn't you take better care of me?"

The negative anima is an affect that casts its shadow over all aspects of life. Even in the case of an intelligent man, this affect can distort an otherwise infallible sense of logic to the point where his argumentation ignores logic altogether and is determined entirely by his objective. We even find this approach creeping into scientific treatises, where it leads to obvious falsifications based on wishful thinking. Animus and anima alike are hypocrites, deceivers, and liars, but from entirely different motives. The animus does it for the sake of appearing to be right or for power. The anima does it out of ambition or vainglory.

Beyond this, the anima has the function in a man of making a connection to the unconscious. In that way it is a counterbalance to the *persona*, the external social adjustment. The woman's animus represents her connection with spirit, which counterbalances her closeness to nature.

A comprehensive account of the manifold manifestations of animus and anima would exceed our present scope. In particular, we would also have to discuss their style of projection onto other people, in which the anima tends to play the seductress and morally inferior person and the animus, the hero or preacher (spiritual seducer), who can sometimes have tremendous, fascinating power and urgency. We would also have to look into the image of the negative anima as succubus and that of the negative animus as incubus in manifestations of the unconscious.* These figures were often depicted in religious art.[6]

Finally, demons are not only negative but figures altogether exceeding the human capacity to relate to them. For this reason, their positive manifestations should also be presented. When I speak here of negative and positive, I am aware that these are my own evaluations. The archetypes are nature, which is divinely exalted and terrifying at the same time. In the same way, the animus and anima demons in human beings are sometimes their most valuable side, lifting them beyond the norm, and sometimes their most fiendish, reprehensible, and evil side. Here, as so often, we see how near opposites really are to each other.

---

*In the demonology of the Middle Ages, the succubus was a demon believed to have sexual intercourse with sleeping men and the incubus a demon believed to have intercourse with sleeping women.

8

The Ancestral Spirits

Often behind the animus and anima demons lies a particularly strong father or mother complex. "Among the possible spirits," says Jung,

> the spirits of the parents are in practice the most important; hence the universal incidence of the ancestor cult. In its original form it served to conciliate the *revenants*, but on a higher level of culture it became an essentially moral and educational institution, as in China. For the child, the parents are his closest and most influential relations. But as he grows older this influence is split off; consequently the parental imagos become increasingly shut away from consciousness, and on account of the restrictive influence they sometimes continue to exert, they easily acquire a negative aspect. In this way the parental imagos remain as alien elements somewhere "outside" the psyche.[1]

Elsewhere, Jung tells us, "the more restricted a person's field of consciousness is, the more psychic contents [*imagos*] appear quasi-externally as spirits or magical potencies projected on living persons (sorcerers, witches)."[2] And again,

> The image [of the parents] is unconsciously projected, and when the parents die, the projected image goes on working as though it were a spirit existing on its own. The primitive then speaks of parental spirits who return by night (*revenants*), while the modern man calls it a father or mother complex.[3]

Jung speaks constantly of *imagos*, images, that we have of our forebears. These images arise in part from the experiences and impressions of our objectively existing parents and grandparents and in part from our typical conception of such experiences. The child has an inborn range of potential conceptions of parental archetypes.[4] Using a term borrowed from the Swiss writer Carl Spitteler, Jung calls this blend of personal experience and inborn potential the *imago*.[5] However, our distinction between the personal and the typical in this image is an abstraction for which there is no corresponding subjective experience. In the image, both elements are inextricably interwoven.

This complicates any inquiry into the extent to which psychological properties are inherited. And from the genetic point of view, we are also products of our forebears. The sum of the lives of his ancestors converges in the life of each individual. In his *Memories, Dreams, Reflections,* Jung expresses it as follows:

> I feel very strongly that I am under the influence of things or questions which were left incomplete and unanswered by my parents and grandparents and more distant ancestors. It often seems as if there were an impersonal karma[6] within a family, which is passed on from parents to children. It has always seemed to me that I had to answer questions which fate had posed to my forefathers, and which had not yet been answered, or as if I had to complete, or perhaps continue, things which previous ages had left unfinished. It is difficult to determine whether these questions are more of a personal or more of a general (collective) nature. It seems to me that the latter is the case. A collective problem, if not recognized as such, always appears as a personal problem, and in individual cases may give the impression that something is out of order in the realm of the personal psyche. The personal sphere is indeed disturbed, but such disturbances need not be primary; they may well be secondary, the consequence of an insupportable change in the social atmosphere. The cause of disturbance is, therefore, not to be sought in the personal surroundings, but rather in the collective situation. Psychotherapy has hitherto taken this matter far too little into account.[7]

"We are the products of our parents" sounds quite banal; taking it seriously in analysis often demands a lot of work and care. The very fact that the separation from our parents is so hard for us shows that it is less a personal problem than an archetypal one. Where archetypes are in play, it is not a matter of "overcoming" something; rather, what is needed is to understand the essence of the contents and integrate them. The ancestors continue to show up as disturbing and subversive elements in the life of the individual as long as they are not able to take part in it. The ancestors are, so to speak, inherited elements that constitute our life in the superpersonal sense; ultimately they merge into the collectivity and historicity of the human psyche. When we speak of the ancestors, we are speaking only to a limited degree of specific individuals. For the unresolved problems they have left to posterity mostly go beyond the personal sphere. When we characterize a person, we usually strongly emphasize their individual features. But it is the collective archetypal problems that actually shape a life in its uniqueness. If an essential question or an essential problem of a life remains unresolved, then it is communicated to the succeeding generations. In my experience, it is not until the third generation that it becomes clearly formulable. It leapfrogs, as it were, the immediately following generation. This is a point that has hitherto been given too little consideration in psychotherapy. Jung tells us that

> Our souls as well as our bodies are composed of individual elements which were all already present in the ranks of our ancestors. The "newness" in the individual psyche is an endlessly varied recombination of age-old components. Body and soul therefore have an intensely historical character and find no proper place in what is new, in things that have just come into being. That is to say, our ancestral components are only partly at home in such things. We are very far from having finished completely with the Middle Ages, classical antiquity, and primitivity, as our modern psyches pretend. Nevertheless, we have plunged down a cataract of progress which sweeps us on into the future with ever wilder violence the farther it takes us from our roots. . . . The

less we understand of what our fathers and forefathers sought, the less we understand ourselves, and thus we help with all our might to rob the individual of his roots and his guiding instincts, so that he becomes a particle in the mass, ruled only by what Nietzsche called the spirit of gravity.[8]

The ancestral spirits represent an extension of our brief life beyond the limited bounds of our lifetime. Our present, determined by the manifold currents of the past, carries within it the germ of the future. In the unconscious, the future of individual lives and of the culture as a whole is prepared long in advance. The problems of the past that have been incompletely dealt with become ancestral demons who cast their shadow over the present and shape the future. This fateful function of the ancestors explains why such an important place is reserved for them in all the cultures of the world and why they become important cult objects.

I experienced the power with which ancestors affect the lives of modern people in connection with the case of a thirty-three-year-old Swiss woman. She recounted to me a series of dreams in which a common theme was apparent:

First dream: "War. I am fleeing from the enemy. It doesn't come to a fight."

Second dream (two months later): I have been put back into the Middle Ages. There are hostilities between the clan I belong to and a powerful neighbor. I am given the mission of bringing the enemy a written peace offer. A couple of boys accompany me through the trackless country.

At last we're on top of the hill where the enemy army camp is. The magnificent tents show the power and wealth of the adversary. Suddenly I'm in a castle. Here I learn that the proposed peace negotiations have been rejected. I and my companions hastily leave the camp.

A little later I'm with my clan or people again. On the instructions of the leader (who might be either a man or a woman), everyone starts off on a strange migration. The goal is not clear, but it might be a journey to sue the enemy for mercy.

The whole clan is together again in its own territory. From a leader we learn that the enemy will soon attack again and that we will lose the battle against the mighty opponent. With a few other women, I flee into nearby but strange territory. Here we hide, fearing that our pursuers will rape us.

Third dream (three months later): On a small plain beneath a castle tower, many people have gathered for a memorial ceremony. A few women I know are driven by curiosity to also have a look at the inside of the ancient tower. A young girlfriend of mine has a special relationship to this building and to the ceremony. An ancestor, for whose memorial we are probably assembled, lived in this castle.

Fourth dream (a month later): I'm in a castle and am running down a lot of long corridors. I want to get outside. Finally, I get into a brighter corner room with windows. The lord of the castle or a son of his have been expecting me here. I look through a window and see that the building is in lonely, barren mountain country. I am anxious to go, since I know that enemies are approaching from below who are going to storm the castle. I learn that I am supposed to stay, because I have been chosen by the lord of the castle. He loves me. I seem to be related to him.

Together with the lord of the castle and his few faithful retainers, I have left the fortress-like castle and am now on a road in the mountains. The men are on horseback and are wearing swords and daggers. For me too, there is a beautiful, frisky horse at the ready. I am ordered to mount. I hesitate and ask if I'm supposed to mount sidesaddle or the other way. The men say I should do it the regular way. Now I feel a bit more secure and follow their instruction. I check to see if my horse obeys me. It reacts to the slightest tug on the reins.

I'm frightened, for in a few moments the enemy is going to appear. I am filled with thoughts of flight. I want to ride my horse up the mountainside to the top and down the other side. It would be a simple and sure way of saving myself. The men sense that I want to run away. They want me to stay with them and defend myself along with them. I stay and am afraid. I see some men fighting with each other. Many of them have bloody stab wounds.

Fifth dream (two months later): The war is on. As a soldier, along with other comrades in suffering, I experience pursuit, hunger, misery, and captivity in Germany. It seems I was able to escape, because I am now in Austria where I and other homeless soldiers are being granted asylum.
Some helpful people give us a pot full of fresh vegetables, bean seeds, and potatoes. Full of hope, I take the seeds out of the pot. They shouldn't be used for food, but should sprout and grow in a field. A new, fresh life begins now.

This vivid dream series began before the woman started analysis. Its scenes contrasted sharply with the plain middle-class existence of the analysand. She had never had ambitions resembling anything in the dreams, but had lived a kind of changeable, unsteady life in which she had tried to be as inconspicuous as possible. She was living below her potential. As a result, she was neurotic, almost bordering on psychotic. She had lost her father in early childhood. Her mother, who had brought her up on her own, had transmitted a strict Catholic worldview to her. As early as junior high school, physical disorders began to show up. Recently, she had had to undergo a difficult operation for a malignant ailment.

Disregarding for the moment the threat of her physical ailment, nothing in her life was sufficiently important to explain the weighty quality of her dreams. This dream series could well represent a kind of night-sea-journey.*[9] A war is in progress that has to be decided, not by any peace negotiations, but by bloody battle. But after pursuit, hunger, and captivity, the analysand acquires the seed for the new future.

In the dreams, the analysand appears as an Amazon in a very masculine world of warriors, which she was unable to explain. I suggested that she do some research into her family history. At

*The mythological motif of the night-sea-journey, which appears all over the world, corresponds to a regeneration in and through the unconscious. This is represented by the image of the journey of the sun from its setting in the west to its dawning in the east.

that point she learned from her mother that on her father's side, her family line went back to the fifteenth century. A *Landvogt* (provincial governor) was recorded in the register for the year 1444. In 1515, one of her ancestors fell at the battle of Marignano. In 1550, another member of the petty nobility from her family, a *Talvogt* (district governor), is recorded.

Her mother's family line went back to an abbess of Muenster in 1190. The family line as such was registered as of 1300. Around 1400, it divided into three. From one warlike line came a brave and pious knight who served the French crown as a high officer for over forty years. His brother was in the Venetian army, and this brother's son fought on many battlefields as a French officer. Some of her mother's forebears were district judges and formed the chief family of the free state of Graubünden. One ancestor was appointed a general and made a knight of the Legion of Honor by Napoleon on the battlefield of Austerlitz. The title of baron became hereditary in the family. The family also boasted some outstanding statesmen, including a governing baron and the chief administrator of an ecclesiastical diocese. We need not enumerate all the notable ancestors in the analysand's family line. The reader is already in a position to gauge to what extent her ancestors' influence persisted in her psyche.

It is true that none of her ancestors appeared in her dreams; nevertheless the dream scenes do fit her family history. They take place in a medieval environment, but without depicting a particular historical situation. The lives of the ancestors are represented in the sense that they partook of the type of scene we find in the dreams. They were country nobles living in castles, entangled in the political and military conflicts of their time. The analysand became neurotic, because she underestimated and undervalued the dimensions of her personal background. She had to acknowledge that problems of her time were manifesting in her in the guise of personal conflicts, and that she owed these problems a response. What could such dreams have to communicate to a young woman living in entirely different conditions and surroundings than those depicted in them? Apparently they point to the fact that, in spite of changed conditions, she has a collective role to play. She attempted to relate to no more than her own personal existence—and became sick. The psychic dimensions of many people point beyond their individual existences. Their life is not just theirs to dispose of freely, but has a certain vocation. They belong not to themselves, but to everyone.

There are people who come to the conclusion from experiences like these dreams that they have remembered the lives of their ancestors.[10] We can say nothing with certainty on this point. That the experiences of our ancestors are deposited in our psyche as inherited elements fully suffices as an explanation without our having to resort to foolhardy and unprovable speculations.

The individual ancestors gradually merge into the collective ancestry. At a Chinese ancestral shrine, the last four generations of the ancestors are venerated individually. When someone in the next generation dies, the little tablet representing the oldest ancestor is put in the "ancestor chest"; it has lost its individuality, being too remote from the consciousness of the current generation. In an agricultural culture, which is the type in which the cult of ancestors plays the greatest role, the individual memory probably does not reach back more than four generations in any case. The experiences of all our ancestors are deposited in the archetypes.[11] "Primitive peoples," Jung observes, "often hold the belief that the soul of the child is the incarnation of an ancestral spirit, for which reason it is dangerous to punish children, lest the ancestral spirit be provoked."[12] Among primitives, because of the reduced level of consciousness, the unconscious plays the decisive role. For that reason, primitives perceive the qualities inherited from their ancestral lineage much more sensitively than we do. But with us also, the immediate forebears, the parents, are often not the ones who provide the governing impulse for the life of their children. As Jung says:

what the child is . . . as an individuality distinct from his parents can hardly be explained by the causal relationship to the parents. We ought rather to say that it is not so much the parents as their ancestors—the grandparents and great-grandparents—who are the true progenitors, and that these explain the individuality of the children far more than the immediate and, so to speak, accidental parents. In the same way the true psychic individuality of the child is something new in respect of the parents and cannot be derived from their psyche. It is a combination of collective factors which are only potentially present in the parental psyche, and are sometimes wholly invisible. Not only the child's body, but his soul, too, proceeds from his ancestry, in so far as it is individually distinct from the collective psyche of mankind.[13]

In the light of this, it is no wonder that ancestors have been referred to as "the mighty dead"; over the centuries the living have feared them, made sacrifices to propitiate them, supplicated them for help, and asked them to make their crops flourish.[14]

"Another case of structural change [of the personality]," says Jung in his essay ("Concerning Rebirth"),

concerns certain unusual observations about which I speak only with the utmost reserve. I refer to states of possession in which the possession is caused by something that could perhaps most fitly be described as an "ancestral soul," by which I mean the soul of some definite forebear. For all practical purposes, such cases may be regarded as striking instances of identification with deceased persons. (Naturally, the phenomena of identity only occur after the "ancestor's" death.) My attention was first drawn to such possibilities by Léon Daudet's confused but ingenious book *L'Hérédo*. Daudet supposes that, in the structure of the personality, there are ancestral elements which under certain conditions may suddenly come to the fore. The individual is then precipitately thrust into an ancestral role. Now we know that ancestral roles play a very important part in primitive psychology. Not only are ancestral spirits supposed to be reincarnated in children, but an attempt is made to implant them into the child by naming him after an ancestor. So, too, primitives try to change themselves back into their ancestors by means of certain rites. I would mention especially the Australian conception of the *alcheringami-jina*,[15] ancestral souls, half man and half animal, whose reactivation through religious rites is of the greatest functional significance for the life of the tribe. Ideas of this sort, dating back to the Stone Age, were widely diffused, as may be seen from numerous other traces that can be found elsewhere. It is therefore not improbable that these primordial forms of experience may recur even today as cases of identification with ancestral souls, and I believe I have seen such cases.[16]

If we in the West were not so apt to project everything onto external reality, but were aware that an ancestral presence in the life of the individual does not necessarily mean a particular ancestor, then we could use this terminology for many important psychological phenomena. In his memoirs, Jung recounts that around the age of eleven, he lived in two realities. One was the schoolboy, the other a man

> not to be trifled with. . . . This "other" was an old man who lived in the eighteenth century, wore buckled shoes and a white wig and went driving in a fly with high, concave rear wheels between which the box was suspended on springs and leather straps.
>
> This notion sprang from a curious experience I had had. When we were living in Klein-Hüningen an ancient green carriage from the Black Forest drove past our house one day. It was truly an antique, looking exactly as if it had come straight out of the eighteenth century. When I saw it, I felt with great excitement: "That's it! Sure enough, that comes from *my* times." It was as though I had recognized it because it was the same type as the one I had driven in myself. . . . The carriage was a relic of those times! I cannot describe what was happening in me or what it was that affected me so strongly: a longing, a nostalgia, or a recognition that kept saying, "Yes, that's how it was! Yes, that's how it was!"[17]

Many people feel an emotional kinship with a particular epoch. They understand it from the inside out, as though they were children of that time. This was also the case with Jung and alchemy, about which he had already had fantasies as a schoolboy on his way to school.[18] They were about the secret of the castle tower where there was a kind of laboratory where he would make gold, in fact, make it out of the secret substance he drew out of the air with a copper root. "It was really an *arcanum* [secret] of the nature of which I did not, and could not, have any notion. Also, there was no imagination about the nature of the transmutation process."

This example makes quite clear how fateful such feelings of kinship can be. They represent the spiritual ancestors or the historicity of the psyche. In primitive cultures, an ancestral spirit often speaks through a medium in a trance. In chapter 4, we saw how much value the tribe places on the instructions of the ancestral spirit that are transmitted by the medium.

Since the dead have been buried in the ground and have vanished into the land of the dead—the unconscious[19]—they work on the living from out of the earth. It is said that if the Chinese were wiped out and an alien race settled on their land, in a hundred years these inhabitants would be Chinese again. The earth, steeped in the heritage of the ancestors, exercises a power of assimilation on the people living on it. For this reason, the Indian is the soul of the Americans.[20] And the reason, it seems to me, that the visions of the Indians resemble each other is not their common tradition—rather, their visions come out of their earth. The chief Black Elk[21] was nine years old when, after a serious illness, he had the great vision that was his vocation. The cosmic images of this vision bear all the earmarks of the religious worldview of the woods Indians of North America.[22] In particular, there were twelve horses of different colors in each of the four cardinal directions, buffalo hooves, deer's teeth, antlers, and geese, all important Indian symbols. Is it possible at his age already to have learned so much of the Indian culture that so strongly marks this vision? On the other hand, experience with horses was quite common and familiar. On the whole, I can only understand the content of this vision as the influence of the earth on the boy, which in this case also saved him from his illness.

In many regions of the earth, for example, in Black Africa, the belief exists that it is not possible to conquer either a particular territory or the powers inhabiting it, only living people. The political domination of the newcomers extends only to the human inhabitants; the first possessors of the ground, even as a subject people, remain the lords of the earth.[23] According to a principle familiar in the history of religions, though conquerors may impose political and social structures on a subject nation, the native gods will undermine them.[24]

The further back in time the death of an important person lies, the more his individual features are lost to the memory of people and the more he is unconsciously mythologized. A pertinent observation was made by J. F. Thiel[25] among the Yansi on the Songo river, a tributary of the Zaire in the Congo, where he knew the great chief Mfumu Bay, who died in 1967. When Thiel returned to this region four years after the chief's death, the number of those visiting the graveyard had greatly diminished, though the grave was still being cared for. On the other hand, the people were telling each other miraculous things about the chief, giving Thiel the impression that Mfumu Bay was on his way to becoming one of the tribal ancestors.

As the individual features of important persons are transformed into legendary qualities, such figures become more and more a common cultural property and are increasingly incorporated into the collective unconscious. For the sake of historical precision, we might lament the loss of these individual details, but nonetheless it is the archetypal features of the person that constitute his or her timeless value. Thus the personality of the historical Jesus can no longer be reconstructed[26] and is also not at all important. What continues to work on in Him are the archetypal features that have been handed down by tradition, perhaps not with historical accuracy, but in the spirit of those times. Our time emphasizes the unique individual destiny and character too strongly over the timeless, archetypal, supraindividual qualities. The more a dead person is removed in time from the living, the more he becomes part of the universal humanity represented by the archetypes. In this way, we come to the idea of the deified dead, or divine heroes. Imhotep of Egypt's Old Kingdom is said to have been a famous builder and physician who was later deified.[27]

The soul or psyche has a historical character. Though it receives its contents only at the beginning of the individual lifetime, there are certain innate potentialities that play a great part in the processing of its experiences. An outlook that fails to do justice to the historical character of the psyche causes the psyche to wither. Destiny-fraught determinants lie within it that give the individual life its uniqueness. Taking into account the role of the ancestral spirits in the individuation process in this generalized way has become imperative. Doing so has a very wholesome effect.

The question of rebirth occupies many people today. The difficulty of proving genuine reincarnation arises from the fact that there is absolute knowledge in the collective unconscious.[28] When objects belonging to a dead person are put before a child and he "recognizes" them, this is not proof but rather a highly interesting suggestion of the possibility of a personal rebirth. Jung left this undecidable question open, but investigated the archetypal aspect of the idea from the psychological point of view.[29] In his autobiography, he expresses himself on the subject:

> I know of no answer to the question of whether the karma that I am living out is the result of my past lives, or if it is not rather the work of my ancestors, whose legacy comes together in me. Am I a combination of ancestral lives who embodies them again? Have I, as a specific person, already lived before, and did I make enough progress in that life so that I can now seek a resolution? I do not know. Buddha left this question open, and I may presume that he did not know the answer with certainty. I can well imagine that I have lived in earlier centuries and there ran across questions

that I was still unable to answer; that I was reborn because I had not fulfilled the task that was laid upon me. When I die—so I conceive it—my deeds will follow after me. I will take along what I have done.[30]

In the dream series I described earlier, as in other dreams with historical content, it has struck me that personal details and dates are absent. We must consider the possibility that an archetypal quintessence of our existence lives on and is reincarnated. What we know about dreams of death and dreams about deceased people fits together with this. Perhaps we put our attention in the wrong place, because the unique features of a human personality are what seem to us to be the distinctive aspect. But we overlook thereby that archetypal features, though they are more general, are the essential aspect of an existence. Thus in memory, the ancestors lose their personal attributes while the archetypal ones remain. The archetypal attributes represent the crux of the problem of being human and constitute the essential aspect of a human life.

Jung tells us:

In this book I have devoted considerable space to my subjective view of the world, which, however, is not a product of rational thinking. It is rather a vision such as will come to one who undertakes, deliberately, with half-closed eyes and somewhat closed ears, to see and hear the form and voice of being. If our impressions are too distinct, we are held to the hour and minute of the present and have no way of knowing how our ancestral psyches listen to and understand the present—in other words, how our unconscious is responding to it. Thus we remain ignorant of whether our ancestral components find an elementary gratification in our lives, or whether they are repelled. Inner peace and contentment depend in large measure upon whether or not the historical family which is inherent in the individual can be harmonized with the ephemeral conditions of the present.[31]

9

The Relationship between Subject and Object

How can a content of consciousness be distinguished at all from an unconscious content?[1] This same question arose in chapter 7, where I related that a person who is possessed by animus or anima insists that he or she is behaving fully consciously. Thus an animus-ridden woman finds her state to be one of the utmost clarity and awareness.

With this question, we come to a central problem of psychology as a whole. There are still people today who deny the existence of the unconscious altogether, or who, like Jean Gebser, explain everything in terms of different intensities or levels of consciousness. And it is not just plain contradictory to speak of unconscious contents? After all, a content can only be distinguished and grasped by consciousness. The moment a content is formulated or construed, it has already been appropriated by and as consciousness. The unconscious seems to be at best negatively definable—as everything that I am not conscious of, of which I know nothing.

But the unconscious is not just ignorance or unknowing, even though it is the not-known. This may sound confusing, but it will become clearer by considering the evolution of consciousness.

In the primordial state, man lives in an archaic identity with his environment, or as the great French philosopher and ethnologist Lucien Levy-Bruhl called it, a *participation mystique*.[2] Primordial man does not distinguish between himself and his environment; since he is not yet aware of himself as a subject, it follows that no such thing as an object yet exists for him. He lives immersed in a flow of events.[3] There is really no time. Everything is present occurrence, everything is focused in the present moment, which is only a narrow timespan; before and after are relative. Stone Age man lived hundreds of thousands of years in this psychological state. He lived a life without history. In this state, everything that occupies or fascinates a man is immediately present. The small beam of his consciousness is confined to illuminating this brief instant. Only what he grasps becomes the subject of his interest and attention (libido). Anything that falls even slightly outside this beam is relegated to the unconscious. In this state, consciousness is restricted to each present moment. There is neither past nor future. It is true that even such a man learns from experience—but he stores experience as such and not as retrievable memory.

In this state, space does not exist any more than does time. There is only the *here* in which the present moment takes place. A later here is not a there, but rather another current here, because there is no relationship between the two. The flow of events is a sequence of infinitely many moments comprised of here and now with no connection. For the unitary consciousness or subject that might entertain this interrelatedness is absent.

For us to have a real sense of this state is difficult. Doubtless even at this stage of consciousness, human beings, whether members of a primitive tribe or infants, behave purposively. As with animals, their instincts provide them with the basis for maintaining their lives.

Instinctive behavior itself shows us what a great gap there is between mere purposive action on the one hand and consciousness of carrying it out and of the reasons for carrying it out on the other. And even when we are occasionally conscious of *what* we are doing, we are still far from knowing *why* we are doing it.

At Christmastime, we put ornaments on an evergreen tree and say that we are doing it for the birth of Christ. Probably only a few people are conscious of what they are doing. Most people do it because everybody does it and because their parents before them did it, because it's the custom. This is the way man lived for a very long time. He did what "is done," what he has seen the adults doing since childhood and therefore imitates. In our everyday life also, we do many things by way of imitation, without questioning what our own motivation is.

In hindsight we are seldom at a loss for reasons for our actions. At least we are certain by then that we are conscious of our motives. In many situations we believe that we made a free decision and chose between various alternatives. We even engage in reasonings concerning the pros and cons of the various alternatives—and yet our unconscious has long since made the decision. We deceive ourselves mightily as to how great a part consciousness plays in our daily life.

I have often brought down on myself the earnest protests of my patients by insinuating that they have done something unconsciously. What we are unconscious of, we do with the firm conviction of not doing it. "But I *never* . . . !" We haven't an inkling of that which we are unconscious of. We claim self-righteously never to have thought or done anything of the kind—and nobody can hold this against us, "for the unconscious is really unconscious" (Jung).

This does not mean, however, that in our unconscious state we were inactive or had no thoughts. On the contrary: the unconscious is highly active, tirelessly functioning on the basis of its rich store of experience. For, as Jung says, "the unconscious is not a nothing, an absence of something, but rather it is the original way of functioning." "Unconscious" here means that the miracle of conscious development has not yet made its appearance. Thus man remains, like the animals, of a piece with nature. The unconscious contains, on the one hand, all the innate behavior patterns (instincts), and on the other hand, all the innate potential ways of apprehending things (archetypes). That is why primitive peoples are such good subjects for researches into instinctual and archetypal patterns. Consciousness has not yet changed them.

If man were to continue to live with this mentality, he would carry out only the will that was placed in him by the creator. But as the myth of the sacrifice of the cosmic man indicates, through the sacrifice of the cosmic man, the gods or the sages of the time before time began put an end to this paradisiacal state. As I have shown elsewhere,[4] the cosmic man represents an all-embracing continuum in which man is embedded. He experiences his psyche in the world around him. He feels part and parcel of the rest of creation, from which he is not yet separated. Stones and trees tell man their story; they are not dead or mute. In his animistic outlook, the whole world is alive.

This state of mind is by no means as strange to us as it may seem. Poets proclaim it in their poetry, and people who are cut off from it get a taste of it as they read—as though they were hearing an echo from a distant time. Our little children still live in a magic world. It is the world of the unconscious, as we encounter it in our dreams. For this reason, it cannot be alien to us, even though it obeys utterly different laws from the daytime world of our consciousness. That world of the unconscious entangles us in a curious confusion. There we meet ourselves as another person, as an animal or plant or even as an aspect of inanimate nature (stone, storm, cloud)—and yet we are also not that. "Who am I really?" we ask ourselves then. At this level of consciousness, I am somehow everything. Nothing is totally alien to me, even when it causes me fear. Everything belongs to me, and I live in everything around me.

To the extent that we are allied with the unconscious, we have never separated ourselves from this archaic world. Every night we plunge back into it, and also during the day we live in it in those places where the light of consciousness has not yet fallen. If somebody scolds my dog unfairly, I feel personally insulted.

The dog is part of me, I live in participation with it. Everything we are attached to is a part of us. When we lose it, we experience a loss of soul. Such dependence on material things to which we have lost our soul can be dangerous, as can a like dependence on other people—for example, when a child has remained a piece of the mother's soul, when a wife represents the soul of the husband or a husband the mind of his wife. Then they become just "one heart and one soul," a questionable ideal state, because a relationship cannot exist where there is an identity. Identity is a connection but no relationship. Real relationships can only evolve between two separated persons. Insofar as we live in an archaic identity, we live in the things and persons around us, but not in relationship with them. They follow our will or we theirs. There exists a magic dependence, a magic compulsion that the objects or persons exert over us or we over them. We have fallen prey to them or they to us. In such cases, the will or consciousness are not really free.

As these examples show, modern man is not so far distant from the state of mind of primitive peoples. That is the reason he can enter into sympathy with this state of mind. In contrast to our children, a member of a primitive tribe is an adult who verbalizes and accounts for his experience. However, he does not account for it in a logical way but rather in a mythological one that is in tune with the unconscious. That makes dialogue with him difficult. The primitive person believes he has given a highly plausible explanation, while from our point of view it doesn't "explain" anything at all. To explain an event means precisely to make it fit into a given worldview. The "primitive" lives in a world that is alive, in which there is neither subject nor object, neither an external world nor an inner world. The external world is just as good as inner world as the other way around. Thus his mode of action is to a great extent determined by the world around him. Nature is his mother. She cares for all his needs, so that he need neither sow nor reap. He enjoys what nature provides, he is a hunter and gatherer. He takes care of himself when he needs to, and because he lives entirely in the present, he keeps no stores. He lives like the fowls of the air, of whom it is written: "For they sow not and neither do they reap, nor gather into barns; yet your heavenly father feedeth them" (Matt. 6:26).

Since his consciousness is not partitioned off from objects, the borderline between human and animal that seems uncrossable for us is a blurry one for him. Many myths tell of animal ancestors, and fairy tales recount marriages between animals and humans.[5] Humans and animals easily change into one another.[6] Man does not yet experience himself as the crowning glory of creation. He has his place somewhere in the animal world; there are animals that are more powerful than he, such as the lion or the elephant. A sorcerer may move about at night in the form of a crocodile and bring injury on ordinary people. If a crocodile devours a child, the bush soul of the sorcerer must have entered into it, since crocodiles do not ordinarily feed on children.

It is this entirely different way of experiencing the world that fundamentally distinguishes the primitive mentality from ours. The magic that is part of the primitive world is based on identity: effects leap directly from one object to another. Magic plays a major role in explaining the unexplainable. On account of *sympatheia*, a causal interrelatedness of things among themselves, magic is omnipresent. Sorcerers, medicine men, and shamans participate in this *sympatheia*. It is within their magical power to bring about unexplainable effects—for example, hurling illness-bearing projectiles—and also to protect against such effects.

In the world of this mentality, possession is a frequent occurrence, because the ego is weak. Also, nearly every member of a primitive society is capable of liberating a possessed person from his condition without having to undertake a special exorcism.[7] This is an indication of how easily consciousness can be dissociated under these conditions, that is, how easily another content can take possession of it. Every human being goes through this stage in the course of his or her development, and many do not get far beyond it, though they do not live as Stone Age men and women.

Though we live primarily at another level of conscious development, we continue to exhibit the characteristics of archaic identity in areas that are unconscious. An *abaissement du niveau mental* accompanies every emotion, opening the way to the intrusion of unconscious contents that may take possession of consciousness. Our emotions make us easy prey for those types of possession discussed in chapter 6. We are possessed by unwholesome ideas or fears (fear of cancer, or nuclear holocaust). We do not recognize these possessions, because we have logical justifications for their effects—they are cloaked by rationalization. The psychosomatically ailing woman of whom I spoke in chapter 6 did believe in the physical examinations of her doctors which showed that no physical ailment was present, and therefore believed the disorder must be psychological in nature. But still she kept asking herself, "What if the physical disease eluded the doctors' methods of detection?" We trust amazingly little in our modern rationality. In point of fact, the animistic mentality has proved its worth over a longer period of our process of humanization than modern reason.

The archaic mentality is hard to recognize as long as one is living in it, because it seems self-evident and is devoid of contradictions. Only when contradictions or doubts arise is there a piercing of the thin skin under which man lives. That is the moment of the sacrifice of the cosmic man.

With this sacrifice, a second stage in the development of consciousness takes place. At this stage, man realizes that the objects in his environment are laden with contents of his psyche. Only when this stage is reached is it possible to speak of projection. The paradisiacal state of unquestioned union with the world is over, and for the first time man stands over against his world as alien to it. Thence arises the distinction between subject and object. Strictly speaking, it is only now that we can speak of the world being populated by gods, spirits, and demons;

for it is only with the sacrifice of the cosmic man that the world is born. Only when the all-pervading continuum of the archaic unity has been broken up is there a subject who sees himself face to face with a world. Development of consciousness means discrimination, making distinctions. The expulsion from paradise (Gen. 3:24) means precisely such a making of distinctions. In paradise, man continued to live in the innocence of the archaic identity. He could not do otherwise. The romantic vision of life in the South Pacific and other such idealizations of life close to nature are expressions of man's longing for the paradisiacal state of unity out of which we primevally emerged. But we cannot go back. Once one has left paradise, one must look for the tree of life elsewhere. Herein lies the problem of the new stage of consciousness: the divine state of innocence has been lost. Man is no longer securely protected as within an egg but instead finds himself in an alien world where he is menaced by many dangers and encounters many powers. Only looking back from this new level of consciousness could he speak of an archaic identification. Only now does he see alien powers and forces in a world he previously experienced as merely alive. He distinguishes between himself and these beings. Thus an outlook of polydemonism or polytheism arises.

In ancient Greece, not only were there many gods, but also the waters swarmed with nymphs, the bushes and trees with dryads, the fields with satyrs, and Pan terrified the solitary shepherd. In sum, nature was peopled with a multiplicity of *numina*. In the heat of noon, Pan took his forty winks and did not wish to be disturbed. The white lady of noon moved through the fields. In the sea, the waves were crowned with the white manes of Poseidon's horses. Out of the white seaspray foam that had formed about the severed member of the father of the Titans, Uranus, Aphrodite was born. During storms, Zeus's thunderbolt split the heavens. Chaste Artemis bathed in the still forest pool with her maidens, tired from the hunt. Nature bedecked itself with its most beautiful flowers and blossoms when Zeus visited Hera's bed.

Man accommodated himself to these powers, recognizing his dependence on them, indeed his subordination to them. A religious attitude toward them acknowledges this subordination. When man entertains a proper relationship to these powers, he enjoys their help. He is at their mercy, therefore his benefit also proceeds from them. Our word *inspiration* still points to the idea that we do not ourselves have good ideas, but that they are "breathed into" us by the spirits or gods. Thus the poet invokes the Muses to bring him the ideas he needs for his work. As with the Old Testament prophets, God speaks through the poet, who is thus a reed or mouthpiece and a proclaimer of great things.

In cultures in which an outlook such as this predominates, many functions of the psyche are projected. This creates difficulties for comparative psychiatry. In investigating such cultures, we cannot simply take a questionnaire conceived in terms of modern Western culture and translate it into the appropriate native language. Those languages would have no words, say, for "depression" or "depressive."[8] A paraphrase would not work either. In such a culture, this condition is not experienced as an inner psychological experience, but rather, for example, as a loss of soul or a spell. Knowledge, which we hold without doubt to be a psychological function, was, in ancient Egypt, personified as the creator god Atum. The seventeenth chapter of the Egyptian Book of the Dead states: "Hu [utterance] and Sia [knowledge] accompany father Atum [the sun] on his every daily journey." In the eighty-fifth chapter, we find: "I am Hu, who in his name soul cannot pass away."[9] Similarly, in the prologue to the Gospel according to Saint John, the creative word (*logos*) is personified and made flesh. As such passages show, in this stage the soul or psyche lives to a great extent in its projections. For this reason, psychological functions tend to become concretized, whereas we tend to make them abstract. Nevertheless, we might still say, "he has a heart for the poor" instead of "he has compassion," and we localize many functions of the psyche in the body.

Many of our old customs are expressions of this second stage of consciousness, for example, the Saint Nicholas processions in certain parts of Switzerland, where vegetation demons are represented, the customs surrounding the maypole, or others dealing with grain demons.[10] In the traditional ceremony for blessing a new house, a fir tree decorated with colorful ribbons is placed on top of the newly framed house to propitiate the domestic spirits.

A particular problem is presented by local spirits. Already at the archaic level there are auspicious places and inauspicious places, as for example among the aborigines of Australia.[11] Many Christian churches or holy places are built on spots where pagan temples earlier stood. Sometimes churches were built with the stones of those temples, since those continued to be regarded as holy. Still in the Middle Ages, people crossed themselves at crossroads, or placed a chapel where gallows had stood or where the bodies of hanged people had been thrown. Such places were regarded as frightening or "spooky." One had to be careful not to get "ridden" or "caught" by a demon. Modern exorcists still cast out demons into such haunted places. The names of some of our meadows and fields recall the gods and spirits that once inhabited them. For example, the name of the Vrenelisgärtli near Glärnisch, Switzerland, means "Garden of Venus."

Altogether, this and the next stage of consciousness are the ones that come to expression in the sagas of the Swiss mountain people and that correspond to their mentality. "Id"-like powers[12] play the decisive role; people in this stage realize their dependency on them and accord them a suitable level of consideration. As *daimonion* or protective spirits, they can guide the individual. As we shall see later, everyone can have his own protective spirit.

The end of this mentality was marked by the story recounted by Plutarch of the "Death of the Great Pan,"[13] in which sailors sailing by an island hear the message of the god's death and have to carry it to another island, from which, after doing so, they hear the sound of lamenting. With that death, not only the animation of nature by spirits ended but also the veneration of this "bespirited" nature, the respect for its mystery, its superhuman power to which human beings were granted only limited access. When the American Indians were advised to use a plow so as to cultivate their corn in a more rational fashion, they rejected it, saying, "How could we injure our Mother Earth?"

The third stage of the development of consciousness is moral discrimination of good and hostile demons. Hitherto, the demons or spirits have been simply superior powers in relation to whom one had to adapt oneself suitably so that they would be helpful, since otherwise they might well be harmful. Yahweh, the God of the Old Testament, shows himself to Jacob on the banks of the river Jabbok (Gen. 32:24) as a mortal danger as Jacob wrestles with Him in the form of an angel, even though Yahweh is not actually evil. In the story of Job, Satan is still one of God's sons and his inner antithesis. As Jung showed,[14] the Christian aeon, as the Piscean age, must particularly confront the problem of the antithesis of good and evil as represented by the fish swimming in opposite directions. In the common prehistoric culture of Iran and India, the word *d(a)eva* meant "celestial" or "day-sky" in a neutral sense; later in India it acquired the meaning "supreme god"; in Iran, on the other hand, it acquired the meaning "demon" in the negative sense.

A new religion always demonifies his former gods. After the conversion to Christianity, this change took place throughout the ancient Greco-Roman world. All through the European Middle Ages, it was forbidden to say the name of the Germanic god Wotan, because it referred to the chief of the devils. A well-documented fact is this: So long as gods remain the object of a cult, they remain relatively close to consciousness. As soon as another religion covers them over, they are relegated to the unconscious, whence they make a nuisance of themselves whenever they collide with the new worldview. Consciousness is exclusive, because it abhors ambiguity. Whatever conflicts with the prevailing consciousness is repressed. Insofar as the psyche moves toward wholeness, these repressed contents also seek a role in life. Since this can only happen over the resistance of consciousness, they in turn set up resistance to consciousness by engaging in demonic machinations. The moment consciousness carries out a moral judgment excluding particular contents, it begins to be subject to demonic influences. The discrimination of moral judgment is part of the evolution of consciousness; from it inevitably arise demons in the negative sense.

This process can be readily seen by examining the Greek terms in question. In Homer and Hesiod, *daimon* can still mean "god." In classical Greek philosophy, from Plato to Plutarch, it designates a power between gods and men that is for the most part beneficent and worthy of offerings and supplications (*Symposium* 202D). Xenocrates systematized Plato's teaching on the demons by assimilating them to the notion of souls. In Middle Platonism and Neoplatonism (Apuleius, Porphyry, Iamblichus) this trend continued. Demons were seen not only as sending pestilence and war, they were also the sources of oracles, dreams, and inspirations—in short, whatever comes from a hidden source.[15] Sometimes they are closer to gods, sometimes to men, in whose passions they participate. They are capable of both good and evil. The definitive distinction occurs in The Book of Enoch (6–9), according to which the angels were created good but took the daughters of men to wife; out of their union the race of giants was born (what an inflation!), and the demons are the souls of the giants. It is they who seduce men into evil and cause them to turn away from God. Then in the New Testament, idol worship, that is, the veneration of the old gods, is attributed to the influence of demons (1 Cor. 10:20; Rev. 9:20). The spiritual battle between God and the archdemon for the souls of human beings dominated the minds of the Church fathers.

Following the third stage comes an enantiodromia, that is, an abrupt switch to the opposite. Having divided the world into good and evil demons, in the fourth stage, the phase of Enlightenment, this opposition is done away with. The existence of demons is denied; they are dismissed as the products of human "imagination." In the Enlightenment phase, psychology degenerates into a subjectivism. Man, the subject, is the only psychic reality. This stage is the antipode of the first. In the first stage, the whole world and the whole psyche were identified with each other as external. In the fourth stage, they are identified with each other as within. The ego acquires the central position in psychology. Gods and demons are considered mere superstition. Nature and the world are entirely desacralized.

This stage of the evolution of consciousness, which is prevalent today, contains two dangers: a one-sided rationalism and the demonification of man. The Enlightenment did not simply make the demons go away, nor did it render them impotent. It is true that they did disappear from the outer world. When man became the only psychic reality, the demons migrated into him. Man has become identified with the demons; he no longer distinguishes himself from them. Man has become the source of all good and evil. For the most part, he is somewhat conscious of being the source of everything good, since that is what he mainly wants to be. But since he identifies with the good, the evil that he does is unconscious. Unconsciously enacted evil is nonetheless bad. For the most part it remains camouflaged by good intentions; and this creates much too heavy a burden for humanity. Today we see the whole world talking about compromise, peace, and disarmament while just the opposite is actually taking place. Despite remonstrances of good intentions, the most hideous acts of cruelty occur. How is that possible? One party thinks the other party is not honest—they will say nice things and do the opposite. That is a typical projection. There are in fact only a few who intentionally act badly while proclaiming their good intentions. When it comes to projections, the influence of the unconscious is present. Such misunderstandings go to show that one is unable to see the active element here—the demons. One cannot see them so long as one is demonic oneself. Man has become demonic to such a degree that he is now in danger of destroying himself and the world. Actually, he is no worse today than he used to be; only, since the demons have fled from him into the unconscious, he is no longer able to fend them off. An invisible foe is far more dangerous than a visible one. It seems that today all the important things have been said, all the clever thoughts have been thought, and all the statements of good intentions have been made—we need no more of these things. However, what we do not yet know and recognize are the demons in us. Only when we begin to track them down will we have prospects of solving the grave problems of our time.

That is why we have to go beyond our "enlightened" approach and seek out the fifth stage of consciousness, that of the objectivity of the psyche, the *unus mundus*. This stage in some sense takes us back to the beginning, for it once again ascribes to both the psyche and its demons their own reality. At this stage the split between psyche and physis is resolved in the One World (*unus mundus*).[16] Beyond the conscious level of experience, psyche and physis rest on a common psyche-like (psychoid) stratum. That is why, in instances of synchronicity, there is a single-intentioned convergence of psyche and physis. The psyche is not less objectively existent than the physis.

With this fifth stage of the development of consciousness, we come, so to speak, full circle. The psyche does not identify with, and is thus not limited by, consciousness; rather, as is the case in the first stage, it is limitless and cosmic. It encompasses both consciousness and the unconscious. The two are interrelated rather than essentially separate realities. Although the unconscious is, as its name says, unknown, it betrays itself in our communications and in other signs enough so that it is possible to say something about it. Myths are examples of communications of the unconscious concerning itself. They express something about how contents of the unconscious wish to be understood—something that otherwise we would know nothing about.

Paranormal manifestations are part of the nature of the unconscious. Insofar as we are not in a position to make statements about the nature of the unconscious, such manifestations require no further explanation. This delimiting of our knowledge is based on the fact that the unconscious lies beyond the range of consciousness; that is, it is (consciousness-)transcendent. When I speak here of the unconscious, I mean the collective unconscious, not the personal unconscious. The latter is much closer to consciousness, and in fact could just as well be conscious. Consciousness and will have no influence over the collective unconscious—other than through very specific means specially suited to relating with it.

Consciousness and the unconscious are interrelated; they are complementary. The unconscious completes consciousness through contents that the latter lacks for its wholeness. Whether the unconscious relates antagonistically or cooperatively with consciousness depends on the attitude of consciousness. A religious attitude of the consciousness makes it possible for the unconscious to play a cooperative role. Good spirits, as for example the shaman's helping spirits, are evidence of this. By contrast, evil spirits, like those the saints faced, are examples of the antagonistic or compensatory function of the unconscious.

Thus spirits and demons are not entirely autonomous beings; in a subtle way they are dependent on the approach of consciousness. This makes it understandable how erstwhile gods, being dominant elements of the collective unconscious (archetypes), transform into evil demons when they are no longer worshipped and represented in consciousness. They are neglected areas of the psyche that evolve their negative effects in order to call attention to themselves. Ceremony, worship, and myth are possible means for maintaining archetypal material at a certain level of consciousness, or gaining representation for it in consciousness. In this way, it can take part in the life of the psyche and provide it with a certain equilibrium. If an important content becomes unconscious—like the dethroned gods—a disequilibrium occurs. This brings about a counterreaction in the unconscious, which manifests as a demon. If consciousness is completely cut off from this, this counterreaction can, as in the case of haunting, intensify to the level of paranormal vividness.

Everything that I have set forth here concerning spirits and demons is based on the viewpoint of this fifth stage of consciousness. Misunderstandings can enter in if these notions are criticized from the point of view of another stage of consciousness.

10

The Stone:
Demon of Procreative Power

For archaic man, stones possessed a *numen* and might belong to a god. Literally, *numen*[1] means a slight movement of the head, a nod, as in the verb *adnuo*, "nod to, wave to." Beyond that, however, it means a divine or supernatural force or influence, a god. An object that seems dead to the rational mind shows by this almost imperceptible movement[2] that it is alive—and this is attributed to a spirit or demon in the object. The feeling that a spirit or demon is present in an object arises from subtle experiences. When walking alone in a still woods, we ourselves sometimes experience what is meant by *numen*. We sense a living presence continually around us, though there is no living being to be seen. These are the forest spirits, the spirits in trees and stones who live in the woods. It was as this kind of presence that Zeus Endendros was worshiped on Rhodes and Paros and Dionysos Endendros in Boeotia.

In Thespiae, a plain stone was a symbol of the fertility-bestowing god Eros. A stone, *herma*, was the primeval image of the Greek god Hermes. As a stone, he stood guard at the gates of house and court.[3] In honor of him, travelers tossed stones on a heap at crossroads, which is, incidentally, an ancient custom found throughout the world. Crudely carved stones called herms with a bearded head and an erect member (*ithyphallos*) represented the god; they stood at many places both in the city and

the country. In addition to their guardian function, they were
also supposed to work apotropaically, that is, they warded off
demons. In Cyllene, the cult image consisted simply of a male
member. Whole processions with phalluses moved through the
streets of Athens and Delos during Dionysiac festivals.[4] Priapos
of Lampsakos,[5] the guardian of gardens and harbors, was always
represented ithyphallically. Donkeys were sacrificed to him,[6] as
were geese. In general in ancient times, there were many local
ithyphallic deities. Their images stood in the workshops of
artisans, in bakeries, and on potters' kilns. They were symbols
of creativity. Later, they were assimilated to one of the three
deities Hermes, Dionysos, or Priapos.

Hermes was worshiped as Terminus, the divine personification
of borders. He was the bringer of wealth and fertility as well as
the mentor of homosexual love. He also guided and protected the
traveler. Hermes in his own form was also regarded as the guide
and protector of travelers. In his three-headed or four-headed
form (*tricephalos, tetracephalos*), he stood at crossroads to show the
way. He was the god of shepherds and itinerants (*demiourgoi*). He
protected by means of clever stratagems and magic; thus he
carried a magic wand with which he caused people to fall asleep.
He appeared and disappeared suddenly in an eerie manner.
When a large group suddenly found itself at a loss for conversation, it was said that Hermes had entered the room. His winged
shoes, which later became a winged hat, permitted him to move
with the speed of the wind. He became a messenger between
gods and men. Thus he assumed a position comparable to that
ascribed by Plato to the demons in his *Symposium*.[7] Finally, he
was regarded as the accompanier of the dead, Hermes Chthonios.
Herms are also found at graves, possibly as a symbol of the
fertility-fostering influence of the dead. Unlike the other gods,
Hermes was not worshiped in a temple or as part of a local cult.
His omnipresence made him more like a demon or spirit, a
quality also expressed by his wings. Later he was called Logios,
god of speech. In Hellenistic syncretism, he became Trismegistos

("thrice great") and Psychopompos ("guide of souls"). With his brother Apollo, he was considered the inventor of the lyre and of music.[8]

The word *daimon* went through a considerable change of meaning. Though Homer does still use the word in the meaning of *theos*,[9] he uses it rather more in the sense of the appearance of a numen.[10] The term *daimon* refers to something superhuman that is still unknown, whereas *theos* refers to the person of a god. The writers of tragedy called *daimon* everything that "strikes" man—a stroke of fate, death, everything good and evil, fate in general, as in the sentence "Happy scion of Atreus, you received a fortunate demon as your portion at birth."[11] In many passages in the epics, the demon is what happens through the will of the gods.[12] In this sense, it approaches the meaning of the *Moira* (from *moros*, "lot"), the goddesses of fate. As mother gods, they represent the lot that falls to a man by fate. Etymologically, *daimon* comes from the Indo-European root *da*, meaning "divide, cut up, tear up."[13] In this sense, it goes well with the *Moira* as an active apportioner of fate. For the writers of tragedy, it was the family curse of a particular house in which an original sin continued to draw further ones in its train.

The *daimon* is that divine power that drives a man on in his actions and thus entangles him in his destiny. Here its meaning touches on that of *tyché*, ("fate, fortune"), an expression stemming from a folk belief combatted by contemporary philosophers for the sake of establishing freedom of moral decision.[14] Though *tyché* might be condemned as blind and regarded as arbitrary, nevertheless the action of the gods lies behind it. In fact, it can even be regarded as the *Moira*. A city has its *tyché*. This gradually becomes personified and venerated as a goddess, to whom a temple is built. What is a concept for us today may often have been a *numen* in ancient times that was later personified and worshiped—as for example *nike* ("victory"). *Tyché*, like a *daimon*, belongs to an individual person and is born with him or her. As *agathos daimon*, it is no longer separable from *daimon*.[15]

No other Greek god is so surrounded by "stones" as Apollo.[16] Apollo Agyieus was initially nothing other than a stone pillar. A pyramid-shaped stone in the Gymnasium of Megara was called Apollon Karinos. In Malea, Apollo as Lethésios stood next to a stone. Pausanias (10.16.2) writes of an oracle of Apollo in Delphi: "What the people of Delphi call *omphalos* is made out of white stone and is regarded as located at the center of the earth."[17] Such a "central stone" is found also in the Celtic tradition. For example, there is Liam Fail, the stone that begins to sing as soon as a future king sits on it. At the Ordal, the Judgment of the Gods, the accused, if he is innocent, becomes white when he climbs on the stone. If a woman is to remain barren, the stone sweats blood; if she is to bear, it excretes milk. There are also phallic variants of these cultic *omphaloi*. The middle and fertility go together. In the French village of D'Amancy (Canton De la Roche), there is still to be found the Pierre du Milieu du Monde (the Stone of the Middle of the World).[18]

Also such a middle was the stone on which Jacob laid his head on the night he dreamed about the ladder to heaven (Gen. 28:11– 22). Beth-el, the "house of God," the stone Jacob erected as a monument, is the place where heaven and earth come together, the "middle" that corresponds to the "gate of heaven." Similarly, Mount Sinai or the black stone, the Kaaba, in Mecca, are the centers of the world. Among the Romans, the "navel of the earth" was a hollow in the ground called *mundus*. On the days it was open, the gate to the underworld was open; at such times, the dead invisibly mingled with the living, who therefore had to be particularly careful.[19]

Stones are also the resort of ancestral spirits. In central Australia, there is a stone called Erathipa with an opening on the side. There the souls of the ancestors lie in wait for a woman to pass by through whom they can be reborn as children. Barren Maidu women touch a rock that in form resembles a pregnant woman. In southeastern New Guinea, on the island of Kai, a woman who wants to have children bastes a stone with fat. In modern Egypt, barren women become capable of bearing children by climbing seven times over a conical stone in the vicinity of the tomb of Sheik Sayyid.[20] In many parts of the world, newlyweds walk over a stone to make their marriage fruitful.[21] According to Indian belief, certain stones are born out of themselves and then reborn (*svayambhū*, "autogenesis"); thus barren women venerate them with offerings. Agdistis, the mother of the vegetation god Attis of Phrygia and Asia Minor, was a rock that bore the divine son out of itself. Mithras, the god of the Roman soldier, was also thought to have been born from a rock. The *petra genetrix* ("stone mother") was worshiped in a temple. In order to bear children, young women slip lengthwise under a consecrated stone.[22] Widely diffused is the ritual custom of barren women rubbing against sacred stones. In the first nights after their marriage, newlyweds pay a visit to a large rock in Saint Renan called *la jument de pierre* ("the stone mare"), and the woman rubs her belly against the rock. A woman who wants to have a baby sleeps on this rock for three nights. In the Middle Ages, there were many ecclesiastical and royal prohibitions against the cult of stones and against the ejaculation of seed in front of stones. There were the *pierre d'amour* and the *pierre de mariage*, stones of love and marriage. In the village of Carnac, women sit with raised skirts on the dolmen Creuz-Moquem. In the French canton of Amance, women kneel to the *pierre percée* and pray for the health of their children and toss a coin through the hole. The custom, still practiced today, of passing a newborn child through the hole in a rock is a kind of baptism by stone; it is supposed to preserve the child from harm and bring good fortune; it is also a kind of rite of rebirth. In India such ring-shaped stones, as sun symbols, are gates of the world (*lokadvara*) through which the soul can be transported away and thus saved. The hole in the stone is called "the gate of liberation" (*muktidvara*). Eliade interprets this as liberation from the cosmos and the cycles of karma.[23]

The stone represents the middle, the place where this world and the beyond, the profane and sacred, consciousness and unconsciousness meet. Death and birth, ancestors and newborn babies belong together in any case. The phallus-shaped stone from Antipolis was regarded as the *therapon aphrodites*, "the servant of Aphrodite."[24] In Naxos in Sicily, in the temple of Aphrodite, representations of both female and male genitalia were displayed. In Samothrace, the two Kabirs were ithyphallic. The ancient Italian god Mutunus Tutunus in Veliae demanded from newlyweds the sacrifice of virginity.[25] In Lavinium, a matron publicly placed a wreath on the phallus so that the crops just sown would flourish. In the temple of the Vestals, a phallus, the *fascinus populi Romani*, was worshiped; as an amulet it was hung around the necks of children, for as a *medicus invidiae* it provided protection against the evil eye and against jealousy.

As we have already indicated, the meaning of *daimon* gradually came nearer that of "fate." This linked it semantically with procreation and the moment of birth. Though the Roman *genius* was phallic,[26] the word *genius* itself derives from *genere*, "procreate, generate"; from that in turn comes *ingenium*, "the innate, natural makeup, temperament, innate ability, understanding, a bright person, talent, genius." Censorinus explains: "The genius is a god under whose protection each person who is born lives. It either makes sure that we are begotten, or it is born with us, or it receives and protects us after our birth. Certainly the word derives from 'generate.' "[27] The genius is the life principle of a man, and has a definite connection with the forehead. It can also be the life principle of a woman, her feminine identity, which is called Juno. Every woman possesses her Juno,[28] which expresses itself especially in the eyebrows. To Juno belong the dark time of the new moon and the subterranean depths. Goats and snakes are sacred to her. Juno Lucina is the goddess of birth. Sometimes *animus* and *genius* are treated as equivalents.[29] In Plautus, *genius* embodies the idea of the well-being and health that are necessary to the complete unfolding of a life. Inasmuch as the bed is related to the birth of children, who owe their existence to the life principle of the parents, it is called *genialis lectus*. While originally the genius belonged to the person, the *lar* by contrast was an earth deity, which according to Pliny the Elder appears as a male member by the hearth in the birth legend of Servius Tullius.[30] The *lar familialis* is the protector of the house. The genius had already in antiquity begun to merge with the lar, especially under Greek influence: "Only the Genius, the companion who rules our birthstar, knows, / God of human nature, dying with each / Individual; changeable of expression, kindly and somber."[31] Eventually this quality of mutability led to the genius being doubled: "When we are born, we each have two genii allotted to us; one urges us on to good, the other seduces us into evil."[32] While for Horace the genius is mortal, for Apuleius (*De deo Socratis* 15), it is immortal: "Although it is immortal, it is nevertheless to some degree born with the individual."[33] On grave monuments, the genius is sometimes reckoned among the *manes*. It is thus not surprising that the genius is frequently associated with the snake, which symbolizes not only fertility, but also the depths of the earth. This is the *genius loci:* "Others think that the genius is the god of any given place."[34] The commentary of Servius on the *Aeneid* (*Aen.* 5.85) confirms this: "There is no place without a genius; it usually makes itself known in the form of a snake." The snake is the *"agathos daimon*, which the Latins call *genius."* Finally, the genius can be a protective spirit and *genius fatalis.* A genius can also be associated with collective bodies such as a college or senate. The Christian guardian angel is a counterpart of the genius. What the Christians called *angelus bonus* was for the ancients the *mercurius psychopompos.* The wings of the angels ultimately derive from the wings of Hermes. Wings symbolically indicate a volatile, that is, spiritual, nature.

In this way the archaic mentality created a symbolic representation of a destiny-fraught spiritual principle in man, his *daimon.* It is born with him but is immortal (according to most writers). It embodies all his innate talents and abilities, but also the qualities of his moment of birth, on which his fate depends. In life it manifests as a kind of soul that leads him on to good or evil. The lives of ancestors also leave their mark on it. Fertility is not only connected with procreation, but is also an expression of vitality.

A peculiar position is occupied by the *daimonion* of Socrates.[35] It is generally thought of as a voice through which the deity made its will and prohibitions known to him. However, according to contemporary accounts Socrates heard "no voice, but rather the utterances of a spirit, which reached the perceiving mind with its revelations by itself without sounds."[36]

In the *Republic* (617E, 620D), Plato has one of the characters tell us that the soul chooses the moment in which it is born into a new earthly life, its *daemon*, which then watches over a man during his life and guides him to Hades. In the *Phaedo* (107D, E; 108B), it is said that the daemon chooses the person. In the pseudo-Platonic *Epinomis*, the visible gods, the stars, are contrasted with the demons. They revealed themselves to men in dreams, oracles, and premonitions (984D, E; 985C). According to the great philosopher and mystic Poseidonios, the demons could make themselves understood without words; their *logos* was propagated through the air. If someone's soul was still, it resonated in the stillness of the soul. During sleep it spoke to men and revealed to them their future. The later Stoics—Seneca, Epictetus, Marcus Aurelius—place the demon in man as his moral makeup; thus a divine nature inheres within him (anthropos). Occasionally, as with Plutarch, this idea tends to merge with the notion of a protecting spirit.[37]

The phallic cult could not have attained worldwide diffusion had it not been the cult of a particularly powerful demon or god. For archaic man his own power of procreation was a major concern because of high levels of child mortality; for cattle breeders and farmers, fertility of the herds and crops was a crucial matter. To the visible signs of fertility were soon added the invisible ones connected with prosperity, good fortune, the prospering of clan, family, and commercial ventures. It is not, as Freud thought, concrete sexuality that is one of the mightiest demons of man, but rather his drive to create. On the biological level, this expresses itself in the miracle of begetting new life and in the mystery of the sexual act. On the mental level, it is the drive to create new things, reshape existing things, to invent, bring forth new ideas, in sum, to create a new order. Geared toward change, it has much to do with the instinct of play.

The compulsion or urge to create is the fate-fraught *daimon* of creative people. It can entirely determine the life of its bearer— and destroy it. Many creative people die young, as though their demon had burned them out. We need only think of Mozart or Schubert. Many, like Hölderlin or Nietzsche, are torn apart by it when they are not able to follow its urgings. In chapter 4, I spoke of the "creative complex." Here it becomes clear what happens when the drive to creation becomes a person's destiny. Not for nothing is the *lingam* of the creator god Shiva venerated throughout India, not only in houses and temples but also in the fields. It is the drive to consciousness that brings the world into existence.[38] Many psychological and physical ailments have their origin in a hindrance to the development of consciousness. In individuation, the potential of a person is realized; at the end of this process stands the higher man (anthropos) or the Self. The daimon of procreative power is ultimately the *principium individuationis*, the drive to individuation. On the biological level, it reproduces the individual, creates new life. On the archaic level it overcomes and renews the old king (in Egypt, Horus as the son of Ra and Osiris). On the modern level, it is the mystery of transformation, the renewal of life in the individual himself.

The most multifaceted and profound symbolism of the stone is found in alchemy, in the image of the *lapis philosophorum*, the philosopher's stone. To give even a relatively full account of the meaning of the stone in alchemy is impossible. It bears a thousand names, it is an *arcanum*, a secret substance about which the most contradictory statements have been made. This marks it as an *ineffabile*, something unutterable, a divine mystery not accessible to man in words. "No matter what name it is given," we find in the *Rosarium Philosophorum*, "it is always one and the same. Of it Merculinus says: 'A stone is hidden, buried in the ground of the source. / Of little worth and despised, covered with muck and mire.' "[39] Along with the idea that the stone is a supreme mystery, it is emphasized that it is cheap, ordinary, available anywhere, despised by men, and trampled in the mire. In a dialogue between an ignorant person (Ignotus) and an ancient one (Antiquissimus),[40] the stone is called *salutaris*, "wholesome." In the "Dicta Belini,"[41] the stone says of itself that it is "the greatest and the cure for all illnesses and all impurities" and that the wise are already acquainted with its qualities and its high worth. In the "Philosophia Reformata" of Johann Daniel Mylius, it is said that "that stone heals nature." Elsewhere it is referred to as poisonous: "They [the philosophers] also call the stone a poison and compare it with basilisks, dragons, vipers, the salamander, the serpent, the lizard and other reptiles, and the toad."[42] The stone also has dark and dangerous aspects, and just for this reason leads to the wholeness and completeness that it itself represents. This wholeness encompasses all aspects of life, including the level of animal instinct. "This divine water (*hydor theon*) is indeed a poison of utmost strength . . . without which nothing is effected. It is called divine, because it is unalloyed with any impurity, and it itself purifies the qualities of the stone and frees it of impurities (*abluit*)."[43]

The alchemical stone is alive. The "Exercitationes" in "Turbam Philosophorum"[44] speak of the *lapis animalis*. Gerardus Dorneus,[45] a Frankfurt physician, student of Paracelsus, and alchemist whose philosophical treatises were highly valued by Jung, states:

> They [the philosophers] confirmed in the strongest way by spirit and reason that their stone was alive. They named it their Adam, who bore his Eve hidden in his body from the moment in which the two were united by the will (*virtute*) of the Creator. . . . In virtue of this position of the best philosophers, one must understand the "adamantine" matter of the stone as the limbus of the microcosm and the homogeneous and only matter of the philosophers.

Limbus is a typical concept of the Paracelsian philosophy. Dorn[46] describes it as the "great and universal world, seed and prime matter of man." In this view, the stone is at once a primal substance or prime matter of the creator and the primal man who is not yet differentiated into man and woman. From the psychological point of view, he represents the *anthropos*, the starting point and final product of the individuation process. Now we understand why the stone is at once physical and spiritual, animate and inanimate, heavenly and earthly, and yet, paradoxically, represents the wholeness of man. Inasmuch as this is not a static state but rather an ongoing process of transformation, the stone simply stands for the creative principle.

The creative principle is a *mysterium magnum*, a mysterious process that goes on in every human life. Even if everyone is not a Mozart or a Picasso, the miracle of the creative process takes place in all of us, to the extent that we do not shut it out through monotonous routine. Everything that we copy from others and do automatically hinders creativity in our lives. Creativity can only unfold when we step out of well-worn ruts. Imagination is an essential factor in creativity and has its source in the unconscious—the stone in the ground of the source. Not only our understanding but also our imagination must be nourished. The folklore we have mentioned satisfies the imagination. For it, the world around us is not dead. Thus it has an enlivening effect on the psyche. In the creative process of individuation, our innate potentialities are realized. Whenever something purely potential becomes a reality, a creative act takes place. This transformation draws upon the very roots of the mystery of life. We shall never be able to fathom this mystery through the medium that itself is the product of the creative process—consciousness.

I I

Hieronymus Bosch: Painter of the Demonic

A psychology of demons would be incomplete without a study of demonic iconography. In the therapeutic process, in order to get a better understanding of a psychic content, we work with the imagery associated with it. Demons are emotions—for example, fear. To grasp an emotion consciously, a patient attempts to create a representation of the image that comes up in connection with the emotion. One cannot deal with an emotion directly; one can only either suppress it or let it happen. Experience shows that it is better to let it happen than to suppress it. Emotions are the dynamic expressions of complexes, and since these are ultimately impossible to keep down, it pays to acknowledge them. For this, they must be commuted to a form that consciousness understands.

Every psychic content has two aspects: an irrational, pictorial one and a rational, mental one. Thus the *I Ching*, a Chinese oracle text thousands of years old, provides a "judgment" and an image for each sign. Dreams are comprised purely of images; these represent a communication. Working with these figurations is a first step on the path toward integrating the unconscious content. Through them, the emotion is objectified, that is, drawn forth from the inner space of the psyche. This is a relief to the psyche, and this object is something one can work with; one cannot work with something one is identified with (the emotion as such). The emotion continues to be obsessive for as long as one has not distinguished oneself from it.

Making the demons visible has an exorcizing effect, as we saw in chapter 5. That is the reason that in every time and among every people there have been depictions of them. Here I will concentrate on a few general points. The reader is referred to more exhaustive analyses of these images elsewhere.[1]

The painter whom I have selected as representative of many others is one who has been repeatedly imitated, even up to the present day. I am referring to Hieronymus Bosch (c. 1450–1516).[2] The purpose for which Bosch created his pictures remains a matter of controversy. They do not belong in a church, although many religious themes are treated in them. They were also not intended for the proper drawing room of a wealthy patron; they are much too unpleasant for that. Evidently what we have here are images from the unconscious that arose out of an inner emotional pressure and from which the painter freed himself by giving them form.

Hieronymus Bosch created his work outside and independent of most traditions. Of course, even he could not fully elude the currents of time; however, parallels with "predecessors" are no more than faintly suggested.[3] His pictures illustrate no known scenes, which is unusual in the pictorial arts. Their titles often contribute little to their understanding. (Moreover, it cannot be affirmed with certainty that of any of the titles originated with the artist himself.) All these points suggest to me that Bosch's images arose spontaneously from the unconscious.

For a psychologist, to be able to interpret images in the formation of which consciousness has played hardly any part is a rare, lucky find. Unfortunately we know very little about the life of the artist. On the other hand, this gives us the freedom to drop any consideration of personal characteristics and to focus interpretation on the collective content of the images.

It is no accident that many commentators have discovered alchemical symbolism in Bosch's work.[4] Of course we have no indication that Bosch took an interest in alchemy, though it was in full flower during his lifetime. But alchemical symbols are to be found in all products of the unconscious, independent of any particular tradition. Their appearance in Bosch's pictures can be regarded as a further indication that the pictures originated in the collective unconscious.

Hieronymus Bosch's painting style had a great influence on succeeding generations.[5] His images were copied, his themes freely varied, and his style has been imitated down to the present time. Obviously, the painter was able to strike a new chord in people. Moreover, the early Dutch painting of his time was very highly bound by tradition and left the artist only limited room for improvisation.[6]

All these facts suggest making use of the same type of interpretation for his images as we do in therapy for the images produced by our analysands.

Already at first glance, Bosch's paintings, with few exceptions, exhibit a confusing multiplicity of figures and scenes. None of his pictures can be grasped in just one glance. One must spend time in front of the painting before getting a sense of the main features; one almost has to "read" it line for line. Bosch's style of composition has been called "scatter patterning."[7] Certainly we find scenes with many figures in early Dutch painting, but they are mostly oriented around a central event.[8] Such a central event is almost always absent in a Bosch painting; therefore, his pictures give the impression of dissociation.[9]

As I showed in chapter 3, the psyche is only a whole in a relative sense. It is comprised of fragmentary personalities, among which the ego personality is only one of many, though it is a central personality. The other fragmentary personalities are either incompatible with the ego or not yet suited for consciousness. Among these fragmentary personalities, there is a kind of cohesion that assures the unified activity of the person. If we consider that for every position in consciousness, there is in the unconscious (as dreams show) a corresponding counterposition, then if all impulses were equally charged with energy, the subject would always be paralyzed by equal opposite tendencies. As individual tendencies cross the threshold of consciousness, they are represented in consciousness and can be selected by consciousness as suitable for total functioning. Whatever does not fit is immediately repressed, that is, pushed down into the unconscious. There it stays until, through further repressions of related material, it becomes sufficiently charged with energy to penetrate into consciousness as a disturbance. A demon of this nature should be understood as a counterreaction of the unconscious to one-sidedness on the part of consciousness. Distinguishing active and inactive complexes as those that do and do not have the energy to obtrude into consciousness, however, does not always work. Especially at times of fatigue or exhaustion, there is a *abaissement du niveau mental;* at such times the selective function of the consciousness is reduced and entirely opposite impulses can arise at the same time. In this way a state of dissociation develops.

We are all familiar from our own experience with passing states of this kind. We have no reason to assume that Bosch painted the images that bear the signs of dissociation while in such a state. While such states do make up part of a normal psychic life, sometimes also chronic states of dissociation are met with. Hyperintuitive persons as well as "borderline cases" are prone to these chronic states. Hyperintuitives suffer from too many ideas seeking to foist themselves off on the subject at the same time; as a result of this "embarrassment of riches," the subject is unable to choose. In "borderline cases," on the other hand, there is too little "mortar" between the individual bricks of the personality. Here the subject is constantly more or less in peril of coming apart. This does not necessarily become visible on the outside; the primary threat is to the inner world. Such people are sometimes noticeable because of their contradictory speech and actions. The inner threat can manifest as nervousness, malaise, irrelevant behavior, restlessness, and lack of equanimity. The presence of such people is tiring, draining.

Since we know little of the life and personality of the painter, pigeonholing him by noting a state of dissociation is inadequate. We must look closer.

On the outside shutters of the triptych *Garden of Earthly Delights* (in the Prado, Madrid), which are painted entirely in grey and depict the creation of the world, and also in the upper part of the central panel of the triptych itself, the most artfully shaped, strangely pointed figures appear. The context of the painting as a whole does nothing to explain them. They either represent meaningless playfulness or the unconscious presentation of a problem. I incline toward the latter alternative. Such pointed forms are quite familiar to us from pictures by our analysands that give form to problems of aggression. The *Garden of Earthly Delights* is not the only painting by Bosch where these pointed forms appear. They are to be seen as the thorns in the *Crowning with Thorns* (National Gallery, London), in the neck-band of the man with the large hat and in the numerous dry branches in the *Temptation of St. Anthony* (Prado, Madrid) and in *St. Christophoros* (Museum Boymans-van Beuningen, Rotterdam). This motif reappears in almost every picture; it seems to reflect a fundamental problem of the painter's.

Bosch's style of painting very much reflects a particular type. With a very fine brush he reproduces the smallest details realistically. Leaving aside his fantastic forms, the artist shows himself to be a very precise observer of nature. For example, he successfully reproduces typical Netherlands landscapes in his backgrounds, often ravaged by famine, war, and fire (*Garden of Earthly Delights*, right panel). He works out even unimportant details with meticulous precision, for example, the design on Balthazar's ball and on Melchior's cloak in *The Epiphany* (Prado, Madrid). From this we can tell that the painter's primary function is sensation.[10] His inferior function is the creative function, which composes the images. The painter belongs to the irrational function type. While the attitude of the extravert is determined by the intensity of the object, the introvert (such as our painter) is oriented toward the intensity of subjective participation in the sensation triggered by the objective stimulus. In the case of introverts, the relation between object and sensation is not balanced and proportional, but arbitrary. Since we have here the rare case of a producing artist who belongs to this type, the irrationality of the type is very striking. The object immediately triggers a subjective reaction, which then has nothing further to do with the reality of the object. This is what makes Bosch's pictures so mysterious. The eye keeps recognizing naturalistically represented objects, which, however, have no understandable relationship to each other. The stimulus of the object only produces the effect of an external show—something seemingly familiar that is nevertheless alien to its surroundings. This alien quality is due to unconscious contents that are imposed from the side of the subject. Ultimately, the paintings depict neither objects nor unconscious images; they mix the two, the unconscious subjective participation in the sensation and the effective impact of the object. From this arises the *illusionary reality* that exercised so great a fascination over succeeding generations and that inspires emulation to this day.[11]

In the course of further development, the individual of this type distances himself increasingly from the reality of the object; he is increasingly given over to his subjective perceptions, which orient his consciousness toward an archaic reality. As Jung tells us,

> actually, he moves in a mythological world in which people, animals, trains, houses, rivers, and mountains appear to him either as gracious gods or as malicious demons. That they appear to him this way he is unaware. . . . If he is more inclined toward objective reason, he will find this discrepancy [between sensation and reality] unhealthy. If, on the other hand, he is prepared, in faithfulness to his irrationality, to attribute reality to his sensation, the objective world will become for him a mere illusion and a comedy.[12]

Bosch's paintings clearly show how he sees the world—as a meaningless merry-go-round like the one in the middle part of the central panel of the *Garden of Earthly Delights*, where naked figures ride phantasmic animals counterclockwise around a pond. The naked figures, which are particularly numerous in this picture, are lacking in any erotic quality. Even though it was very daring to paint naked figures—except Adam and Eve—at all at that time, they are not exciting; they are wan, one-dimensional figures with no other individual character. They cast no shadows, like most of the other objects. This is not due to the inability of the painter but rather to his intention to devalue the object. Bosch is depicting an inner reality in the form of external objects; thus they are only a semblance of external objects.

The unconscious of the painter is characterized by the extraverted and archaic character of his intuition. Through it, he senses all the ambiguous, sinister, sordid, and dangerous background qualities of reality. In this, there is something dangerously undermining, which often stands in stark contrast to the benevolent harmlessness of consciousness.[13]

What Jung notes about the inferior function of the introverted sensation type is applicable to Bosch to a particularly great degree. While extraverted intuition as a primary function gives a person a "good nose" for all the possibilities of objective reality, as an inferior function it is much more archaic. The introverted intuition as a primary function is quite frequently met with in artists;[14] it enables them to structure perceptions that are sometimes quite remote from the tangible level of reality. Through it, the artist, who may thus become quite enigmatic to his audience, acquires a kind of prophetic quality. His art shows us "extraordinary things, remote from the ordinary world, shimmering in all colors, fraught with meaning or banal, beautiful and grotesque, sublime and bizarre." At this point, it would be the task of every creative person to bring his creative function and his primary function to a synthesis. Critique of the creative inferior function by the primary function would make the latter lose a great deal of its archaic, negative character. Bosch's painting shows us very penetratingly how unconscious the painter was. He must have been under tremendous and relentless inward pressure to come to grips with his creations consciously.

The artist would have had sufficient leisure for this. Our sources tell us that Bosch came from the van Aken family, who had migrated in the thirteenth century from Aachen to 's-Hertogenbosch. There in 1478 he married a wealthy patrician's daughter. Presumably he was not dependent on his artistic handiwork for income.[15] Thus it is likely that a few of his paintings were commissioned. In that case, he would have had plenty of time to meditate on the finished pictures (as we advise our analysands to do) in order to bring their contents nearer to consciousness. In this way he could have undergone a process of maturation.

Bosch scholars are pretty much in agreement as to which pictures of his are to be ascribed to his early, middle, and late periods, even though none of them is dated and the differences in the artistic style from period to period are quite slight. The painter did not pass through major phases of development. This shows that his art did not serve him as a means for the evolution of his consciousness. I am inclined to the view that he was beset by fantasies, which he spontaneously painted.

I was led to this view by an analysis of the left wing of the *Garden of Earthly Delights*. There Bosch depicts the earthly paradise and the creation of Eve. In the middle, an extraordinarily artfully painted fountain rises, with numerous pointed tubes sprinkling water into a pond. In front of the fountain, there is a heap of sludge out of which birds are picking shiny objects that might be glass balls or eggs. If we move to the right, the direction of conscious development, we see a colorful host of amphibian-like creatures creeping out onto the land; some of them are deformed, having three heads or missing their hindlegs. The heap of sludge symbolizes the *prima materia*, the original material, which contains the seeds for the development of consciousness.

Eventually, these seeds creep up onto the land of consciousness as formed living beings. They want to become conscious.

Below the scene of God with Adam and Eve, there is a cut-out pond in which strange fish move about. Frogs, which because of their humanlike form can be regarded as premature forms of humans, are trying to climb out of the pond onto the land in order to become conscious. But on the edge of the pond, fantastic birds, one of them with three heads, are waiting to devour the frogs as soon as they come within reach.

What does this mean? Figures, still having very strange forms, detach themselves from the unconscious of the painter and approach consciousness. But instead of letting these creatures gradually ripen into a form that can be integrated into consciousness, they are prematurely snapped up by intuition—the birds. The artist does not give himself time to carry around and brood on the ideas long enough for them to be assimilated by his conscious personality. He was a kind of "first-thought" painter: he put his ideas on canvas in a few sessions. This trait also, in my view, confirms the notion that he was under great inward pressure and was unable to wait.

Indubitably Bosch was a gifted painter who understood the techniques of his trade. But he must have had an ambivalent attitude toward the images that he painted, for he did not take them entirely seriously. The marks of the Trickster can be seen everywhere. We need only look at the figures in the lower part of the middle panel of the *Garden of Earthly Delights*. We do not find depictions of perverse sexuality as might be expected; the naked figures are just involved in various forms of silly play. Here a number of humorous or playful ideas have been painted with a fresh quality. All the figures have a light, playful, or at least noncommittal air. It seems as though the painter regarded his creative fantasies as no more than an inconsequential, entertaining game. That also explains why he drew no profit from them for his conscious life. Perhaps his material independence had the drawback that it permitted him not to take his artistic vocation seriously, but to regard it simply as a pastime.

I have repeatedly stressed how important the creative drive in man is. When a painter of the dimensions of a Hieronymus Bosch does not take his creative impulses seriously, there can be catastrophic consequences. The creative complex is an unconscious content that cannot yet be integrated by consciousness. It behaves like a demon. If consciousness makes no effort to integrate it, but shuns it instead, then it turns destructive.

Such a process can be clearly detected in Bosch's paintings. We can see it most blatantly in the two "Fall of the Angels" portrayals (on the left panels of *The Hay Wagon*, in the Prado, Madrid; and of *The Last Judgment*, Academy of Fine Arts, Vienna). Late Judaism and nearly all the early Church writers saw in the sons of God who took daughters of men (Gen. 6:2, 4) fallen angels. According to a widespread view, the sin of the devil and the angels who fell with him was arrogance. The words of Isaiah 14:13–14 are put in the devil's mouth:

> How are thou fallen from heaven, O Lucifer, son of the morning! how art thou cut down to the ground, which didst weaken the nations!
>
> For thou hast said in thine heart, I will ascend into heaven, I will exalt my throne above the stars of God: I will sit also upon the mount of the congregation, in the sides of the north:
>
> I will ascend above the heights of the clouds; I will be like the Most High.

In his arrogance, the devil is said to have brought other angels to sin.

From the time of the early Middle Ages, Acts 12:7 has been read—taking no account of the context—as meaning that Satan with some of the angels revolted against God, and that Michael with his angels threw Satan out of heaven.

> And there was war in heaven: Michael and his angels fought against the dragon; and the dragon fought and his angels,
>
> and prevailed not; neither was their place found any more in heaven.[16]

This may well have been the religious background for Bosch when he painted the fall of the angels above the scene in paradise where the Temptation was taking place. The earthly Fall is, so to speak, prefigured by the fall of the angels.

If one takes a closer look at depictions of the fall of the angels, one notices that the dark angels, as they are falling from heaven, transform into winged, insectlike demons. They become the same type of hideous demon that can be seen in many of the paintings torturing people. We find such scenes in the middle panel of *The Last Judgment* (Academy of Fine Arts, Vienna) and in the right panel of *The Garden of Earthly Delights*. From the psychological point of view, we might say that the artist's arrogance has conjured up destructive demons in opposition to his ideas. This highly sensitive artist must have suffered from awful nightmares, because he did not possess the humility to take his fantastic ideas seriously. That is the reason why we also find so much nonsense in his pictures. He was unable to make use of his primary function and his moral judgment to distinguish meaningful unconscious images from meaningless ones. The inward pressure did not leave him the equanimity for this. In other words, the artist was unable to assert himself in relation to his inner images. The stream of images carried him away. Thus he could not find the time to build up his pictures layer by layer, as was then customary.

I am convinced that, fundamentally speaking, Hieronymus Bosch did not live up to his gift. Had he worked intensively to develop his power of expression, as later Rembrandt and Rubens did, he would have been capable of a whole new level of work. However, we must content ourselves with the work of his that we actually do have and can only surmise what he might otherwise have been capable of.

In the context of the endless struggle of man against the demons and the excruciating pain that they inflict on him, Bosch provides us with a picture of the inwardly torn individual. Perhaps as a product of his time, he also gave expression to transpersonal problems of the period. In this way, he could be accounted a seer of his epoch. Still, he had no solutions. The artist was so little able to cope with his own problems that his insight into the times could scarcely have brought better results. Yet to the extent that he was attuned to the contemporary zeitgeist, his paintings express something of general validity and worth. That is why they are still imitated down to our own day.

Now let us have a closer look at the tormenting demons. Many of them resemble insects (middle panel of *The Last Judgment*; Academy of Fine Arts, Vienna) and ride on humans—an expression of possession—whom they torture and dismember. Particularly numerous are amphibian- and toadlike monsters, often with only two legs and pointed snouts. Dragon- and fishlike monsters menace humans, who are being fried or boiled in pots—a hell of the most hideous pain. If we try to make a bit of sense out of this place of retribution, a real purgatory, then we note that most of the subhuman beings we find there are transitional forms, forms in transformation. On the whole, they are incomplete creatures, retarded at an early stage of development, who are transforming into malevolent mongrels.

Amphibians are transitional forms from water to land beings. They make the leap from gill to lung breathing, as a result of which they are able to establish themselves on the dry crust of the earth. The two-leggedness here—for an observer as acute as Bosch, was something monstrous—anticipating the erect human way of walking. The misshapen things with fishheads or fish as steeds in the air are to be understood in a similar fashion: as a tendency toward evolution of consciousness. We also find rodent-like creatures with sharp teeth in their mouths and coarse snout hairs. In dreams, these are indications of the presence of gnawing unconscious impulses. Knives, symbols of discriminating consciousness, are not here instruments of consciousness but are in the hands of demons.

Many of these demons resemble those who, in the Paradise panel of the *Garden of Earthly Delights*, were trying to creep out

onto the land. As we saw there, they represent inchoate unconscious contents. Since they encounter no understanding from the
side of consciousness, they transform into the monstrous spawn
of hell. The insectlike beings[17] are engendered in the fall of the
angels. They are particularly remote from consciousness and
represent unconscious motivations of the type that can manifest
as stimuli to the autonomous nervous system. To perceive them
requires a very special effort of empathic attention on the part of
the conscious subject. But in this case, the subject was not only
not prepared to offer this, but, on the contrary, for moral reasons
banned them from the wholeness of the psyche. The unwholesome consequences are to be observed in every painting of
Bosch's middle period.

Demons—psychologically speaking, complexes—are part of
the natural makeup of the psyche. Their tendency to dissociate
the personality and to lead an independent life within the psyche
is balanced by the *mysterium coniunctionis*, the mystery of the
union of opposites. With the Self as its starting point, this Eros
aims at bringing the disparate fragments of the psyche into an
ordered and cohesive whole. This whole is actually logically
impossible and to this extent is a mystery of the psyche. In it, all
opposites are related to each other, subsumed by a larger unity.
This wholeness is the goal of the individuation process.

I cannot, with the best will in the world, discover this tendency to unity in the panels of Bosch's paintings. Isolated
symbols of the Self are present, but they are not powerful enough
to reconcile the glaring opposites in the pictures. From this, I
draw the conclusion that the artist must have been an inwardly
torn, unbalanced, unharmonious, uneasy person. The demons
are, after all, much more colorfully, graphically, and vividly
depicted than the pale and insipid human beings whom they
torture. The human standpoint seems to have been quite weak,
yet this was the cultivated and evolved aspect of the painter's
psyche. The archaic elements were dominant. Certain motifs in
the paintings could be described as perverse, but to me they

seem really more to be expressions of something very archaic that conscious understanding was never able to help evolve. In Bosch's pictures, a relationship between the various motifs building toward a sense of unified meaning seems to be lacking. This had already been a source of difficulty for earlier commentators, who could interpret the paintings of the middle period only as a scattering of symbols and suggestions of meaning—never as a whole.[18] It is indeed to be doubted that there is an integral meaning in these pictures. In no case are we sure that the title comes from the artist himself. We are merely groping in the dark as to the nature of the creative process within the artist. I see the middle period in terms of a free and aimless play of fantasy. Exceptions to this are the left panels in a few of the triptychs where the creation of Eve and the Fall are depicted. We can only wonder about the haunting by ghosts around the saint on the right panel of the *Saint Anthony* triptych. There are really very few references to the saint's life in the painting. That the artist stopped painting this kind of work in his later period might simply be due to his getting tired of this kind of meaninglessness.

In the late period, by which time the personality of the painter may have matured, the demons are introjected. In *The Bearing of the Cross* (Musée des Beaux-Arts, Ghent)—perhaps his last picture, consisting almost entirely of portraits—apart from Christ and Saint Veronica, one finds nothing but devil's heads. These are the demonic faces of possessed beings, whether it is the evil thief below right, being admired for his abysmal badness; or the fanatical monk above right, who is castigating the good thief. We already encounter similar faces in the early period, for example, in the *Mocking of Christ* (Städel Institute, Frankfurt), but these faces still express something within the ordinary range of the human character. In *The Bearing of the Cross*, we see the faces of madmen.

Hieronymus Bosch is a psychologist among painters. He ruthlessly pulls his characters' masks away. But he only reveals, he does not synthesize. He saw the ghastly abyss in people. Perhaps he was also criticizing his time. But he was no healer; even for himself he had no remedy. He did indeed suffer from the moral contradictions and hypocrisy of his time. But his pictures lack any confidence or consolation. He has always been admired, because he mercilessly exposed whatever was merely empty show. He must have had a very negative and cynical understanding of the world. He was perhaps disappointed by reality and longed for a better world.

Could Christianity have been a fortress for him against the onslaught of the demons? Let us consider the representations of Christ or God in his pictures as an expression of his Christianity. The table platter with the seven deadly sins in the Prado in Madrid shows in the middle the resurrected Christ with his wounds in the pupil of the gigantic eye of God, and the inscription *Cave, cave, Deus videt!* ("Beware, beware, God sees!"). It is an emaciated, wan Christ figure with childlike features. Here it seems to suggest a kind of childish faith, the faith of a child who follows the rules like a good boy. According to the sources, Bosch belonged to the Brotherhood of Our Lady, which does not necessarily mean that he was especially pious. Such brotherhoods had a social function; their members helped each other in times of need. Or consider the cold, despondent, broken-down Christ figure being led before Pilate by a colorful crowd of people in *Ecce Homo* (Städel Institute, Frankfurt). This is supposed to be the savior corresponding to the cry of the people: *Salva nos Christus Redemptor!* ("Save us, Christ our Redeemer")? Yes, precisely this abased, abject, weak Christ could become the savior (think of the suffering servant of God in Isaiah 53), if consciousness would fully participate in him. "As many were astonished at thee; his visage was so marred more than any man, and his form more than the sons of men" (Isa. 52:14). "He hath no form nor comeliness; and when we shall see him, there is no beauty that we should desire him. He is despised and rejected of men; a man of sorrows, and acquainted with grief; and we hid as it were

our faces from him; he was despised, and we esteemed him not"
(Isa. 53:2–3).

We find in the Bible a basis for solving the problem of
Hieronymus Bosch, which is not just his problem but in some
sense the problem of our time. Precisely that which seems
despicable, weak, low, and without significance can become a
savior from the demons. The alchemists made claims of this
nature on behalf of the philosopher's stone, which for them was
the savior and which they thought of in terms perilously close to
the Christ principle.[19] It was a truism for them that the philosopher's stone is originally unesteemed, scorned, and trodden in
the mire. This corresponds to Bosch's amphibious monsters,
who are trying to creep up on the land. If he had understood
what he was depicting and what an opportunity was being
presented to him there, then that which was alive and quick in
the demons could have become a saving force for him. To realize
this, he would have had to take his pictures seriously and
meditate on them; in this way their positive significance would
have come out. But instead, apparently he remained fixed at a
childish level of belief, thus enlarging the gap between his demon
world and his consciousness.

This childishly innocent faith comes to expression on the back
side of *The Bearing of the Cross* in the Academy of Fine Arts in
Vienna. There the Christ child pushes with his left hand a
child's walker and in the right hand holds a pinwheel. Are these
the first innocent steps of life? Does this represent the longing
for innocence? Is the painter unable to bear the thousand devils
inside him—as the cross laid on him?

We should not neglect at least to mention the Christ in the
clouds over the hay wagon in the triptych of the same name in
the Prado, Madrid. Bosch may well have been inspired to paint
this image by the Flemish proverb: "The world is a haystack,
and everyone takes from it what he can hold." Around the wagon
is a colorful hurly-burly: even the pope and the king with their
retinues are following it; some people are trying to get hold of

some of the coveted hay by using ladders or hooks. In their efforts, some of them end up under the wagon wheels; a wife is attacking her husband with a knife. The wagon is being set in motion by demons, for they are the driving force behind the whole scene. A helpless Christ looks down on this vain and meaningless expenditure of energy with outstretched arms, as though he wants to cry out: "And for this I died on the Cross!"

Bosch's pessimistic worldview is revealed here all too clearly. His world is full of discord, power struggles, and deceit. Yet the artist cannot except himself from this scene of hollow striving. He should have recognized within himself the treachery of the collective values he depicted; he should have seen that they suppress the first springings of individuation so that, denatured, they become demons.

Bosch made fun of the world and the vain machinations of mankind—and failed to notice that he was depicting his own inner state. Instead of mocking the depravity of the world, he should have asked himself in earnest what his so very cynical worldview could be based on. Is it possible that it proceeded from his own attitude? Instead of reproaching his fellow men for their demonic carryings-on, he might have done better to discover through introspection his own unseemly condition. He was indeed a child of his times, and these were perhaps not very far different from our own. We also live in such an extraverted fashion that we believe the essential is to save others from ignorance rather than cast a light into our own inner depths. If we do not have the courage to face our own demons, we have no right to point to other people's demons. It is true as Bosch depicted it: the demons keep the world in motion. But whether they propel us into the abyss or lead us to wholeness is up to our attitude and the nature of our understanding. Bosch's example might stand as a warning to us.

12

The Spirit in Matter

"Go to the streams of the Nile; there you will find a stone that has a spirit. Take it, cut it in two, put your hand into it and take out its heart, for its soul is in its heart."[1] Here a Greek alchemical text of Zosimos cites the legendary Ostanes, said to have been a Persian alchemist.

That their mystery-shrouded philosopher's stone was a living being seemed natural to the alchemists—but seems quite odd to us. Yet a citation like the above is by no means exceptional. The much later *Rosarium Philosophorum* (Rose Garden of the Sages) attributes to the philosopher "Rosinus" (a highly retailored form of Zosimos) the following statement: "This stone is indeed the key [to the work]; without it, nothing happens. Our stone is of the strongest spirit, bitter and brazen, with which bodies may not blend until it has been dissolved."[2] Here the stone seems rather to be inanimate matter, though it is strong of spirit. It is of central importance in the work; however, to begin with it is unworkable—before it goes into solution. A later passage of the same text mentions a philosopher Tudianus, who is supposed to have said: "Know that our stone is airy and volatile. . . ."[3] This again seems to conflict with the notion of a stone that dissolves. However, it does concord with the previous quote in that spirit is of an airy and volatile nature. Alchemy always sees steam as a manifestation of spirit. As we know, spirit was once thought to be of the nature of wind; still, such a property in a material thing like a stone seems odd.

These few conflicting and confusing citations may already be sufficient to give us an impression of the paradoxical nature of the *arcanum* that is referred to by the code word *lapis*. "Thus the stone is also called *rebis*, that is, a thing that is made of two things, that is, of body and spirit, or of sun and moon, or of a purified and a fermented body."⁴ The opposites are resolved in the *rebis*, their unity. Only something exhibiting the most paradoxical properties could be the sought-after One in which all possible opposites are present. For the alchemists, the *lapis*, the philosopher's stone, is this miraculous thing—spirit and body in one.

With this background, the citation from Ostanes becomes more comprehensible. In an Arabic text attributed to him, Ostanes says: "It is a stone bound within a stone, a stone set within a stone, a stone fused into a stone, a stone placed within a stone."⁵ Here Ostanes is alluding to the "two-thing" (*rebis*). Only its simultaneous opposed and self-same qualities make it possible for the citation to make sense. This is the One, which contains a variety of qualities and aspects and yet remains self-identical. The cited passage continues: "The philosophers poured forth tears over the stone, and when it was thus moistened, its blackness disappeared, its dark color became brighter, it appeared like a rare pearl." Whatever the properties of this double-natured thing with a hundred names—alive or just substance—might be, the emotional participation of the experimenters in their work is essential. Thereby it changes its color and quality and transforms into an entity of unsurpassed worth. Its initial form is black. This corresponds to its unconscious and doubt-enshrouded nature and to a depressed state of mind on the part of the adept. The right attitude is sadness over this unresolved situation. Whether it is the blackness of the stone that moves the alchemist to tears or whether it is his own need of salvation that is thus expressed is hard to say.

In his letter to Euthiciam (Theosebeia), which survives in dialogue form, Rosinus (Zosimos) says: "It is thus because the soul of fire is hidden in his [the stone's] soul. And she [asks]: Is this stone then spiritual? He replies: Did you not know that the spiritual strengthens the spiritual, since it devours its impurities and separates superfluities from it?"[6] Not only does the stone possess a spirit within its material substance—it is altogether spiritual. As we saw in chapter 4, the spiritual aspect has something to do with the emotional quality, symbolized here by fire. This fire spirit is what "enflames" the stone, what gives it the living quality that has always been associated with the soul. The spirit of the stone strengthens the spirit of the alchemist and does away with all its inessential elements. Psychologically speaking, the impurities and superfluities stand for egoistic tendencies and shadow aspects, which in the spirit of the stone become completely extraneous. Sooner or later, communities based on a conscious purpose fail because of shadow intrigues, whereas real communities formed around the symbol of the Self overcome such shadow tendencies to a great extent. The Self is stronger than the shadow. The spirit of the Self casts out the deceiving spirit and at the same time strengthens the spirit of the weak and undecided in its own cause. In this way, it develops a powerful influence.

Anyone even a little familiar with Jungian psychology and its interest in alchemy knows that what the alchemists referred to through the symbol of the philosopher's stone is what we call today the Self, the indescribable wholeness of the human being.[7] The fire that lies within the stone as its soul is the *principium individuationis*, which animates the seemingly dead stone. This is the motivating force that radiates from the stone.

The tractate *Rosinus [Zosimos] ad Sarratantam Episcopum* deals with the stone in detail:

> This is a stone and yet not a stone, for it has soul, blood, and reason, and is similar to both. Muhammad spoke thus: The stone that is in this work is necessarily an animate thing. It is found everywhere in the plains and in the mountains, and in all waters. The rich have it as well as the poor. It is at once the most

inconsiderable and the most cherishable. It grows from flesh and blood. . . . Out of it, armies come together and kill kings. . . . There is impurity in this stone, wherefore men think little of it, and they believe that it [the impurity] cannot be separated from it. . . . This stone that is not a stone is projected into things and raised up onto the mountains; it lives in the air, and in the rivers it is fed on quicksilver; and on the mountaintops it is at rest. Its mother is a virgin who has not cohabited with its father. Moreover, feet trample this stone into the dung, and often foolish ones made excavations to try to draw it out, but were unable to find it. . . . It is called the "small world," not because it is a microcosm, but because the world is governed by it."[8]

This long citation gives us a clearer impression of what the alchemists meant by this "stone that is not a stone." If it possesses soul and blood and reason, it must be a living being with a soul. It is found throughout the world and with all men, whether rich or poor. It is a being resembling a human, of flesh and blood and so powerful that it can gather armies and bring down kings. It is at once the most negligible and the most precious of things. Stupid people trample it into the mire, and yet, as a small world, it rules the world. The impurity that is within it is inseparably a part of it, as a result of which many hold it in small esteem.

Before we despair or get irritated over these contradictions and obscurities, we should consider that here the alchemist is groping in territory unknown to him, in which the object he is dealing with slips beyond the grasp of language.

A phrase that is quite difficult to understand tells us that "the stone is projected into things." The alchemical concept *proiectio*[9] is different from the "projection" of the psychologists, the transference of a subjective process into an external object.[10] The *proiectio* of the alchemists relates to the end of the alchemical process. In his "Fragments," Isaak Hollandus says: "The stone is without as well as within and in the middle. Whatever thing it is projected on, in it it accomplishes its perfect work; its inside changes to its outside and vice versa."[11]

What the alchemists meant by *proiectio* was something long familiar in the East: *consciousness frees itself from the distinction between outside and inside, subject and object.* "In looking, consciousness dissolves," says the "Hui Ming Ging."[12] What comes closest to this in Jungian psychology is active imagination,[13] a technique in which, in the waking state, consciousness permits unconscious contents to come into it and treats them as *the* reality. In that way, "the inner becomes the outer and vice versa." Active imagination is a kind of mystical journey in which inner images are taken as the equals of external reality, often with magical or clairvoyant results. In that the unconscious is allowed to enter, a vantage point outside the ego arises from which the ego can be objectively seen. A dream that Jung had after a serious illness illustrates this phenomenon most clearly:

> Then I came to a little wayside chapel . . . and I went inside. . . . But then I saw that in front of the altar, on the floor, a yogi was sitting, in the lotus position and in deep meditation. As I looked at him more closely, I realized that he had my face. I was profoundly startled and awoke thinking: Aha, so that's who it is who is meditating me. He has a dream, and that is me. I knew that when he awoke, I would no longer exist.[14]

Jung himself provided a commentary on this dream:

> It is a metaphor. A Self enters into meditation, as it were, like a yogin, and meditates my earthly form. One could also say: it takes on human form in order to enter into three-dimensional existence. . . . In the earthly form it can gain experience of the three-dimensional world and can attain a bit more realization through this further awareness. The figure of the yogin represents to a certain degree my prenatal wholeness. . . . Like the magic lantern [in a later dream], the meditation of the yogin "projects" my empirical reality. As a rule, we become aware of this causal relation the other way around: we discover in the products of the unconscious, mandala symbols—that is, circle and quaternity figures—that express wholeness. . . . Our vantage point is ego consciousness, a field of light centered on the ego-point that

represents our world. From here, we look out on an enigmatic, tenebrous world and do not know to what extent its shadowy lineaments are caused by our consciousness or to what extent they possess their own reality. . . . However, more precise observation shows that as a rule the images of the unconscious are not made by consciousness but possess their own reality and spontaneity. The reversal [of the roles of ego consciousness and the unconscious] suggests that, according to the view of the "other side," our unconscious existence is the real one and the world of our consciousness is a kind of illusion or represents an apparitional reality created for a particular purpose, somewhat like a dream that continues to seem like reality for as long as one is in it. It is obvious that this state of affairs has a great deal in common with the Oriental worldview based on the notion of *maya*. The unconscious wholeness thus appears to me as the real *spiritus rector* of all biological and psychic events. It seeks total realization, that is, in the case of man, the total development of consciousness. The development of consciousness is culture in the broadest sense and self-knowledge is thus the heart and essence of this process. The East undoubtedly attributes a "divine" meaning to the Self, and according to an ancient Christian view, self-knowledge is the way to the *cognitio Dei*.[15]

This radical reversal of our vantage point and of our view concerning what we call reality seems to me to be expressed by the alchemist's *proiectio*. The *proiectio* of the stone on all things then has the following meaning: only through it do things acquire their "true" existence, that is, an existence liberated from the unconscious intermingling resulting from the *participation mystique*. Through this, the stone becomes the real creator and ruler of the world. But this is the *cognitio matutina*, the knowledge of the morning, and not the *cognitio hominis*, the knowledge of man; that is, it is the world in the light of God and not of man, as Augustine expressed it.[16] But the *cognitio matutina* is self-knowledge, *cognitio sui ipsius*, which Augustine equated with *scientia creatoris*, is the knowledge of the Creator,[17] the knowledge of the Self, that is, of objective appearance.

The *Rosinus* text continues by saying that the stone is raised up onto the mountain, lives in the air, feeds in the water, and rests on the mountaintops. An alchemist would understand these enigmatic allusions at once. For one thing, they are supported by the unassailable authority of the so-called *tabula smagdarina*,[18] in which it says: "(4) His father is the sun, his mother the moon, the wind bore him in its belly, his nurse is the earth." His parents are the cosmic eminences—the sun as the archetype of consciousness and the moon as the archetype of the unconscious, the anima, are, so to speak, primordial opposites, between which the stone is begotten. In our text, this aphorism is transposed into Christian metaphors: His mother is a virgin and the father has not had intercourse with her. In this way, the alchemical stone comes to resemble Christ, who was transfigured on the mountain (Matt. 17:1–13). "And his face did shine like the sun, and his raiment was white as the light" (17:1), and "behold a voice out of the cloud, which said, This is my beloved Son. . . ." (17:5). For the stone is the "son of the philosophers" (*filius philosophorum*). This might sound like a blasphemous comparison, but the alchemists did not mean it this way at all. On the contrary, to point out this parallel was a matter of great satisfaction for them. They were surely not conscious of how far removed they were from orthodox Christian doctrine. From time immemorial, mountaintops have been considered seats of the divine *numen*.

From all these hints and suggestions, we may infer that the *lapis* is a god in some ways similar to Christ,[19] but who at the same time is far more archaic than the latter. For the stone is, as the alchemists say, a *deus terrenus*, a god of the earth. So Benedictus Figulus tells us in the *Rosarium novum olympicum*:

> It is a single thing with a body in it tinged at once with the spirit and the soul . . . and which figure the prophet Ezekiel saw as one wheel within another and as a spirit of life which was in the midst of the wheels. And because of this he was known by some as the god of the earth.[20] In contrast to Christ, the stone is entirely

163

earthly, material. In this sense, it is the god that is hidden in matter. In the "Oxyrhynchos Papyrus I," which shows certain parallels to the *Gospel according to Thomas* (Log. 77), we find, "Turn to the stone, there will you find me; split the wood, and I am there."[21]

The *Gospel according to Thomas* expresses an idea similar to the precedent: "But the Kingdom is within you, and it is outside of you. When you recognize yourselves, then you will be recognized, and you will know that you are the sons of the living Father. But if you do not recognize yourselves, then you will be in poverty, and you will be poverty."[22] Clearly there were attempts made to put forward a view that neither overvalued the object nor suppressed the subject. However, far too few people understood these subtleties for such texts to be adopted as part of the canon. Instead, in the first centuries after Christ, the extraverted approach, which was based on the more conspicuous aspects of the outer reality and was supportive of the papal authority, came to prevail. In this way there arose a fundamental break between outside and inside, subject and object.

For us, matter is dead. Thus we believe that we may do anything with it that we like. We exploit matter for our ends and according to our whims. Dead matter has no feelings and cannot defend itself. We take this so much for granted that it does not occur to us that there is anything more to discuss. However, from the point of view of the psychologist, who examines man's epistemological process critically, the state of affairs is not that simple. On the one hand, we have the ideas of the alchemists outlined above, and the alchemists were not merely charlatans. On the other hand, there is the relationship between subject and object described in chapter 9. Something that appears dead to consciousness is an object that consciousness is not entering into relationship with. No relationship is possible with objects with which the subject is still archaically identical, since subject and object are not yet differentiated. Knowledge or consciousness can only develop—to stress this point once again—once the subject separates itself from the object. We suppose that we automatically distinguish ourselves from matter and thus recognize it as something else. But this happens only on a very superficial level. Consider the case of the South American Indians who perceive themselves as human beings, but are nevertheless red parrots, because they belong to the red parrot clan.[23]

Because we are still caught up in our archaic identity with matter, we are unable to become aware of it. We can, however, become unconscious of it if we give heed to how we deal with matter and how it behaves toward us. As long as we presume it to be inanimate, we notice nothing. Why are we not struck by all the things that happen to us in connection with matter? It is too much of an easy way out merely to categorize disasters caused by chemical spills and atomic accidents in causal terms, merely as failures of security measures or results of human error. It is not enough just to find something or someone on which to place the blame. We have to take the question of their meaning much more seriously.

As soon as we are willing to ascribe a meaning to the action of matter and cease to see it purely in terms of accident or coincidence, then we are already beginning to free ourselves a bit from the *participation mystique;* we begin to respect it as an equal partner. Men have done this since time immemorial. Only in our industrial-technical age have we turned away from this approach; had we maintained it, the technical revolution would scarcely have been possible. Modern man had to be free himself from his timid deference to matter. But nowadays we are beginning to see hints that matter is striking back. We hear news of some technical disaster, great or small, nearly every day. Doubtless in each case, looking at things causally, this or that failed to function. But such an approach is just as superficial as saying that since the Empire State Building is made out of stone, the proper way to study it is mineralogically. A deeper analysis, which takes into account contexts as well as causes, must inevitably consider man's fundamental attitude toward the spirit in matter.

In our daily life, this spirit usually makes itself felt as the notorious "deviousness of objects," whereby objects behave as though they were alive. Moreover, we inadvertently treat them that way, frequently as though they possessed a roguish personality fully equipped with consciousness. We shout insults at sharp corners that we have bumped into as though they were responsible for our pain. We kick objects into the corner that we have stumbled over as though they had deliberately placed themselves in our path. Doubtless this style of reacting is primitive; yet try to suppress it though we will, we have still not gotten over it.

What is it that makes us behave this way? Of course it is the "animate object." Whether it is primitive or not, we have always basically experienced objects as alive. We might speak in terms of projection, but that still fails to explain why matter behaves so strangely toward us. Those artisans who treat their materials with respect precisely because their materials reward them for it are becoming ever rarer. In this connection, I am reminded of the story of the stonemason who wanted to build a wall out of large stones from a river. He would strike one of the round stones with his hammer and then lay it aside for a while so that it had a chance to make up its mind in which direction it wanted to be split.[24]

Recently, during a skiing outing, I was reminded that we are sometimes not so far from the right attitude. A new lift station had just been built, and the lift itself had already been in operation for a while. As we were enjoying ourselves on the slopes and the lift with many other people, we saw a priest, sprinkling holy water and accompanied by his young acolytes, making his magic circle around the lift station. It seemed as though for a moment two different centuries were meeting. No doubt official government inspectors had tested the lift for safety and reliability before allowing it to be put in operation. Nonetheless, sometimes dreadful accidents take place on lifts and cable cars. Is it not more prudent to accommodate the unpredictable as well by means of a blessing?

The "residual risk" of accident remaining after technical security measures have been taken has lately become a major topic of concern. Modern man employs terms of this sort to designate the spirit in matter or the behavior of animate objects. The residual risk is the unpredictable and incalculable aspect of our technology, which we are unable to bring under our control. How great this risk is depends on our attitude toward it. If we relate to the materials that our technology makes use of with suitable respect, a religious attitude, and the awareness that some time our life may depend on it, then we can hope for it to be minimal.

We speak of "human error" when a train accident takes place because the engineer has gone through a stop signal. We do not need to explain to the engineer what he should do when he comes to a signal that says Stop; we need not even rely on the engineer, since automatic safety devices to prevent this type of accident are usually also present. So why, despite all this, does the accident still happen?

We all make mistakes from time to time, not being infallible automatons. We would never dare place ourselves in the hands of pilots or surgeons if we dwelled on the fact that nobody is proof against error, especially in critical situations. We take it for granted that everybody in a responsible position will do his best, will do everything in his power to prevent mishap. Nevertheless, the human element represents a risk of unknown proportions. There is no technology that is not at some point dependent on people. Even in nuclear installations where there are many layers of automatic security, it is people who set the machinery in motion and thus also create the risk.

Even at the highest level of technical development, there is a constant relationship of exchange between the people and the technology. After all, technology never exists purely for its own sake. It is there to serve people, to make their lives easier. All the same, it carries a demon within it, something that eludes human intervention. This is something we must be conscious of to be able to deal with it responsibly. Nowadays, our danger lies either in further embracing an optimistic belief in the increasing perfection of technology or of pessimistically condemning all technology as the work of the devil. We cannot return to the dubious idyll of the Stone Age. We have no choice but to go forward with a life in which humanity can coexist with technology. One of these two aspects must not be allowed to stifle or diminish the other. Such a harmonious relationship of these two elements must begin in our everyday situations, not in the world of large-scale politics. The demonic forces in matter can, like a medicine, prove salubrious or deadly, depending on how they are applied.

The alchemists were on the track of this secret. Because of that, we can learn from them. Their starting point was the mystery of matter. What they were able to learn and experience about it is something we must discover again for ourselves today. They were convinced that the salvation of Christianity did not go far enough, since it did not include the dark, sublunar, material world.[25] This is a result of archaic identity, also the collective unconscious. What revealed itself to the alchemist in his laboratory, without his being aware of it, was the collective unconscious, uninfluenced by his consciousness. Thus, for modern depth psychology, alchemy provides a unique field of study. Now at last we understand what the alchemists were talking about when they said that in the end their stone would be projected on all things: if we follow the behavior of external material things with attention, they will become for us a mirror of what is taking place within us. This is good advice for contemporary man, if he would like to find the meaning behind inexplicable accidents. As soon as he ceases merely to seek the causes and begins to look for the meaning, then seemingly lifeless things begin to speak to him. The "big world" suddenly stands in a curious state of correspondence to the "small world" in himself.[26] Everything that happens externally has a mysterious relationship to our own psychological situation. Such meaningful coincidences or *synchronistic occurrences* can be helpful to us. They happen much more frequently than we think. They give the individual a sense of once again belonging to a great all-encompassing whole.

Members of primitive tribes saw the whole world as animated by spirits, for the world was a soul. In the course of the evolution of consciousness, this soul found a new placement—within man. A parallel process was the de-demonification—but at the same time, desacralizing—of the world around him. The modern approach, which in some ways had its predecessors in alchemists like Gerard Dorn,[27] is to some extent returning to the starting point by asking the question: What could have caused people to experience matter as animate? as having a soul? In asking this question, we make the startling discovery of a parallelism between *psyche* and *physis*. In each meaningful coincidence, psychic and physical events take place in correspondence with each other—not in terms of cause and effect but in terms of meaning. In the case of individuated people, the two spheres develop an increasing parallelism until finally they merge. From the experience of the unity of the outside and the inside, a new sense of the world arises, that of the *unus mundus*. This stands as a theoretical concept behind every case of synchronicity. According to it, beyond the level of consciousness, *physis* and *psyche* are part of one and the same reality. To the extent that the individuated man lives out of this wholeness, he participates in the *unus mundus*. This is the basis of the modern interpretation of the "stone that has a spirit," or of the living quality of the object.[28] In an uncanny fashion, the living quality of the object makes itself felt in paranormal phenomena: in the case of "haunting."

13

Dead People in One's Head: Parapsychological Apparitions

Despite our rationalism, we can still be fascinated by ghost stories. Perhaps it is precisely because of the "enlightened" attitude of our consciousness that we seek out repressed irrational material in the form of ghost stories, science fiction, or fantasy stories. For there is no doubt that the irrational, the mysterious, the unexplainable, and the incalculable are all part of life. When these elements are systematically excluded from participation in our life, they take on a form acceptable to consciousness in order to do so. A life without mystery is a spiritually impoverished one.

The mysteries of the church are more and more being lost. We do not know how to relate to them any more. They no longer connect with anything living and numinous for us. The miracles of the Bible, once a proof of the truth of Jesus' message, are now ridiculed by some as superstitious leftovers. Others would like to authenticate them on the basis of parapsychology. Modern man is caught in the conflict between a rational conscious attitude and an instinctive need for the miraculous. This greatly boosts the stock of all manner of quasi-religious movements that, with their hocus-pocus, promise to fulfill this need. Jung alluded to the subjective profit, the aggrandizement of one's own personality, experienced by a person who in his free time is the grand master of some lodge or other.[1] This raises him above the ordinariness of his everyday life. He feels a sense of special importance. He does not speak in ordinary, everyday language; instead he makes use of elevated diction, feeling that thus he recaptures some kind of lost secret.

Someone who lives entirely within the confines of a sensible rationalism is by no means proof against this kind of pseudospirituality. Quite the contrary; he easily falls prey to any irrational demon. Consciously he struggles to do away with whatever is unreasonable—and for that very reason falls into the clutches of the deceitful spirit. For this spirit cloaks itself in the apparent reasonableness of any "ism." Ideologies do not arise from an authentic spirit, but rather some unconscious impulse cooks them up using logical ingredients. Such forms of irrationality are not only ludicrous, they are dangerous, because ideologies can "legitimize" the basest wrongs. The end is used to justify the means so that we do not feel frightened to apply it. Our century might go down in history as the century of terrorism. It has indeed been reserved for our century to come up with the depravity that permits a few to cast fear and panic over the many. If the many can be blackmailed, the few win the power struggle. They can impose their conditions on the majority.

Transferred from the outside to within us, in the psyche, terrorism is precisely the means used by the demons. A fragmentary personality gone wild demands total power over the psyche and brings it under its thumb. In an earlier chapter, we learned to recognize this phenomenon as possession. A situation in which an important part of the psyche is prevented from participating in the life of consciousness always ends in possession. Terrorism is, as it were, "possession from the outside." Here also, special interests, neglected because of the overwhelming power of the majority, give vent to their frustration through acts of terror.

Demonic problems are always minority problems, problems with incidental, inobtrusive, neglectable elements. At least this is the way it appears. But in fact the reality is more that of "powerful things that come in small packages." In my view, terrorism is the counterpart of the demons in the external world. The irrational side of us is the one that produces the most demons, because we are too rational. Genuine respect (in the sense of a religious attitude) toward the irrational, of which the numinous is part, is a demand of our time.

However, this does not mean falling for every display of hocus-pocus we encounter. When we meet with something genuine in the sphere of the irrational, a numinous awe arises. That which inspires this kind of response cannot be converted to social currency, as is so often done in occultist circles. One cannot appropriate it by hanging catchy labels of ineffability on it. As far as parapsychology is concerned, it makes the worst of this problem by going back and forth between simpleminded gullibility and techno-progressive show. On the one hand, it insists on the authenticity of phenomena that are easy to see through. On the other hand, it is much too little affected by a sense of wonder. It cannot endure the tension and suspense of the inexplicable, so it forces it into a gridwork of concepts, tries to manipulate it with tests and experiments. That is the old attitude of magic, which is not content to let the miraculous simply happen, but must somehow control it.

Why this longwinded introduction to our theme? Here, as elsewhere in analytical psychology, taking the right attitude is of the essence. If we approach the phenomena with the wrong attitude, we falsify them. The phenomena we are concerned with here are rare and arise spontaneously. To those who experience them, they seem peculiarly meaningful, extraordinary, and fateful. To the investigator gathering accounts of such experiences, the uniformity of the events, amid all the variations, is striking.[2] The investigator will attempt to approach the phenomena in question in a cool and objective manner, because that is what science demands of him. But in so doing, he divests the phenomena of one of their essential properties—they cease to be emotionally gripping.

Investigators are amazed again and again to discover how many people have experiences of this nature. People almost never talk about them, and the investigators know why. These accounts are only given when the subject sees that the person he is talking to has the right attitude. Often it is a matter of a once-in-a-lifetime experience, one that is remembered a whole life long fresh as though it had happened yesterday, because it was bound up with a powerful emotion. Such an experience buries itself deep in the soul. The subject feels absolutely convinced about it. This feeling, however, as intense as it may be, tells us nothing about the nature and cause of the experience. It only confirms the veracity of the experience and resists any attempt to interpret it reductively. Any attempt at explanation must take this feeling into consideration. It is the same consideration and respect that is due to any numinous experience.

Among the best known phenomena are those in which dying people see dead relatives coming to fetch them. Such experiences often indicate that death is imminent. The brother of Miss Hattie Pratt told the famous parapsychologist Hyslop that even in the midst of her death struggle with diptheria his sister remained completely calm and apparently without pain. Her mind seemed clearer and more reasonable than ever before. She knew that she was about to die, and gave her mother instructions concerning the distribution of certain possessions of hers among her girl-friends. Suddenly, she directed her eyes toward the farthest corner of the room as though she heard someone speaking there. At last she said: "Yes, Grandmother, I'm coming, I'm coming, please just wait a minute." She expressed her amazement that the others in the room could not see her grandmother, and finished giving her instructions. Then she again gave her attention to her grandmother and said her good-byes to those present. "Now I'm ready, Grandmother," she said and departed without struggle or suffering.[3] Instead of puzzling over such events and proposing speculative hypotheses, we should first let these accounts work on us. This particular experience comes to us from a dying person who was in full possession of her powers; to dismiss it as a pathological result of the agonies of dying would explain too little.

Jean Vitalis was suffering from inflammatory arthritis of the joints accompanied by high fever. When, on his sixteenth day in the hospital, the doctor found him smiling and without a trace of fever, the patient explained to him that his father had visited him the previous night, not in a dream but as he lay fully awake. His father had entered the room through the garden window, approached him, touched him all over lightly to take away the pain and fever, and then announced to him that that evening at exactly nine o'clock he would die. His father hoped he would prepare himself for death as befitted a good Catholic. Vitalis called for his confessor and had himself given the last rites. As tested by the doctor, at that time his pulse was strong and even his temperature normal. Cheerful and composed, Vitalis said good-bye to his family in the presence of the doctor. One minute before nine, he lay down on his bed and never moved again. The doctor could do no more than confirm his death.[4]

To "explain" such an account, we must remind ourselves of the reality of the Father archetype; aside from this, we would do better to drop any attempts to investigate such cases from a causal point of view. The archetype is a superpowerful psychic reality, which can manifest in a variety of ways. It belongs to the collective unconscious and is therefore experienced as outside the ego. In this sense, it is a manifestation of the objective psyche. Thus an explanation of it should not be based on the viewpoint of the subjective role of the psyche. This is the mistake of most attempts at psychological explanations—they take the appearance of the subject's personal father as a subjective event. That the perceiver related to the appearance of the father as that of a spirit shows just how objective it was. "Objective" means independent of the will of the conscious personality. For the most part, persons who have such things happen to them are not at all prepared. The very idea that such-and-such "happened to me" already expresses that the event was objective. Such an interpretation is especially supported by cases in which the dying person could not have known that the person represented as an apparition had already died.

In June 1889, two girls had become ill with diptheria, and one of them had already died. As the second now also lay dying, medical prudence dictated that the death of the other child (three days previously) be kept secret from her. On her dying day, the survivor sent her friend a farewell message and picked out two pictures for her. The sick child seemed to have no fear of death and talked about dying. She seemed to see some girlfriends of hers who she knew were dead. Suddenly she called to her father in a voice of utter astonishment: "But Papa, I'm going to take Jenny with me. Why didn't you tell me that Jenny is here?" With outstretched arms, she called out, "Oh Jenny, I'm so happy you're here."[5]

A teleological consideration of this experience is more appropriate than an ordinary causal one. Rather than ask why, we are better off asking "What is the goal?" "Where to?" "What for?" The appearance of the dead to the dying makes the transition between life and death easier by taking away fear and giving confidence. Is it the dying person consoling himself with these images—or do they appear to him independent of his will? The former would be a subjective consolation, the latter an objective one. Given that death is a natural part of life, perhaps we may presume that nature herself takes measures to enable us to face this transition without panic. Perhaps the appearance of the dead at the deathbed is among these.

However, there are also phenomena that require a view other than the teleological one. Mrs. Rogers, a seventy-two-year-old crippled woman, lay unconscious in bed. The night before her death, between two and three in the morning, her nurse saw through the door from an adjoining room the figure of an unknown man of medium size, with broad shoulders, a ruddy face, reddish-brown hair, and a beard. He wore a buttoned-up overcoat. His facial expression was serious. He stood there totally motionless. The nurse took him for a real man and was wondering how he could have entered the building with the doors locked. She turned away, and when she looked again the apparition was gone. When a niece of the dying person came to visit in the morning, the nurse asked her if the apparition resembled the late Mr. Rogers. She said no, but that the description did fit Mrs. Rogers's late first husband, a Mr. Tisdale. Besides the niece and Mrs. Rogers, no one in the vicinity had known him.[6]

In a letter to the parapsychologist Hans Bender,[7] C. G. Jung asserted that all the distinctions and categorizations related to parapsychological phenomena are artificial. All these phenomena, he indicated, are examples of synchronicity. (Jung used the term *synchronicity* to refer to the relative simultaneity of a physical event in the outside world and an inward psychic event that arises causally independently of each other but are connected with each other through their significance.)[8] Parapsychological apparitions are part of the nature of the collective unconscious. They do not "prove" anything, including life after death. In times of crisis (death, accident), apparitions are common. The nineteenth-century work *Phantasms of the Living* (see note 2, above) contains numerous case records in which people in unexpected life-threatening situations have appeared as apparitions to other people. Only secondary importance is laid on whether the threatened person appeared in a dream or as an apparition in the outside world. This seems to me an important indication that in both cases we are dealing with the same type of psychic event. Possibly whether the experience can manifest in a dream or whether it needs an external apparition in order to impress itself on consciousness depends on how open the consciousness is. There is no essential difference between dreams and parapsychological events.

To understand apparitions, we must get away from overt or covert causal explanations, which is what most parapsychologists attempt. The psyche is a reality that can bring about a tremendous variety of effects in both the outer and inner worlds. The two worlds are connected with one another through the principle of synchronicity, which in turn is ultimately based on the *unus mundus*, or one world. The dispute between animists and spiritists as to whether apparitions have psychic causes or arise because of the presence of a real spirit is an idle one. We can only perceive apparitions psychically. They appear to be real no matter whether they arise in the outer or the inner world. This is a matter not of extrasensory perception (ESP), but rather of psychic experiences that become conscious through the senses.[9] Their only extraordinary quality lies in the fact that they cannot be produced by consciousness deliberately, but arise spontaneously.

Haunting or phenomena connected with ghosts can manifest much like the phenomena in question, but they are much more loosely related to life-threatening situations. The gardener Alfred Bard was on his way home from work as usual through the Hinxton cemetery. There he saw straight ahead of him, in the rectangular mausoleum where Lord Fréville was buried, the latter's wife, who had formerly been his employer. She was leaning on the railing and was wearing the clothes in which he had most often seen her. She was looking directly at him. Her face was extraordinarily pale. He presumed that she had come to the crypt in order to have it opened. He walked around the grave at a distance of five to six meters without losing her from sight. She followed him with her head. He stumbled over a clump of grass and looked for an instant at his feet. The apparition disappeared. Only on the following day did Alfred Bard learn that Lady Fréville had died about seven hours before the apparition had taken place.[10]

A confirmed case of haunting was that involving a Mrs. O'Donnell,[11] who had rented rooms at the British seaside resort of Brighton for herself and her daughter. The very first night she was disturbed by the loud sound of steps from the floor above. Her room appeared to her to be full of people. The following morning she learned that the upper floor was unoccupied. The following night the steps were so loud that she was unable to sleep. The third night, there appeared on the wall opposite the fireplace a ghastly figure that pointed with one arm into the vacant adjoining room and with the other toward herself. She pulled the bedclothes over her, hoping that the apparition would disappear. But when after a while she looked again in that direction, it was still there. She screamed. Involuntarily, she stretched her left hand toward the apparition as though to feel if it was really real. To her horror, an icy dead hand gripped her. She had no recollection beyond this point. The next night she spent in her daughter's room. In the middle of the night the door opened and a stocky young man entered and said: "Oh, you're living in the Scot's room!" Then he went back out, smiling in a friendly way. Later it turned out that a twenty-four-year-old man with the appearance of the nocturnal apparition had committed suicide a few weeks before by throwing himself out the window of the adjoining room. The daughter's bedroom had been occupied by a friend of the suicide, a young Scot.

There are many examples of this kind of occurrence. Some people assume that hauntings take place whenever there is a case of a violent death. It almost seems that the unconsumed life-force of the life that has not been lived out to the full remains attached to the place of death. This fits in with the concept of *biothanati*, those who have violently died without fulfilling their life span.[12] For that reason, places of execution also have a haunted quality. There are auspicious places and inauspicious places without it being possible to confirm in every case that an act of violence has taken place in one of the latter. Curiously enough, irrespective of this, there are places that are conducive to violence. Ghosts connected with a particular spot are among the most difficult to explain. In earlier times, people paid careful attention to whether a place was an auspicious one, that is, whether it emanated good influences or not. In order to find this out, someone would sleep on the bare ground and note what kind of dreams he had. Of course, there has been no lack of attempts at explanation, but on the whole they are pretty unsatisfying. In the case of haunted houses, generally the approach has been to try to prove that some particular special event has taken place there. But is there a single place on earth that has never been sullied by blood? If this hypothesis is correct, many more places would be haunted than is the case. Jung himself was the witness of a very vivid ghost phenomenon that left him rather speechless.[13] He suspected that subliminal perceptions played a part in the matter. He understood ghost phenomena as an exteriorization of unconscious processes:[14] since the attitude of consciousness denies them an entry point, they turn up in the external world. This is very much the case with psychokinesis, the movement of objects from a distance. Here an unconscious process manifests in a physically tangible fashion.

Spirit apparitions can touch all our senses. In fact they are more often heard than seen. A cold ghostly breath is a typical experience, or, as in the example given above, the touch of a ghostly hand. In Jung's incident, he smelled an indefinable unpleasant smell in the room, which disappeared as soon as he woke up.[15] He felt that quite possibly odor hallucinations have more to do with an intuitive sense of the psychic quality of a place than with real odors. In this connection, he pointed out that primitive medicine men can smell not only thieves but spirits (cf. chap. 4). In cases of possession and exorcism, it has frequently been stressed that a hellish stench arises when a devil leaves its host. By contrast, the Holy Ghost is associated with a fragrant odor. It is no accident that we say so-and-so is "in bad odor," thereby expressing a psychological state of affairs.

The notion of a *genius loci* in connection with a place-bound ghost actually belongs in the same category. In this connection the symbol of the snake often crops up—the creature of the spinal cord (*kundalini*), of the peripheral physical unconscious. Thus the snake might well suggest subliminal perceptions of a particular place. Expressions such as "earth-rays," "waves," and "radiation" are nothing but pseudoscientific explanations for the fact that there are good and bad places. Where Christian churches have been built in the place where pagan temples once stood, the building was probably done in both cases for the same reason: the spot seemed auspicious. Probably place-related parapsychological factors play a much greater role than we think. Many stretches of highway are well-known death zones, where for inexplicable reasons large numbers of fatal accidents occur. Parapsychological factors must be involved when an accident victim gets into a car as a hitchhiker, tells the story of his accident and then suddenly disappears.

We can make no progress with this enigmatic material unless we examine the psyche of the perceiver more closely. The outer circumstances surrounding apparitional phenomena have been thoroughly investigated; related inner constellations, on the other hand, have been largely neglected. For example, Charles Emmons[16] investigated spirit apparitions among the Chinese in Hong Kong, focusing entirely on the associated cultural background and entirely failing to consider the psychological circumstances in which they arose.

These psychological circumstances are important, because they help to distinguish "normal" from "pathological" apparitions. Unlike pathological apparitions, normal apparitions, although they do shock us, impair the perception of external reality only momentarily. In both types of cases, a constellated archetype clarifies its form to the point of a sensory perception. What is normal or pathological is the reaction of the personality. This depends to a great extent on the cultural context and the level of development of consciousness. Among primitive peoples inner images are continually being placed on top of outer ones with equal vividness, so that it is difficult for them to tell the outer from the inner.

Some people are especially receptive to the perception of parapsychological processes. It is said that they are gifted as mediums or that they have "the second sight." In this, they differ from us normal folk only in degree. Mediums do not possess a "sixth sense"; for the most part, their consciousness is rudimentary, and as a result they relate more deeply to unconscious processes. Their unique personalities can be somewhat on the borderline of normalcy, since they are continually in the high-pressure situation of being in contact with archetypes. Neurotic and psychotic patients often have mediumistic talents. This is a further indication of the fact that synchronistic phenomena arise in connection with constellated archetypes.

"Supernatural phenomena" are out of the ordinary ("super") in that they are not intentionally produced and thus cannot occur regularly. Since the unconscious is the purely natural part of man, they are natural phenomena. This also includes feats that conscious man is incapable of.

Because time is relative, the unconscious knows about things that for consciousness lie in the future (precognition). Because space is relative, the unconscious knows about things that for consciousness are occurring in a distant place (telepathy and clairvoyance). Unconscious perceptions have no spatial or temporal limits. These perceptions come to consciousness through the usual senses, though, as in dreams, there are no external sense stimuli. We can evaluate the reality value of images conveyed by the psyche by considering the reality value of dreams. The psychic structures needed to convey a sense stimulus and to convey an inner image are ultimately the same.

The message of sense stimuli is not a photographic representation of the world. For example, we do not see light waves of different lengths, but rather see colored light. Perception to a great extent includes processes of knowledge based on comparison with previous sense impressions. Memory plays a major role in this. In connection with memory, we must distinguish between knowledge available to voluntary recall (for example, knowledge recalled for an examination), knowledge that is there but not retrievable at present (for example, things we have forgotten), and absolute knowledge, which is not accessible to consciousness but is accessible to the unconscious (for example, in a dream). Absolute knowledge includes absolute memory, in which everything that was ever known remains stored, as well as knowledge that has never before been known. Knowledge of this sort is, for example, knowledge of internal bodily processes. Thus the unconscious may know about a physical ailment that has not yet become manifest or about a pregnancy that has not yet been confirmed.

Only in its personal aspect does the unconscious resemble consciousness. It includes everything that was ever conscious and later forgotten or repressed. In its collective aspect, it is an entirely different, incommensurable medium. This is something one feels when one has to translate a dream into the language of consciousness in order to write it down. The unconscious has entirely different properties from consciousness. The unconscious is too often misunderstood as merely a reduced, dimmed, twilight version of consciousness. Not the unconscious but consciousness is the derivative, secondary phenomenon. The unconscious is the matrix and ground of consciousness.[17] Unconsciousness is not, however, as it might seem, a void, a vacancy. It is a living, functioning something that is not known and does not appertain to any conscious personality. Thus it cannot be localized; it is equally inside and outside, filling the entire cosmos.

Some parapsychological explanations do take the reality of the collective unconscious into account, but one senses that behind these explanations there is no concrete experience. As a result, certain questions are asked, such as whether "an unconscious projection" may have caused an apparition. First of all, this question is once again being conceived in causal rather than synchronistic terms. Second, it implies a misunderstanding of the nature of projections. For everything that is unconscious is also projected.[18] Thus an unconscious projection provides no explanation here. It is of the nature of the collective unconscious that it can manifest itself anywhere.

A more fruitful question concerns the meaning of an apparition. Well known are those apparitions that have had far-reaching effects, because they were regarded by those who experienced them as extraordinarily meaningful, even as a signal from God. Among these were the apparitions experienced by Joan of Arc.

In the vicinity of her home town of Domrémy was a renowned forest, known as Bois Chenu ("the hoary forest"), about which all kinds of miraculous stories were told. There was also apparently a prophecy in circulation to the effect that a maiden who would accomplish wondrous things would come from the region of a small forest. Near Joan's home there was a "ladies' Tree," also called "the Fairies' Tree," a great beech close to a spring. (The tree of life at the spring of life is an archetypal conception.[19] This spring is said to cure illness.) In the shadow of the tree, according to the old people of the village, fairies moved about. The girls of the neighborhood hung wreaths of flowers in the branches of the tree and danced around it. Asked about such pagan customs at her trial, Joan of Arc set no particular importance on them, but knew of them. They are an indication of the numinosity of a place.

From the records, we can only reconstruct the general lineaments of Joan's story. When she was barely thirteen years old, a shining cloud (*nubes praelucida*) appeared before her eyes, out of which a voice said to her: "Joan, you have been chosen to lead another life and to accomplish wondrous things; for you are the chosen one of the King of Heaven to restore the kingship of France and to help King Charles, to protect him who has been driven from his lands. You must put on man's clothing; you must bear weapons and become the leader of an army."[20] At her trial, Joan tersely recounted that around midday in the summer, a voice called to her from the direction of a church, accompanied by a brilliant light. At first she was confused and doubted this miracle.

In the Old Testament, God reveals himself to Moses in a cloud (Ex. 14:19, 20:21). The phenomenon of a voice out of a cloud or accompanied by a light is again a genuine, spontaneously arising archetypal idea. Later Joan of Arc attributed the voice to the archangel Michael, which is already an interpretation. Interpreting in this fashion is typical: mysterious phenomena are made to fit into a cultural context with the help of consciousness. This is by no means meant as a falsification of the original experience, but is an attempt to assimilate an unconscious content.

The archangel advised Joan that Saint Catherine and Saint Margaret, at God's behest, would thenceforth give her instructions that she must follow. She often saw her three familiars with her earthly eyes. They always came out of a cloud, accompanied by a heavenly light. She could touch and embrace them. The spirits addressed her as *Johanne la Pucelle, fille de dieu* ("Joan the Maid, daughter of God.") Pleasant odors surrounded the apparitions; on their heads they bore magnificent crowns of light rays. They appeared to her several times a day, especially in the forest, and brought her guidance and consolation.[21]

It would be utterly inappropriate to try to explain such psychic experiences in a personalistic fashion. The simple farm maid was animated by the spirit of the century, the zeitgeist. Soldiers reported apparitions of Joan of Arc even in the trenches of the world wars. She deeply impressed herself on the French psyche. Following her guides, she fulfilled not an individual but an archetypal destiny. The case of Joan of Arc tells us a great deal about the collective background of apparitions.

The visions of Saint Perpetua[22] indicate the significance and meaning of such apparitions, which appears to me to lie more in their content than in their parapsychological mode. Three types of apparition should be distinguished:

1. hallucinatory apparitions (visions, auditory and tactile phenomena, etc.)
2. apparitions in the context of crisis situations
3. place-related apparitions

Apparitions of the first type tend to be cases of the collective unconscious giving expression to its own contents, whereas apparitions of the other two types convey information about external events. In her book *On Dreams and Death*,[23] Marie-Louise von Franz calls attention to a series of dreams about a deceased person in which, in some of the dreams, the deceased person appeared as an inner image of the dreamer (subjective phase), and in others, as a spirit (objective phase). The question parapsychologists ask—whether an apparition is to be understood in an animistic or spiritistic sense—is wrongly formulated. Such a formulation fails to take into account the objectivity of the psyche. If the archetype, as Jung stressed,[24] is psychoid in nature, it has the potential to manifest in consciousness psychically as well as materially. What is important is the reality of the apparition and not the medium in which it appears. Behind the old dispute is the idea that if the spiritists are right the apparition is more objective, and if the animists are right, it is a mere subjective figment.

Often the dead are feared because they might come back as ghosts and harm the living. There is a widespread custom of informing a deceased person that he is now dead and must travel to the beyond. To prepare him for this, since the most ancient times, it has been the custom to provide him with food for the journey and even to go so far as to send his entire household— wives, servants, and animals—to the grave with him. Psychologically there must be some process of separation that permits them to take leave of the deceased.

The closer the psychic connection with the deceased and the more unexpected his death, the longer this process takes. I recall a man of middle age who came to see me with his new wife, because he was unable to rid himself of the image of his former wife who had died. He had gone through a decade of strife-torn marriage with her, and they were just on the verge of reconciliation when she became ill with a brain tumor and shortly thereafter died. After the usual mourning period, he became acquainted with a nice woman whom he wanted to marry. However, he was unable to focus his feelings entirely on his new wife, since he kept experiencing this as disloyalty toward the old.

This became such a weight on the new relationship that the two had to consider whether they should separate. For the man, his dead wife had become a jealous ghost who begrudged him all happiness in life. I advised him to set up a corner in the bedroom where he could keep her memory alive. He had, after all, obstinately tried to drive her out of his memory; for this, she was taking her revenge.

Ceremonies for the dead and masses held in memory of deceased persons are meaningful rituals that make it possible for survivors to work through the experience of a death. Reformed churches, in particular, leave people who have just lost near relatives completely to themselves. Ministers' condolence calls are valuable in the human sense, but psychologically speaking they are inadequate expressions of feeling. The labor of mourning should be gone through consciously, so that the deceased person does not become a harmful complex.

This unfortunate process was one I saw developing in one of my analysands. Her father, to whom she had been very close, became ill and died. After the burial, she had dreams in which she once more met her father. She knew in the dreams that he was dead and avoided any physical contact, such as shaking hands. As time went on, he appeared in her dreams more and more frequently. The analysand could not free herself from him emotionally. Pretty soon she began almost to enjoy his reappearances. In the course of the dream series, the father became more and more negative, until finally it reached the point where death heads were dancing in front of her. At this point, the whole thing became too much for me, and I quite vehemently lost my temper with her. After that, she did not dream about her father any more. The emotional ties that had turned him into a destructive vampire had been broken by my emotional reaction.

These examples show that we should not repress the memory of a dead person, but through the work of mourning we must loosen the bonds of sentiment that are based on projections. Such bonds contain psychic energy (libido) that is drawn out of our lives and wanders with the deceased in the beyond. This energy animates the images that as apparitions rob the survivor of his or her peace of mind.

An undissolved *participation mystique* is often the reason that with older couples the death of one is soon followed by the death of the other. The libido of the survivor wanders with the dead partner in the beyond and is no longer available for his or her own life. Such a dearth of energy manifests not only in depression but also in a diminution of physical resistance and heightened vulnerability to illness.

Ghosts can make the living sick: they are out for blood. Therefore, there are countless defense mechanisms for warding off the harmful influence of the undead. The dead are dangerous for the living, because they may well draw them in the direction of a degeneration of consciousness. Consciousness is constantly under threat of slipping back into unconsciousness. A strong regressive influence emanates from the dead, because they represent the past. This undertow from beyond has always been felt to be dangerous, because it is hostile to life. Through it the dead person becomes a parasite.

Dying is an archetypal situation, as a result of which synchronistic events often occur in the period surrounding it. Appearances of ghosts, which occur particularly in connection with death or the dead, make entirely clear that complexes or demons are realities of mysterious origin. They represent the psychic reality itself, which cannot be reduced to anything else. We must recognize that the psyche is *the* reality per se. This reality consists of images. These images have an effect, thus they are real, whether they represent so-called outer or inner realities. We can no more distinguish between apparitions of animistic or spiritistic origin than we can differentiate subjective pain with organic causes from pain of psychic origin. Our mental representations are reality, as we experience anew in every dream, and we react to them. Here our knowledge meets its limits; beyond them is a boundless field of mystery, which ultimately feeds into the mystery of life as a whole. Hopefully, scientific investigators, despite all their drive for knowledge, will have the sense to feel awe at the impenetrability of this mystery.

14

Evil

The question of evil has woven like an unbroken thread in and out of our inquiry. It is a basic theme connected with all aspects and activities of demons and man's way of relating with them. Are demons what evil is? No, neither from a psychological nor a theological point of view is that the case. Many theologians assert that the devil and the host of demons bring about evil on earth. That is already a more acceptable formulation, even from a psychological point of view.

Are complexes evil, since, as we have shown, complexes are demons? All psychic factors are capable of both good and evil. Brilliance and darkness, light and shadow—both are part of life, of nature, and of human beings. Where one is, the other must also be. Nature and life are beyond these opposites. They are neither good nor evil. Creation and destruction are necessary aspects of the eternal flow of the life process. One is as indispensable as the other; without either the process would come to a halt.

But are we not relativizing evil to a dangerous degree? In point of fact, we have no objective vantage point outside the world from which we could pass judgment on good and evil. Our judgment is subject to the subjective conceptions connected with our personal development.

Tolerance is a modern need. But does tolerance mean that I must renounce all moral judgments on the acts of others? My position is not too far removed from this, since in my view it is not the act alone that is to be judged, but also the person, the circumstances, and the motives and intentions. Modern jurisprudence respects these, which I consider a great step forward, though it is not yet widely understood. Carried to its ultimate conclusion, this would mean that jurisprudence itself would disappear, for there would be no more deeds to be avenged by the penal code; there would only be the psychology of the doer, in consideration of which his deed would become understandable and perhaps appear inevitable.

But must we then drop the qualifications of good and evil altogether, because they are man-made and relative? Had we continued to live like animals, it would show that we have no moral function in our psyche. A lion that eats a missionary is not an evil lion, just a carnivore. That is, to the extent that we are purely natural (like the lion), we have no moral sense. Only with consciousness do we acquire something of this nature. Is it then an invention of consciousness? Is it man who establishes what is good and what is evil? Is it an arbitrary human convention to call one thing good and another evil? In other words, are good and evil culturally conditioned? This is quite certainly to some extent the case. For example, certain sexual practices, such as the ritual union known as *hieros gamos*, are considered quite repulsive in some cultures, in others sacred. A great part of our moral code is culturally conditioned; it is a general consensus that changes over time. It is inculcated in young people through their education. All collective moral notions about what "one" should do or refrain from are of this nature.

The real moral question begins neither here nor with the penal code; both of these have big enough loopholes to let a crafty reprobate slip through. The penal code is a social institution with the function of regulating our life together. True ethics begin on a level beyond these collective and periodically changing man-made rules—at the level of the conscience. Jung called the conscience the voice of God (*vox dei*).[1] It is the moral function of the Self. This, however, only comes into play when conventional morality has to some degree been transcended and a relationship to the Self has been established. As long as collective norms are still regarded as irrefutable standards, the quiet *vox dei* remains inaudible in the background.

Only when a critical period in life arises in which the conventional norms are no longer adequate, does man begin to orient himself toward the *vox dei*. This is an objective authority, since its judgment is independent of the ego's wishes and desire, indeed often goes against them. This is the judge who presides day and night over our deeds.[2] Only here do we find ourselves on the sure ground of a judgment of good and evil that is not subject to the limitations of our humanity. But it is also precisely here that the real problem of the evil of the demons arises. As complexes the demons correspond to an unconscious side of the psyche. Everything that is unconscious is also projected. It was thus already a forward step in the development of consciousness when the early Christian hermits withdrew into the desert in order to fight matters out with their demons. For most of the time we are fighting matters out with the alleged demons of our fellow men and do not recognize them as our own demons. A great part of the unhappiness in our world arises through these projections.

We cannot prevent projections. As long as an unconscious content has not been assimilated by the personality, the latter also cannot recognize it. It can then be as easily perceived in the environment. The reason that such a content is still unconscious is that it is incompatible with the attitude of consciousness. If, as a result, it appears in the environment, this has the advantage that the moral conflict that could mean sleepless nights for the subject is shifted to the outside. Unfortunately, with the momentary advantage of regained peace of mind comes a much greater disadvantage: the conflict remains unresolved. Any genuine conflict only becomes resolvable when the subject recognizes its own part in it. It can only do this if it tries to become aware of its complexes. The result of remaining unconscious is that—with the best of intentions—we do evil.

It is rare that someone intentionally does evil. We all want the good. Our Christian culture is so steeped in an insistence on the good that we *should* do, that we dare not recognize the evil that we do. We would sink into a slough of despair and misgivings about the good in man if we genuinely and soberly recognized how much evil we bring about. Therefore we prefer to lay the emphasis on the good intentions with which we do evil. This good intention seems to excuse us for all the bad things that we will still do. We are full of good intentions; we have far too many good intentions to be able to see clearly what we actually do. What good are the best of intentions if we are not capable of doing as much good as we intend? On the other hand, too much good is also demanded of us. The Christian goal of perfection, even if one is expected to fulfill it only to a degree, causes everything to be repressed that stands against it. We simply demand too much of ourselves, and there is no place for all the bad of which we are capable. It shouldn't be, it mustn't be. But when it nevertheless is?

The doctrine of *privatio boni*—evil exists, if at all, only negatively, as an absence or attenuation of the good—surely arises from the fact that evil has no place in our conceptions. Since the question of evil brings about a painful conflict, it is cursorily dismissed as nonexistent.

Where, then, does that leave evil? Because it often appears as something unconscious that is independent of, and often counter to, my conscious intentions, it is experienced as something happening outside of me. That is the demons. As Paul says, they cause me not to do the good that I would do and to carry out the evil that I would not (Rom. 7:19). Since they often thwart my will, I experience them as alien to my ego. Thus there is a strong tendency to set them up outside of myself. The danger there, of course, is that they then elude my ability to deal with them. In that case, they can easily transform into my neighbor.

But our demons are not the principle of evil. They are a precious good, an opportunity to become whole, that somehow, somewhere got stuck—through an unfavorable stroke of fate or a trauma. Demons are our neglected and unacknowledged side. But they also want their part in our life. Since consciousness does not allow them that, they force their participation on it. In doing that, however, they show us their negative side, since they are now in the role of enemies to the conscious personality's well-being. Since consciousness identifies with the good, everything that opposes it acquires a negative value. Our natural but unaccepted side then really does end up "bedeviled."

The church shared this view when in the demons it saw angels that had fallen away from God. If we speak psychological language and replace God with the Self, the indiscernible wholeness of the person, then the demons do become negative to the extent that they oppose this wholeness. In this view, evil would be anything that stands against the realization of one's wholeness, against individuation. Of course, anything that transcends the level of consciousness can hardly be defined. And evil is consciousness-transcendent, for neither does the urge to evil come from consciousness nor does the impetus necessary for the judgment of it come from the *vox dei*. As something transcendent, evil cannot be defined by consciousness. It is something living that, as it appears, is treated as such by the *vox dei*. If the conscious personality would have the Christian compassion to accept its complexes, then they would not do all that much harm. But in an extraverted culture like the Western one, we tend to prefer to spend our Christian virtue on the outside world, where it can come rewardingly to public notice. The poor devils within us get the short end of the deal.

It is to this extraverted Christian conduct, this chronic undervaluation and neglect of our psyche that we owe the daily atrocities of the demons in our ordinary situation and in the world at large. There lies the practical origin of evil. Demons are not by nature evil. Our neglect of them and denial of their requirements has made them evil. Unfortunately, the evil quality that they thus acquire is by no means harmless. It makes the demons into willing tools of the Devil.

But has the Devil not long since been done away with? That is the case with the Devil as an external reality, but not with his effectiveness within people. The more we give ourselves enlightened airs, the more obdurately we dismiss evil or the Devil as superstition, the harder he attacks us. There is even the danger that we may identify with the Devil. When matters reach that point, he is no longer there confronting us: he disappears. That is the danger of the Enlightenment, in which all demons are dismissed as nonexistent creatures of superstition. When that happens, they usurp human consciousness. It becomes demonified. It no longer identifies itself with the good. In its likeness to God, it stands above good and evil. Through this hybris, it loses its moral function. It becomes an amoral criminal. Nowadays, all talk of an unconscious separate from consciousness is often discarded as unprovable speculation. The consequence is that ego identifies with the whole of the psyche. The result of this is an inflated ego—and a deflated Self.[3]

To acknowledge the demons or complexes as a reality independent of our opinion is a first step toward the needed development of consciousness and a first step toward putting evil in its place. If evil gets outside the field of our awareness and understanding, then it becomes destructive. Integrated evil is perhaps not less evil, but is less destructive. The integration of evil has become an inalienable duty. But it depends on having first recognized the objectivity of evil. The path of integration requires a fortified ego that does not panic when it encounters the darkness of its own personality. If we could be content with less lofty ideals concerning our humanity, we would be less frightened by its darker sides. Thus we would be able to face fully the reality of our being, which is made up of fairly equal parts of light and darkness.

Do I improve the world by integrating my poor devils? Yes,

because I relieve them of the evil that I have constantly projected on the world. I take on myself that portion of evil—perhaps an infinitesimal fraction of the evil of the world—that belongs to me. This evil no longer goes about unnoticed as a free-roving demon causing harm hither and yon, for it has been exorcised into my psyche.

But what significance does that have considering the unutterable amplitude of evil existing in the whole world? A person who has integrated evil becomes a kind of focal point—evil cannot take effect in his environment; he has exposed and neutralized it. This casts an influence that goes far beyond the person in question. That is why Jung could say that a catastrophe for mankind could only be avoided by enough people becoming conscious of their own darkness. Integrating one's own darkness is a lifelong work, which is capable of shaping our future and filling it with meaning. The demons are the hidden guides of history. Perhaps, for one's own sake and the sake of the world, it is worthwhile taking up the psychology of demons.

Notes

The German edition of Jung's collected works (*Gesammelte Werken*) is cited in the following notes as *GW*. Where an extract has been taken from the English edition (*The Collected Works of C. G. Jung*), the note citation is to *CW*. (See Bibliography for full listings.)

PREFACE

1. "Face to Face," an interview with C. G. Jung by John Freeman, in *C. G. Jung Speaking: Interviews and Encounters*, ed. W. McGuire et al. (London: Pan Books, 1980), p. 436.

CHAPTER 1. THE DEMONS OF THE SAINTS

1. All Bible quotations are taken from the King James version.

2. O. Bardenhewer, *Geschichte der altkirchlichen Literatur*, vol. 3, (Darmstadt: Wissenschaftliche Buchgesellschaft, 1962), pp. 44ff., 67.

3. R. Reizenstein, *Des Athanasius Werk über das Leben des Antonius*, (Heidelberg: C. Winters, 1914), p. 32.

4. L. T. Le Fort, ed., *Oeuvres de S. Pachôme et ses Disciples*, (Louvain: Imprimerie Orientaliste, 1956).

5. *The Lausiac History of Palladius*, ed. C. Butler, 2 vols. (Cambridge: Cambridge University Press, 1898/1904); *Palladius*, "*Historia Lausiaca*" ed. J. Laager (Zurich: Manesse Verlag, 1987).

6. A.-J. Festugière, trans., *Historica monachorum in Aegypto* (Paris: Editions du Cerf, 1964).

7. Jean Cassien, *Conférences*, 3 vols. (Paris: Editions du Cerf, 1956–1959).

8. Cf. *Das Leben der Heiligen Melania von Gerontius*, trans. S. Krottenthaler, BKV 1912.

9. *Evagrios of Pontus, Traité pratique ou Le Moine*, ed. A Guillaumont and C. Guillaumont (Paris: Editions du Cerf, 1964).

10. See further C. Guillaumont and A. Guillaumont, "Demon," in *Dictionnaire de la spiritualité ascétique et mystique*, vol. 3 (Paris: Beauchesne, 1957), p. 191, and J. J. Moser, "Aspects psychologique de la ruse," thesis presented to the C. G. Jung Institute, Zurich, 1976.

11. R. Draguet, ed., *La Vie primitive de S. Antoine conservée en Syriaque* (Louvain: Secretariat du Corpus SCO, 1980), vol. 1, vol. 2, p. 18.

12. Ibid., pp. 9–10.

13. Cassien, *"Conférences II, V,"* in *Sources Chrétiennes*, vol. 42: 116–117.

14. C. G. Jung and P. Radin, *Der Göttliche Schelm: Ein indianischer Mythen-Zyklus* (Zurich: Rhein Verlag, 1954).

15. E. Pichéry, *Sources Chrétiennes*, vol. 42, p. 273.

16. Ibid., p. 258.

17. Draguet, vol. 2, p. 10.

18. Mark 9:43–44: ". . . it is better for thee to enter into life maimed, than having two hands to go into hell, into the fire that shall never be quenched. Where their worm dieth not, and the fire is not quenched."

19. The last part of this sentence I have translated very freely. The French translation of the Syriac is ". . . fut cherchée cette pensée adverse et elle ne fut pas trouvée" ["this untoward thought was sought and it was not found"].

20. Festugière, *Historia Monachorum in Aegypto* p. 18.

21. J. Laager, ed., *Palladius: Historia Lausiaca*, p. 136.

22. "A Review of the Complex Theory," *CW* 8, §§201–204.

23. "Symbols of the Mother and of Rebirth," *CW* 5, §388.

24. The same thing happened when, as a reaction to the movement of *minnesingers*, the church overemphasized veneration of the Virgin Mary. Cf. C. G. Jung, "Das Typenproblem in der Dichtkunst," *GW* 6, §447.

25. "Symbole der Mutter und der Wiedergeburt," *GW* 5, §337ff.

26. C. G. Jung, "Der andere Gesichtspunkt: Der Wille zur Macht," *GW* 7, §35.

27. L. Friedländer, *Sittengeschichte Roms*, (Stuttgart: Parkland Verlag, 1901).

28. Evagrios of Pontus, pp. 100, 139.

29. Laager, *Palladius*, p. 234.

30. C. Guillaumont and A. Guillaumont, "Demon," in *Dictionnaire de la spiritualité ascétique et mystique*, vol. 3, p. 206.

31. Ibid., 193.

32. Festugière, *Historia Monachorum in Aegypto*, p. 26.

33. Draguet, *La Vie primitive de S. Antoine*, vol. 1, p. 41 (chap. 40).

34. Laager, *Palladius*, pp. 141–143.

35. " 'The Face to Face' Interview," in *C. G. Jung Speaking*, p. 390.

36. On this problem, see also C. G. Jung, "Der Schöpferhymnus," *CW* 5, §112.

Chapter 2. Demons in Early Christianity

1. R. C. Thompson, *The Devils and Evil Spirits of Babylonia . . .* (London: Luzac, 1903/1904).

2. C. G. Jung, "Antwort auf Hiob," *GW* 11, §607.

3. For a psychological interpretation, see B. Hannah, *The Religious Function of the Animus in the Book of Tobit* (London: Guild of Pastoral Psychology, 1960).

4. O. Böcher, *Christus Exorcista: Dämonismus und Taufe im Neuen Testament* (Stuttgart: Kohlhammer, 1972).

5. Ibid., p. 171.

6. A. von Harnack, *Die Mission und Ausbreitung des Christentums in den ersten drei Jarhunderten*, 4th ed. (Leipzig: Hinrichs, 1924); K. S. Latourette, *A History of the Expansion of Christianity*, vol. 1.

7. Von Harnack, vol. 1, p. 154.

8. Ibid., p. 157.

9. Justin, *Dialog mit Tryphon 2*, 1–2, in N. Hyldahl, *Philosophie und Christentum* (Copenhagen-Protant apud Munksgaard, 1966), p. 112.

10. "Huius [= philosophiae] opus unum est de divinis humanisque verum invenire." Epistula 90:3, cited in Hyldahl, p. 135.

11. Hyldahl, p. 136.

12. Von Harnack, vol. 2, p. 559.

13. C. G. Jung, "Über die Beziehung der Psychotherapie zur Seelsorge," *GW* 11, p. 488ff.

14. C. G. Jung, *Erinnerungen*, p. 334.

CHAPTER 3. THE FRAGMENTABILITY OF THE PERSONALITY

1. "On the Nature of the Psyche," *CW* 8, §370.

2. H. F. Ellenberger, *Die Entdeckung des Unbewussten (The Discovery of the Unconscious)*, p. 186.

3. Ibid., p. 190.

4. "Zur Psychologie und Pathologie sogenannter occulter Phänomene," *GW* 1, §§1–98.

5. We know her identity today through Stefanie Zumstein-Preiswerk's study *C. G. Jungs Medium: Die Geschichte der Helly Preiswerk* (Munich: Kindler, 1975).

6. "Zur Psychologie und Pathologie," *GW* 1, §59.

7. M. Birchere Benner, *Der Menschenseele Not, Erkrankung und Gesundung* (Zurich: Wendepunkt-Verlag, 1933), pp. 288–310.

8. H. F. Ellenberger, *Die Entdeckung des Unbewussten*, pp. 439–442, 1042–1044; J. Witzig, "Théodore Flournoy: a Friend Indeed," *Journal of Analytical Psychology 27 (1982):* 131–148 (1982).

9. Ellenberger, pp. 193–209.

10. "Zur Psychologie und Pathologie, *GW* 1, §116.

11. Ibid., §81.

12. *GW* 2.

13. Morton Prince, *The Dissociation of a Personality* (New York: Meridian Books, 1957).

14. *CW* 8, §202.

15. Cf. the examples given by Freud in *Zur Pathologie des Alltagslebens (Psychopathology of Everyday Life)*.

16. *CW* 8, §202.

17. Ibid., §204.

18. Ibid., §397.

19. Ibid., §385.

20. Ibid., §388.

CHAPTER 4. THE WORLD OF SPIRITS

1. C. G. Jung, "Zur Phänomenologie des Geistes im Märchen," *CW* 9, I §385.

2. J. V. Andreae, in Dülmen, ed., *Valentin Andreae* . . . (Stuttgart-Calwer, 1981), p. 45ff.

3. H. Silberer, *Probleme der Mystik und ihrer Symbolik* (Vienna, 1914), p. 7.

4. S. S. Walker, *Ceremonial Spirit Possession in Africa and Afro-America* (Leiden: Brill, 1972), p. 74.

5. C. G. Jung, *Briefe, vol. 2*, pp. 396 and 455.

6. J. Beattie and J. Middleton, eds., *Spirit Mediumship and Society in Africa* (London: Routledge and Kegan Paul, 1969).

7. Ibid., p. 71.

8. Ibid., pp. 134f.

9. R. Passian, "Sind brasilianishche Trance-Chirurgien Instrumente verstorbener Ärzte?" (Conference lecture, Basler Psi-Tagen 1985).

10. M. Lambek, *Human Spirits: A Cultural Account of Trance in Mayotte* (Cambridge: Cambridge University Press, 1981).

11. M. Ninck, *Wotan und Germanischer Schicksalsglaube*, (1935; reprint, Darmstadt: Wissenschaftliche Buchgesellschaft, 1967), p. 179.

12. L. Marshall, *The !Kung of Nyae Nyae* (Cambridge: Harvard University Press, 1976), p. 179.

13. *GW* 8, §627.

14. Ibid., §628.

CHAPTER 5. THE WORLD OF SHAMANS AND MEDICINE MEN

1. Knud Rasmussen, *Rasmussens Thulefahrt* (Frankfurt am Main: Societäts-Drückerei, 1926), pp. 230–231.
2. D. and B. Tedlock, *Über den Rand des Tiefen Canyon* (Düsseldorf and Cologne: Diederichs, 1982), p. 42ff.
3. Rasmussen, p. 237.
4. Ibid., p. 239.
5. F. G. Speck, *Naskapi: The Savage Hunters of the Labrador Peninsula* (Norman: University of Oklahoma Press, 1977), pp. 72ff.
6. Rasmussen, p. 242.
7. Ibid., p. 245.
8. Ibid., p. 247.
9. Ibid., pp. 72–73.
10. Ibid., p. 253.
11. Ibid., p. 73.
12. M. Eliade, *Schamanismus und archaische Ekstasetechnik* (Zurich and Stuttgart: Rascher, 1957), pp. 33–42.
13. W. G. Jilek, *Indian Healing: Shamanic Ceremonialism in the Pacific Northwest Today* (Surrey, Canada: Hancock House, 1982), p. 132.
14. Eliade, *Schamanismus*, pp. 93, 95.
15. J. Halifax, *Shamanic Voices: A Survey of Visionary Narratives* (New York: Dutton, 1979), pp. 63–126.
16. Ibid., pp. 74–75.
17. Eliade, *Schamanismus*, p. 97.

CHAPTER 6. THE SORCERER'S ARROWS

1. Cf. Luke 4:31–41; 5:12–26; 6:6–11, 17–19; 7:1–17; 8:25–26; and many other biblical passages.
2. H. Sigerist, *A History of Medicine*, vol. 2, (New York: Oxford University Press, 1961), pp. 57–58.
3. C. G. Jung, *Mysterium Coniunctionis* II, GW 14/II, §§328, 413.

4. "Synchronizität als Prinzip akausaler Zusammenhänge," *GE* 8, §§956–958.

5. "Die praktische Verwendbarkeit der Traumanalyse," *GW* 16, §§342–350.

6. Cited by S. Freeman in "Etiology of Illness in Aboriginal Australia" (Thesis, Ethnologisches Seminar, Zurich, 1981), pp. 31–32.

7. F. E. Clements, *Primitive Concepts of Disease* (Berkeley: University of California Press, 1932).

8. H. B. Wright, *Zauberer und Medizinmänner* (Zurich: Orell Füssli, 1958), p. 49.

9. L. Honko, *Krankheitsprojektile: Untersuchung über eine urtümliche Krankheitserklärung* (Helsinki: Academia Scientarium Fennica; 1967).

10. Freeman, *"Etiology of Illness,"* p. 71.

11. Ibid.

12. Marie-Louise von Franz, *Spiegelungen der Seele*, p. 28. (Published in English as *Projections and Re-collection in Jungian Psychology.*)

13. Freeman, *Etiology of Illness*, p. 71.

14. Older literature in J. G. Frazer, *The Golden Bough*, part 2, "Taboo and the Perils of the Soul," pp. 20ff., and L. Lévy-Bruhl, *Die Seele der Primitiven*, pp. 134ff.

15. C. G. Jung, *Mysterium coniunctionis*, *GW* 14, II, §365.

16. M. Eliade, *Schamanismus und archaische Ekstasetechnik*, pp. 177–207.

17. A. Hultkrantz, *Conceptions of the Soul Among North American Indians* (Stockholm: Caslon Press, 1953), p. 459.

18. Ibid., p. 454.

19. Freeman, *Etiology of Illness*, pp. 130ff.

20. J. Cawte, *Medicine is the Law: Studies in Psychiatric Anthropology of Australian Tribal Societies* (Honolulu: University of Hawaii, 1974).

21. A. Rodewyk, *Die Dämonische Besessenheit in der Sicht des Rituale Romanum*, 2d ed. (Aschaffenburg: P. Pattloch, 1975).

22. T. K. Oesterreich, *Die Besessenheit* (Langensalza: Wendt und Klauwell, 1921).

23. J. Beattie and J. Middleton, eds., *Spirit Mediumship and Society in Africa*.

24. Ibid., p. 82.

25. S. Maderegger, *Dämonen: Die Besessenheit der Anneliese Michl im Licht der Analytischen Psychologie* (Weis: Ovilava Libri, 1983).

Chapter 7. The Demons Animus and Anima

1. Emma Jung, *Animus und Anima* (Zurich: Rascher, 1967; C. G. Jung, "Anima und Animus," *GW* 7, pp. 207ff.; M.-L. von Franz, *Die Erlösung des Weiblichen im Manne* (Frankfurt am Main: Insel, 1980); Körner, "Die Rolle des Animus bei der Befreiung der Frau" (Thesis, C. G. Jung Institute, Zurich, 1981).

2. "Über die Archetypen des Kollektiven Unbewussten, *GW* 9, I, §64.

3. C. G. Jung, *Aion*, *GW* 9, I, §§20–42

4. "Die Psychologie der Übertragung, *GW* 16, §278.

5. Ibid., §423.

6. H. Mode, *Fabeltiere und Dämonen in der Kunst: Die fantastische Welt der Mischwesen*, 2d ed. (Stuttgart: Kohlhammer, 1983).

Chapter 8. The Ancestral Spirits

1. "Anima and Animus," *CW* 7, §296.

2. "The Function of the Unconscious," Ubewussten," *GW* 7, §294, p. 186.

3. Ibid., §294.

4. C. G. Jung, "Die Psychotherapie in der Gegenwart," *GW* 16, p. 103, n. 2.

5. C. G. Jung, "Der Schöpferhymnus," *GW* 5, §65, n. 5.

6. On the notion of karma, see J. Gonda, *Die Religionen Indias*, vol. 1, pp. 206–207; C. G. Jung, "Persönliches und überpersönliches Unbewusstes," *GW* 7, §83, n. 15.

7. Jung, *Memories*, pp. 233–234.

8. Ibid., p. 235f.

9. Jung, "Symbole der Mutter und der Wiedergeburt," *GW* 5, pp. 265–266.

10. With astoundingly unscientific naiveté, Thorwald Dethlefsen has interpreted his retrospective journeys under hypnosis "as recollections of previous incarnations" *(Das Erlebnis der Wiedergeburt; Heilung durch Reinkarnation.)* The sole merit of his method may lie in its ability to resurrect repressed affects. In any case, conflict in the psyche is projected on the external world in a typical Western way.

11. C. G. Jung, "Zum psychologischen Aspect der Korefigure," *GW* 9, I, §316.

12. Jung, "Introduction to Wickes's 'Analyse der Kinderseele'," *CW* 17, §96.

13. Ibid., §93.

14. G. van der Leeuw, *Phänomenologie der Religion*, p. 134.

15. Literally, the eternal ones, the never-created ones; totem gods of the Alcheringa time, mythical ancestors of the Aranda in Australia.

16. *CW* 9, I, §224.

17. Jung, *Memories*, p. 34.

18. C. G. Jung, *Erinnerungen (Memories)*, p. 87.

19. Ibid., 195.

20. C. G. Jung, "Komplikationen der amerikanischen Psychologie," *GW* 10, §977.

21. J. Neihardt, ed. *Black Elk Speaks* (Lincoln: University of Nebraska Press, 1979).

22. W. Müller, *Die Religionen der Waldland-Indianer Nordamerikas.*

23. J. F. Thiel, *Ahnen-Geister—Höchste Wesen* (Bonn: Anthropos Institut, 1977), p. 26.

24. H. von Beit and M.-L. von Franz, *Symbolik des Märchens*, vol. 1, p. 114.

25. Thiel, *Ahnen-Geister*, p. 138.

26. E. Stauffer, "Geschichte Jesu," in *Historia Mundi*, vol. 4, p. 129.

27. H. Bonnet, *Reallexikon der Aegyptischen Religionsgeschichte*, p. 322.

28. C. G. Jung, "Synchonizität als Prinzip akausaler Zusammenhänge," *GW* 8, §921.

29. "Über Wiedergeburt," *GW* 9, I, p. 125ff.

30. *Erinnerungen*, p. 320.

31. *Memories*, p. 237.

Chapter 9. The Relationship between Subject and Object

1. Cf. my article "Demons: Psychological Perspectives," in *Encyclopedia of Religion*, ed. M. Eliade et al. (New York: Macmillan, 1987), vol. 4, pp. 288–292.

2. A. Ribi, *Anthropos* (Munich: Kösel, forthcoming).

3. C. G. Jung, *Briefe* II, 180 (To Marie Ramondt).

4. Ribi, *Anthropos*, chapter entitled "Der kosmische Mensch."

5. M. Gusinde, *Nordwind-Südwind: Mythen und Märchen der Feuerlandindianer* (Kassel: E. Röth, 1966), p. 38.

6. K. Völker, ed., *Von Werwölfen und anderen Tiermenschen* (Munich: Hanser, 1972).

7. L. Marshall, "The Medicine Dance of the !Kung Bushmen," *Africa* 39 (1969): 347–381.

8. J. Leff, *Psychiatry around the Globe: A Transcultural View* (New York: M. Dekker, 1981), p. 42ff.

9. P. Barguet, *Le livre des morts des anciens egyptiens*, pp. 59, 123.

10. Cf. W. Mannhardt, *Wald- und Feldkulte* (Berlin, 1905; reprint, Darmstadt: Wissenschaftliche Buchgesellschaft, 1963), which brings together examples from all over Europe.

11. A. P. Elkin, *The Australian Aborigines*, 3d ed. (Garden City, N.Y.: Doubleday, 1964).

12. E. Renner, *Goldener Ring über Uri* (Zurich: Metz, 1941).

13. Plutarch, *De defectu oraculorum*, 17.

14. C. G. Jung, *Aion, GW* 9, II.

15. Von Franz, *Spiegelungen der Seele*, p. 141ff.

16. C. G. Jung, *Mysterium Coniunctionis, GW* 14, II, §413.

Chapter 10. The Stone

1. P. G. W. Glare, ed., *Oxford Latin Dictionary*.

2. C. G. Jung, "Psychologische Deutung des Trinitätsdogma," *GW* 11, §222.

3. U. von Wilamowitz-Moellendorf, *Der Glaube der Hellenen*, vol. 1 (2d

ed., 1955; reprint, Darmstadt: Wissenschaftliche Buchgesellschaft, 1959), pp. 155ff. On the symbolism of stones, see also Jung, "Die Visionen des Zosimos," *GW* 13, § 126ff.

4. Cf. Aristophanes, "The Acharnians," 242.

5. Wilamowitz-Moellendorf, vol. 2, 320ff.

6. F. Colonna, *Hypnerotomachia Poliphili*, m iiii ff. (Priapos festival).

7. Plato, *Symposium*, 202.

8. Cf. von Franz, *Spiegelungen der Seele*, p. 141.

9. G. Kittel, *Theologisches Wörterbuch zum Neuen Testament*.

10. G. Tavard, "Dämonen," in *Theologische Realenzyklopädie*, vol. 8 (Berlin and New York: de Gruyter, 1981), p. 270.

11. Wilamowitz-Moellendorf, vol. 1, p. 356.

12. Ibid., p. 357.

13. J. Pokorny, *Indogermanisches Etymologisches Wörterbuch* (Bern and Munich: Francke, 1959), pp. 175f.

14. Wilamowitz-Moellendorf, vol. 2, pp. 295ff.

15. Cf. von Franz, *Spiegelungen der Seele*, p. 103ff.

16. Mircea Eliade, *Die Religionen und das Heilige* (Salzburg: O. Müller, 1954), p. 270.

17. Ibid., p. 266.

18. Ibid., pp. 267–268.

19. Ibid., p. 266; see also J. Rykwert, *The Idea of a Town* (London: Faber & Faber, 1976), p. 59.

20. R. Kriss and H. Kriss-Heinrich, *Volksglaube in Bereich des Islams*, vol. 2, p. 209.

21. Eliade, *Die Religionen und das Heilige*, p. 253.

22. Ibid., p. 254.

23. Ibid., p. 259.

24. *Reallexikon für Antike und Christentum* (hereafter cited as *RAC*), vol. 10, p. 13.

25. Ibid., p. 15.

26. Ibid.

27. Ibid., vol. 10, p. 53. "Genius est deus, cuius in tutela ut quisque

natus est vivit. Hic sive quod ut genamur curat, sive quod una genitur nobiscum, sive etiam quod nos genitos suscipit ac tutatur certe a genendo genius appellatur."

28. K. Kerényi, *Die Religionen der Griechen und Römer* (Zurich: Buchclub Ex Libris, 1963), p. 236.

29. *RAC*, vol. 10, p. 58.

30. Ibid., p. 59.

31. Horace (Quintus Horatius Flaccus), *Sämtliche Werke*, trans. J. H. Voss (Leipzig: Recam, n.d.), Epist. 2.2, pp. 187–189, cited in *RAC*, vol. 10, p. 61. ". . . scit Genius, natale comes qui temperat astrum,/ naturare deus humanae, mortalis in unum/ quodque caput, vultu mutabilis, albus et alter / . . ."

32. *RAC*, vol. 10, p. 61 (Servius, *Aen.* 6, 743).

33. Ibid.

34. Ibid., p.67. "Alii genium esse putarunt uniuscuiusque loci deum." On this whole theme, see also von Franz, *Spiegelungen der Seele*, p. 136.

35. Andres, "Daimon," in *Pauly's Real-Encyclopädie der classischen Alter-tumswissenschaften*, Suppl. 3 (Stuttgart: Metzler, 1918), col. 293.

36. A. O. Prickard, *The Return of the Theban Exiles*, 379–378 B.C. (Oxford: Clarendon, 1926), p. 46.

37. Cf. von Franz, *Spiegelunen der Seele*, p. 136. The pertinent texts are also to be found here.

38. Ribi, *Anthropos* (forthcoming).

39. *Artis auriferae* . . . , vol. 2 (Basil: Conr.Waldkirch, 1593), p. 369: "Sed quocunque nomine nominetur, semper tamen est unus et idem, et de eodem. Unde Merculinus: Est lapis occultus, et in imo fonte sepultus,/ Vilis et ejectus, fimo vel stercore tectus."

40. *Theatrum Chemicum* . . . , vol. 3 (Strasbourg: Heredum Eberh. Zetzner, 1660), p. 740.

41. Johannes Jacobus Mangetus, *Biblioteca chemica curiosa*, vol. 1 (Genf: Ritter & de Tournes, 1702), p. 478.

42. Ibid., p. 350: T. de Hoghelande, *De Alchemiae Difficultatibus*.

43. Mangetus, *Biblioteca chemica curiosa*, vol. 1, p. 467 (Allegoria Sapientum).

44. Ibid., p. 502 (Exercitationes XIV).

45. "Congeries Paracelsicae Chemiae de Transmutationibus Metallorum," in *Theatrum chemicum*, vol. 1, p. 509, 1602.

46. Paracelsus, *Dictionarium Theophrasti . . .* (Frankfurt, 1584; reprint, Hildesheim-Olms, 1981), p. 60.

CHAPTER 11. HIERONYMUS BOSCH

1. H. Mode, *Fabeltiere und Dämonen in der Kunst.*

2. In a projected work (Jungiana B3), I shall make a more thorough analysis of Bosch's works based on methods of interpreting unconscious pictures. For this, it will be necessary to compare individual motifs from the whole of the artist's work. Such an analysis is beyond the scope of the present book, which mentions only a few basic points.

3. D. Hammer-Tugendhat, *Hieronymus Bosch: Eine historische Interpretation seiner* (Munich: Fink, 1981).

4. L. S. Dixon, *Alchemical Imagery in Bosch's Garden of Delights* (Ann Arbor, Mich.: UMI Research Press, 1981); M. Bergman, *Hieronymus Bosch and Alchemy: A Study on the St. Anthony Triptych* (Stockholm: Almqvist & Wiksell, 1979).

5. G. Unverfehrt, *Hieronymus Bosch: Die Rezeption seiner Kunst im frühen Sechszehnten Jahrhundert* (Berlin: Gebr. Mann, 1980).

6. E. Panofsky, *Early Netherlandish Painting* (Cambridge: Cambridge University Press, 1953).

7. Hammer-Tugendhat, *Hieronymus Bosch*, p. 57 and n. 11.

8. M. J. Friedländer, *Die Altniederländische Malerei* (Berlin: P. Cassirer, 1924–1937).

9. C. G. Jung, "Die Dissoziabilität der Psyche," *GW* 8, §365ff.

10. C. G. Jung, "Allgemeine Beschreibung der Typen," *GW* 6, §721ff. The analysis that follows refers to various features in Jung's system of psychological types. (Translator's note)

11. G. Unverfehrt, *Hieronymus Bosch.*

12. C. G. Jung, "Psychological Types," *CW* 6, §724.

13. Ibid., §725.

14. Ibid., §730ff.

15. C. de Tolnay, *Hieronymus Bosch* (Baden-Baden: Holle, 1973), p. 411; R.-H. Marijnissen et al. *Hieronymus Bosch* (Ghent: Weber, 1972), p. 16ff; H. Goertz, *Hieronymus Bosch in Selbsterzeugnisse und Bilddokumenten* (Reinbek bei Hamburg: Rowohlt, 1977), p. 15.

16. *RAC*, article "Engel IV" (Christian), V, pp. 190ff.

17. A. Spiro-Kern, "Die Welt der Insekten—Ein Spiegel des Psychischen," thesis, C. G. Jung Institute, Zurich, 1985.

18. Dixon, *Alchemical Imagery*; Bergman, *Hieronymus Bosch and Alchemy*.

19. See chapter 12 and C. G. Jung, "Die Erlösungsvorstellungen in der Alchemie," *GW* 12, §332ff.

CHAPTER 12. THE SPIRIT IN MATTER

1. M. Berthelot, *Collection des anciens alchemistes grecs*, vol. 3 (1888; reprint, Osnabrück: Zeller, 1967), p. 129.

2. *Artis Auriferae*, vol. 2, p. 248: "Hic enim lapis est clavis; eo namque excepto nihil fit, lapis enim noster est fortissimi spiritus, amarus et aeneus, cui corpora non miscentur quousque dissolvatur."

3. Ibid., p. 259: "Scias quod lapis noster aereus et volatilis."

4. Ibid., p. 271. "Item: praedictus lapis dicitur rebis: id est, una res quae fit ex duabus rebus: id est, corpore et spiritu, vel ex sole et luna, ex corpore mundato et fermentato."

5. M. Berthelot, *La Chimie au Moyen Age*, vol. 3, p. 118.

6. *Artis auriferae*, vol. 1, p. 265: "Eo quod anima ignis in anima eius occultatur. Et illa: Hic igitur lapis spiritualis est. Respondit: Non nosti hoc, quia spirituale spirituale roborat, cum eius sordes, et eius superfluitates comedit et separat ex eo?"

7. Further support for equating the stone with the Self may be found in C. G. Jung, "Die Lapis-Christus Parallele," *GW* 12, §395.

8. *Artis auriferae*, vol. 1, pp. 308–309: "Hic est lapis non lapis, habet animam et sanguinem et rationen similem duobus. Sic dixit Mahomet, Lapis qui est in hoc opere, necessarius de animata re est, hunc invenies ubique in planitie, in montibus et in aquis omnibus: habentque eum tam divites quam pauperes, estque simul vilissimus,

carissimus, crescit ex carne et sanguine . . . : ex illo possunt congregari exercitus, et interfici reges. . . . Immunditia est in hoc lapide propter quam ipsum homines vilipendent, et tenent quod non possint eam sequestrare . . . Item hic lapis non lapis, proiectus est in res, et in montibus exaltatus est, et in aere habitat, et in flumine pascitur argentum vivum . . . et in cacumine montium quiescit: cuius mater virgo est, et pater non concubuit. Idem lapis in sterquiliniis calcatur pedibus, et saepe stulti fodiunt, ut eum extrahant, et non possunt eum invenire . . . dicitur minor mundus, non quod sit microcosmus, sed qui mundus regitur per ipsum."

9. J. Fabricius, "The Symbol of the Self in the Alchemical 'Proiectio,' " *Journal of Analytical Psychology* 18 (1973): 47–57.

10. "Definitionen," *GW* 6, §500.

11. *Theatrum Chemicum*, vol. 2, 1659, p. 128: "Lapis qualis est in extrinseco, talis est in intrinseco et in medio, supra quamcunque rem projicitur, in eo perfectum opus exercet, eiusque intrinsecum in extrinsecum, et econtra mutat."

12. "Kommentar zu *Das Geheimnis der Goldene Blüte*," *GW* 13, §64.

13. *GW* 14, II §§ 365, 407.

14. *Erinnerungen*, p. 326.

15. Ibid.

16. C. G. Jung, "Der Geist Mercurius," *GW* 13, §301.

17. *De Civitate Dei*, lib. XI, C. VII.

18. J. Ruska, *Tabula Smaragdina: Ein Beitrag zur Geschichte der Hermetischen Literatur* (Heidelberg: Winter, 1926).

19. C. G. Jung, "Psychologie und Alchemie," *GW* 12, §§447ff.

20. *Benedictus Figulus, Rosarium novum olympicum* (Basel, 1608), p. 18.

21. Neutestamentliche Apokryphen; ed. W. Schneemelcher, 5th ed. (Tübingen: Mohr, 1987), vol. 1, p. 104, lines 28–31.

22. Ibid., p. 98, Log. 3.

23. Cited in C. G. Jung, "Symbole und Traumdeutung," *GW* 18, §465.

24. For this story I am indebted to the late president of the C. G. Jung Institute in Zurich, Dr. Franz Riklin.

25. C. G. Jung, "Einleitung in die religionspsychologische Problematik der Alchemie," *GW* 12, §§1–43.

26. A. Ribi, *Anthropos*, (Munich: Kösel, forthcoming), chapter, "Mikro-Makrokosmos.

27. Marie-Louise von Franz, *Alchemical Active Imagination* (Dallas: Spring Publications, 1979).

28. Marie-Louise von Franz, *Zahl und Zeit: Psychologische Überlegungen zu einer annäherung von Tiefenpsychologie und Physik* (Stuttgart: Klett, 1970).

CHAPTER 13. DEAD PEOPLE IN ONE'S HEAD: PARAPSYCHOLOGICAL APPARITIONS

1. "Individualität und Kollektivpsyche," *GW* 7, §264.

2. See the voluminous collection in E. Gurney et al., *Phantasms of the Living*, 2 vols. (1886; reprint, Gainesville, Fla.: Scholars' Facsimiles and Reprints, 1970).

3. E. Mattiesen, *Das persönliche Überleben des Todes* (1936/1939; reprint, New York: de Gruyter, 1987), vol. 1, p. 81.

4. Ibid., pp. 81–82.

5. Ibid., p. 86.

6. Ibid., pp. 95–96.

7. In H. Bender, ed., *Parapsychologie: Entwicklung, Ergebnisse, Probleme* (Darmstadt: Wissenschaftliche Buchgesellschaft, 1976), p. 747.

8. C. G. Jung, "Synchronizität als Prinzip akausaler Zusammenhänge," *GW* 8, §858.

9. C. G. Jung, *Briefe*, vol. 3, p. 234. To Stephen I. Abrams, 5 March 1959.

10. Mattiesen, *Das persönliche Überleben des Todes*, p. 103.

11. Ibid., p.132.

12. *RAC*, vol. 2, pp. 391–394.

13. Fanny Moser, *Spuk—Irrglaube oder Wahrglaube?* (Baden bei Zurich: Gyr, 1950), pp. 253ff.

14. Ibid., p. 11.

15. Ibid., p. 254.

16. C. F. Emmons, *Chinese Ghosts and ESP: A Study of Paranormal Beliefs and Experiences* (Metuchen, N.J.: Scarecrow Press, 1982).

17. C. G. Jung, "Theoretische Überlegungen zum Wesen des Psychischen," *GW* 8, §§343ff.

18. C. G. Jung, "Die Archetypen des Kollectiven Unbewussten," *GW* 7, §§152ff.

19. G. Widengren, *The King and the Tree of Life in Ancient Near Eastern Religion* (Uppsala: Universities Arsskrift, 1951).

20. V. Sackville-West, *Jeanne d'Arc, die Jungfrau von Orleans* (Hamburg: Wegner, 1937), p. 72.

21. Ibid., pp. 76–77.

22. M.-L. von Franz, "Die Passio Perpetuae," in C. G. Jung, "Aion: Psychologische Abhandlungen," *GW* 8 (Zurich: Rascher, 1951), pp. 387ff.

23. M.-L. von Franz, *Traum und Tod* (Munich: Kösel, 1985), p. 17.

24. "Theoretische Überlegungen zum Wesen des Psychischen," *GW* 8, §440.

CHAPTER 14. EVIL

1. "Das Gewissen in psychologischer Sicht, *GW* 10, §§839, 853.

2. Jung, *Erinnerungen*, p. 347.

3. C. G. Jung, "Theoretische Überlegungen zum Wesen des Psychischen," *GW* 8, §430.

Bibliography

Andres. "Daimon." In *Pauly's Real-Encyclopädie der classischen Altertumswissenschaften.* Suppl. 3, cols. 267–322. Stuttgart: Metzler, 1918.

Artis auriferae, quam Chemiam vocant. 2 vols. Basil: Conr. Waldkirch, 1593.

Augustine. *Vom Gottesstaat* [The City of God]. Translated by W. Thimme. 2 vols. Munich: Deutscher Taschenbuch-Verlag, 1978.

Bardenhewer, O. *Geschichte der altkirchlichen Literatur.* Vol. 3, *Das vierte Jahrhundert.* 2d ed., 1923. Reprint. Darmstadt: Wissenschaftliche Buchgesellschaft, 1962.

Barguet, P. *Le livre des morts des anciens egyptiens.* Paris: Editions du Cerf, 1967.

Beattie, J., and J. Middleton, eds. *Spirit Mediumship and Society in Africa.* London: Routledge and Kegan Paul, 1969.

Bender, H., ed. *Parapsychologie: Entwicklung, Ergebnisse, Probleme.* Wege der Forschung, vol. 4. Darmstadt: Wissenschaftliche Buchgesellschaft, 1976.

Bergman, M. *Hieronymus Bosch and Alchemy: A Study on the St. Anthony Triptych.* Stockholm Studies in History of Art 31. Stockholm: Almqvist & Wiksell, 1979.

Berthelot, M. *Collection des anciens alchimistes grecs.* 3 vols. 1888. Reprint. Osnabrück: Zeller, 1967.

———. *La Chimie au Moyen Age: Historie des Sciences.* 3 vols. 1893. Reprint. Osnabrück: Zeller, 1967.

Bircher-Benner, M. *Der Menschenseele Not, Erkrankung und Gesundung.* Zurich: Wendepunkt-Verlag, 1933.

Böcher, O. *Christus Exorcista: Dämonismus und Taufe im Neuen Testament.* Stuttgart: Kohlhammer, 1972.

Cassien, Jean. *Conférences.* 3 vols. Sources Chrétiennes, 42, 54, 64. Paris: Editions du Cerf, 1956, 1958, 1959.

Cawte, J. *Medicine Is the Law: Studies in Psychiatric Anthropology of Australian Tribal Societies.* Honolulu: University of Hawaii, 1974.

Clements, F. E. *Primitive Concepts of Disease*. Publications in American Archaeology and Ethnology 32, no. 4. Berkeley: University of California Press, 1932.

Colonna, Francesco. *Hypnerotomachia Poliphili*. Venice, 1499. Reprint. Padua: Antenore, 1980.

Dixon, L. S. *Alchemical Imagery in Bosch's Garden of Delights*. Ann Arbor, Mich.: UMI Research Press, 1981.

Draguet, R., Ed. *La Vie primitive de S. Antoine conservée en Syriaque*. 2 vols. Corpus Scriptorum Christianorum Orientalium, vol. 417. Louvain: Secretariat du Corpus SCO, 1980.

Dülmen, R. van, ed. *Valentine Andreae, "Fama Fraternitatis" (1614), "Confessio Fraternitatis" (1615); Christiani Rosencreutz, "Chymische Hochzeit," Anno 1459 (1616)*. Stuttgart: Calwe, 1981.

Eliade, M. *Le Chamanisme*. Paris: Editions Payot, 1949. German ed., *Schamanismus und archäische Ekstasetechnik*. Translated by Inge Köck. Zurich and Stuttgart: Rascher, 1957.

———. *Traité d'historie des religions*. Paris: Payot, 1949. German ed., *Die Religionen und das Heilige: Elemente der Religions geschichte*. Translated by M. Rassem and I. Köck. Salzburg: O. Müller, 1954.

Elkin. A. P. *The Australian Aborigines*. 3d ed. Garden City, N.Y.: Doubleday, 1964.

Ellenberger, H. F. *The Discovery of the Unconscious: The History and Evolution of Dynamic Psychiatry*. New York: Basic Books, 1970. German ed., *Die Entdeckung des Unbewussten*. Translated by G. Theusner-Stampa. Bern: Huber, 1973.

Emmons, C. F. *Chinese Ghosts and ESP: A Study of Paranormal Beliefs and Experiences*. Metuchen, N.J.: Scarecrow Press, 1982.

Evagrios of Pontus. *Traité pratique ou Le Moine*. Edited by A. Guillamont and C. Guillamont. Paris: Editions du Cerf, 1971.

Fabricius, J. "The Symbol of the Self in the Alchemical 'Proiectio.' " *Journal of Analytical Psychology* 18 (1973): 47–57.

Festugière, A.-J., trans. *Historica monachorum in Aegypto*. Les Moines d'Orient, vol. 4/1 (Enquête sur les moines d'Egypte). Paris: Editions du Cerf, 1964.

Foerster, W. "Daimon, daimonion." In *Theologisches Wörterbuch zum Neuen Testament*, edited by G. Kittel. Vol. 2. Stuttgart: Kohlhammer, 1935.

Bibliography

Frazer, J. G. *The Golden Bough: A Study in Magic and Religion.* 3d. ed.
Part 2, "Taboo and the Perils of the Soul." London: Macmillan, 1966.

Freeman, J. "The Face to Face Interview." In C. G. *Jung Speaking:
Interviews and Encounters,* edited by W. McGuire et al. London: Pan
Books, 1980.

Freeman, S. "Etiology of Illness in Aboriginal Australia: Its Psychological Significance and Cultural Shaping." Thesis, Ethnologisches Seminar, Zurich, 1981.

Freud, S. *Zur Psychopathologie des Alltagslebens: "Über Vergessen, Versprechen, Vergreifen, Aberglaube und Irrtum.* Frankfurt: Fischer, 1961.

Friedländer, L. *Sittengeschichte Roms,* edited by G. Wissowa. Authorized
ed. Stuttgart: Parkland Verlag, 1901.

Friedländer, M. J. *Die Altniederländische Malerei.* 11 vols. Berlin: P.
Cassirer, 1924–1937.

Goertz, H. *Hieronymus Bosch in Selbstzeugnisse und Bilddokumenten.* Reinbek bei Hamburg: Rowohlt, 1977.

Guillaumont, A., and C. Guillaumont. "Demon." In *Dictionnaire de
spiritualité ascétique et mystique,* edited by M. Viller et al. Vol. 3. Paris:
Beauchesne, 1957.

Gurney, E., et al. *Phantasms of the Living.* 2 vols. London: Society of
Psychical Research, 1886. Reprint. Gainesville, Fla.: Scholars' Facsimiles and Reprints, 1970.

Gusinde, M. *Nordwind—Südwind: Mythen und Märchen der Feuerland
indianer.* Kassel: E. Röth, 1966.

Halifax, J. *Shamanic Voices: A Survey of Visionary Narratives.* New York:
Dutton, 1979.

Hammer-Tugendhat, D. *Hieronymus Bosch: Eine historische Interpretation
seiner Gestaltungsprinzipien.* Munich: Fink, 1981.

Hannah, B. *The Religious Function of the Animus in the Book of Tobit.*
London: Guild of Pastoral Psychology, 1960.

Harnack, A. von. *Die Mission und Ausbreitung des Christentums in den ersten
drei Jahrhunderten.* Leipzig: P. Hinrichs, 1902. 4th ed., 1924.

Herter, H. "Genitalien." In *Reallexikon für Antike und Christentum,* edited
by T. Klauser. Vol. 10. Stuttgart: Hiersemann, 1978.

Honko, L. *Krankheitsprojektile: Untersuchung über eine urtümliche Krankheitserklärung.* F. F. Communications, no. 178. Helsinki: Academia
Scientiarum Fennica, 1967.

Horace. *Sämtliche Werke* [Collected Works]. Translated by J. H. Voss. Leipzig: Reclam, n.d.

Hultkrantz, A. *Conceptions of the Soul among North American Indians: A Study in Religious Ethnology.* Stockholm: Caslon Press, 1953.

Hyldahl, N. *Philosophie und Christentum: Eine Interpretation der Einleitung zum Dialog Justins.* Copenhagen: Protant apud Munksgaard 1966.

Jilek, W. G. *Indian Healing: Shamanic Ceremonialism in the Pacific Northwest Today.* Surrey, Canada: Hancock House, 1982.

Joly, R. *Christianisme et philosophie: Etudes sur Justin et les apologistes grecs du deuxieme siècle.* Brussells: Editions de l'Université, 1973.

————. *Erinnerung, Träume, Gedanken.* Edited by Aniela Jaffé. Zurich and Stuttgart: Rascher, 1962. English ed., *Memories, Dreams, Reflections.* Translated by Richard Winston and Clara Winston. New York: Pantheon Books, 1963.

————. *Gesammelte Werke.* 18 vols. Zurich and Stuttgart: Rascher; Olten and Freiburg im Breisgau: Walter, 1966–1981. English ed., *The Collected Works of C. G. Jung.* 20 vols. Translated by R. F. C. Hull and edited by Gerhard Adler, Michael Fordham, and Herbert Read. Princeton: Princeton University Press, 1957–1979.

Jung, C. G. *Briefe.* 3 vols. Olten and Freiburg im Breisgau: Walter, 1972–1973.

Jung, Emma. *Animus und Anima.* Zurich and Stuttgart: Rascher, 1967.

Kennedy, E. W. "The Alchemy of Death: Dreams of the Psychic Origin of Death." Thesis, C. G. Jung Institute, Zurich, 1988.

Kerényi, K. *Die Religionen der Griechen und Römer.* Zurich: Buchclub Ex Libris, 1963.

Körner, W. "Die Rolle des Animus bei der Befreiung der Frau." Thesis, C. G. Jung Institute, Zurich, 1981.

Kriss, R., and H. Kriss-Heinrich. *Volksglaube im Bereich des Islam.* Vol. 3, *Amulette, Zauberformeln und Beschwörungen.* Wiesbaden: O. Harrassowitz, 1962.

Lambek, M. *Human Spirits: A Cultural Account of Trance in Mayotte.* Cambridge: Cambridge University Press, 1981.

Lecouteux, C. *Geschichte der Gespenster und Wiedergänger im Mittelalter.* Cologne and Vienna: Böhlau, 1987.

Lee, R. B., and I. De Vore. *Kalahari Hunter-Gatherers: Studies of the !Kung San and Their Neighbours.* Cambridge: Harvard University Press, 1976.

Bibliography

Leff, J. *Psychiatry around the Globe: A Transcultural View.* New York: M. Dekker, 1981.

Le Fort, L. T., ed. *Oeuvres de S. Pachôme et ses disciples.* Corpus Scriptorum Christianorum Orientalium, vol. 150/160. Louvain: Imprimerie Orientaliste, 1956.

Lévy-Brühl, L. *L'Ame primitive.* Paris: Alcan, 1927. German ed., *Die Seele des Primitiven.* Translated by Else Werkmann. Düsseldorf and Cologne: Diederichs, 1956.

Maderegger, S. *Dämonen: Die Besessenheit der Anneliese Michl im Licht der Analytischen Psychologie; Ein Beitrag zur Diskussion über die Personalität des Teufels.* Wels (Austria): Ovilava Libri, 1983.

Mangetus, Johannes Jacobus. *Bibliotheca chemica curiosa, seu rerum ad alchemiam pertinentium thesaurus instructissimus.* 2 vols. Genf: Ritter & de Tournes, 1702.

Mannhardt, W. *Wald- und Feldkulte.* Vol. 1, *Der Baumkultus der Germanen und ihrer Nachbarstämme: Mythologische Untersuchungen.* Vol. 2, *Antike Wald- und Feldkulte aus nordeuropäischer Uberlieferung erläutert.* 2d ed. Berlin, 1905. Reprint. Darmstadt: Wissenschaftliche Buchgesellschaft, 1963.

Marshall, L. "The Medicine Dance of the !Kung Bushmen." *Africa* 39 (1969): 347–381.

———. *The !Kung of Nyae Nyae.* Cambridge: Harvard University Press, 1976.

Mattiesen, E. *Das persönliche Überleben des Todes: Eine Darstellung der Erfahrunsbeweise.* 3 vols. New York: de Gruyter, 1936/1939. Reprint. New York: de Gruyter, 1987.

Michl, J. "Engel IV (christlich)." In *Reallexikon für Antike und Christentum,* edited by T. Klauser. Vol. 5. Stuttgart: Hiersemann, 1962.

Mode, H. *Fabeltiere und Dämonen in der Kunst: Die fantastische Welt der Mischwesen.* 2d ed. Stuttgart: Kohlhammer, 1983.

Moser, Fanny. *Spuk—Irrglaube oder Wahrglaube? Eine Frage der Menschheit.* 2 vols. Baden bei Zurich: Gyr, 1950.

Moser, J.-J. "Aspects psychologiques de la ruse." Thesis, C. G. Jung Institute, Zurich, 1976.

Neutestamentliche Apokryphen in deutscher Ubersetzung [Apocrypha]. Edited by W. Schneemelcher. Vol. 1, *Evangelien.* 5th ed. Tübingen: Mohr, 1987.

Ninck, M. *Wotan und Germanischer Schicksalsglaube*. Jena, 1935. Reprint. Darmstadt: Wissenschaftliche Buchgesellschaft, 1967.

Oesterreich, T. K. *Die Besessenheit*. Langensalza: Wendt und Klauwell, 1921.

Oxford Latin Dictionary. Edited by P. G. W. Glare. Oxford: Clarendon Press, 1976.

Palladius of Helionopolis. *Palladius: "Historia Lausiaca." Die frühe Heiligen in der Wüste*. Translated and edited by J. Laager. Zurich: Manesse Verlag, 1987.

————. *The Lausiac History of Palladius*. 2 vols. Edited by C. Butler. Texts and Studies, vol. 6, no. 1/2. Cambridge: Cambridge University Press, 1898/1904.

————. *Des Palladius von Helenopolis Leben der Heiligen Väter*. Bibliothek der Kirchenväter, "Griechische Liturgien." Translated by S. Krottenthaler. Kempten and Munich: Kösel, 1912.

Panofsky, E. *Early Netherlandish Painting, Its Origins and Character*. 2 vols. Cambridge: Harvard University Press, 1953. 4th ed., 1966.

Paracelsus. *Dictionarium Theophrasti Paracelsi, continens obscuriorum vocabulorum, quibus in suis scriptis passim utitur, definitiones. Dorneus Geardus collectum*. Frankfurt, 1584. Reprint. Hildesheim: Olms, 1981.

Passian, R. "Sind brasilianische Trance-Chirurgen Instrumente verstorbener Arzte?" Conference lecture, Basler Psi-Tagen 1985.

Plokker, J. H. "Das Weltbild des Hieronymus Bosch." In *Hieronymus Bosch*, edited by R. H. Marijnissen et al. Genf: Weber, 1972.

Plutarch. *De defectu oraculorum*. In *Plutarch's Werke* [Collected Works]. Vol. 10. Translated by J. C. F. Bähr. Stuttgart, 1858.

Pokorny, J. *Indogermanisches Etymologisches Wörterbuch*. Bern and Munich: Francke, 1959.

Prickard, A. O. *The Return of the Theban Exiles, 379–378 B.C.: The Story as Told by Plutarch and Xenophon*. Oxford: Clarendon, 1926.

Prince, M. *The Dissociation of a Personality: A Biographical Study in Abnormal Psychology*. 1905. New York: Meridian Books, 1957.

Radin, P., K. Kerényi, and C. G. Jung. *Der Göttliche Schelm: Ein indianischer Mythen-Zyklus*. Zurich: Rhein Verlag, 1954.

Rasmussen, K. *Rasmussens Thulefahrt: Zwei Jahre im Schlitten durch unerforschtes Eskimoland*. Frankfurt am Main: Societäts-Drückerei, 1926.

Reitzenstein, R. *Des Athanasius Werk über das Leben des Antonius: Ein*

Bibliography

philosogische Beitrag zur Geschichte des Mönchtums. Heidelberg: C. Winters, 1914.

Renner, E. *Goldener Ring über Uri: Ein Buch vom Erleben und Denken unserer Bergler, von Magie und Geistern und von den ersten und letzten Dingen.* Zurich: Metz, 1941.

Ribi, A. "Demons: Psychological Perspectives." In *The Encyclopedia of Religion,* edited by Mircea Eliade et al. Vol. 4. New York: Macmillan, 1987.

————. *Anthropos.* Munich: Mösel, forthcoming.

Rodewyk, A. *Die dämonische Besessenheit in der Sicht des Rituale Romanum.* 2d ed. Aschaffenburg: P. Pattloch, 1975.

Ruska, J. *Tabula Smaragdina: Ein Beitrag zur Geschichte der Hermetischen Literatur.* Heidelberg: Winter, 1926.

Rykwert, J. *The Idea of a Town: The Anthropology of Urban Form in Rome, Italy, and the Ancient World.* London: Faber & Faber, 1976.

Sackville-West, V. *Joan of Arc.* London: Leonard and Virginia Woolf, 1936. German ed., *Jeanne d' Arc, die Jung Frau von Orléans.* Hamburg: Wegner, 1937.

Schilling, R. "Genius." In *Reallexikon für Antike und Christentum,* edited by T. Klauser. vol. 10. Stuttgart: Hiersemann, 1978.

Sigerist, H. E. *A History of Medicine.* Vol. 1, *Primitive and Archaic Medicine.* 2d ed., 1955. Vol. 2, *Early Greek, Hindu, and Persian Medicine.* 1961. New York: Oxford University Press.

Silberer, H. *Probleme der Mystik und ihrer Symbolik.* Vienna, 1914. Reprint. Darmstadt: Wissenschaftliche Buchgesellschaft, 1969.

Speck, F. G. *Naskapi: The Savage Hunters of the Labrador Peninsula.* Civilization of the American Indian Series, vol. 10. Norman: University of Oklahoma Press, 1977.

Spiro-Kern, A. "Die Welt der Insekten—Ein Spiegel des Psychischen." Thesis, C. G. Jung Institute, Zurich, 1985.

Tavard, G. "Dämonen." In *Theologische Realenzyklopädie.* Vol. 8. Berlin and New York: W. de Gruyter, 1981.

Tedlock, D., and B. Tedlock, eds. *Teachings from the American Earth: Indian Religion and Philosophy.* New York: Liveright, 1975. German ed., *Über den Rand des Tiefen Canyon: Lehre indianischer Schamanen.* Translated by J. Eggert. 3d ed. Düsseldorf and Cologne: Diederichs, 1982.

Theatrum chemicum, praecipuos selectorum auctorum tractatus de chemiae et lapidis philosophici antiquitate, veritate, jure, praestantia, et operationibus continens . . . 6 vols. Strasbourg: Heredum Eberh. Zetzner, 1659–1661.

Thompson, R. C. *The Devils and Evil Spirits of Babylonia, Being Babylonian and Assyrian Incantations against the Demons, Ghouls, Vampires, Hobgoblins, Ghosts and Kindred Evil Spirits, Which Attack Mankind*. London: Luzac, 1903/1904.

Tolnay, C. de. *Hieronymus Bosch*. German ed. Translated by L. Voelker. 2d ed. Baden-Baden: Holle, 1973.

Unverfehrt, G. *Hieronymus Bosch: Die Rezeption seiner Kunst im frühen sechszehnten Jahrhundert*. Berlin: Gebr. Mann, 1980.

Völker, K., ed. *Von Werwölfen und anderen Tiermenschen: Dichtungen und Dokumente*. Munich: Hanser, 1972.

von Franz, Marie-Louise. "Die Passio Perpetuae: Versuch einer psychologischen Deutung." In C. G. Jung, "Aion. Psychologische Abhandlungen." *GW*, vol. 8. Zurich: Rascher, 1951. Pp. 387ff.

———. *Zahl und Zeit: Psychologische Überlegungen zu einer Annäherung von Tiefenpsychologie und Physik*. Stuttgart: Klett, 1970.

———. *C. G. Jung: Sein Mythos in unserer Zeit*. Frauenfeld/Stuttgart: Huber, 1972.

———. *Alchemical Active Imagination*. Dallas: Spring Publications, 1979.

———. *Die Erlösung des Weiblichen im Manne*. Frankfurt am Main: Insel, 1980.

———. *Traum und Tod: Was uns die Träume Sterbender sagen*. Munich: Kösel, 1984.

———. *Spiegelungen der Seele: Projektionen und innere Sammlung*. Munich: Kösel, 1988. Published in English as *Projection and Re-collection in Jungian Psychology: Reflections of the Soul* (Peru, Ill.: Open Court, 1985).

Walker, S. S. *Ceremonial Spirit Possession in Africa and Afro-America: Forms, Meanings and Functional Significance of Individuals and Social Groups*. Leiden: Brill, 1972.

Waszink, J. H. "Biothanati." In *Reallexikon für Antike und Christentum*, edited by T. Klauser. Vol. 2. Stuttgart: Hiersemann, 1954.

Widengren, G. *The King and the Tree of Life in Ancient Near Eastern Religion*. Uppsala: Universities Arsskrift, 1951.

Wilamowitz-Moellendorff, U. von. *Der Glaube der Hellenen*. 2 vols. 2d ed., 1955. Reprint. Darmstadt: Wissenschaftliche Buchgesellschaft, 1959.

Witzig, J. "Theodore Flournoy: A Friend Indeed." *Journal of Analytical Psychology* 27 (1982): 131–148.

Wright, H. B. *Witness to Witchcraft.* New York: Funk & Wagnalls, 1957. German ed., *Zauberer und Medizinmähner.* Translated by S. Ullrich. Zurich: Orell Füssli, 1958. Zumstein-Preiswerk, S. C. G. *Jungs Medium: Die Geschichte der Helly Preiswerk.* Munich: Kindler, 1975.

Index